MW00789797

December 23, 2019

To Dixie
A sister from
hello ♡
Sandy

JUST BECAUSE
YOU'RE DEAD DOESN'T
MEAN YOU'RE GONE

— A MEMOIR —

sandy foster morrison

Wilma Flewellen Miller Foster
in 1937 at age fourteen
"I was grown"

This book is dedicated
to my mother,
my best enemy,
my friend

ACKNOWLEDGMENTS

No memoir can be told without the willingness of living characters, and the support of reassuring listeners. As much as possible, I have shared the facts, ordered truly and represented without embellishment. Out of respect for their privacy, the only exceptions are the invented names of my mother's late-in-life husband, and the men I have loved. In other cases I refer to someone by a title, and not a name.

I am forever grateful to my daughters, Lacie and Sarah, for not only agreeing to reveal their stories, but also for walking by my side. I thank their husbands, John and Brian, for their unexpected encouragement and hands-on involvement with the publication end-game. I especially appreciate my sister, Jo, who knowingly agreed to the revelation of tales from our childhood, and still supported the contemporary story, even though adult relationships between sisters in a flawed family are sometimes unattractive. And I thank my girls' father for graciously encouraging the sharing of our history "so that others don't make the same mistake."

To my word-spinning sisters — Cecelia, Deb, Gail, Jenny, Kate, Knoel, Linda and Pam — I am forever in your debt. Without your faithful attention, honest feedback and encouragement, this story might never have come into being.

To my childhood friends Ann, Cheri and Cousin Gail, and soul sister, Beverly, without your expert attention to detail and nitpicking hours of crossing every *t* and dotting every *i,* this final version of the book would be shabby indeed.

Most of all, I am eternally grateful to my ancestors, who are the gatekeepers, the generations of my blood where this story began.

Best yo' can do is jes be yo'self.
God don' 'spect no mo' from any of us.

— *Annie*

I

DEAD BUT NOT GONE

Wilma in 1936 at age thirteen

THE SCREEN DOOR SLAPPED SHUT behind me. My sister's late-night phone call echoed in my head, "She's gone, Sandy." I walked out into the brittle stillness. It was midnight and a full harvest moon rose high and white, casting fingers of light through the oak trees.

"Mama? Where are you?"

Silence answered.

I was alone tonight, at home in the Texas Hill Country halfway between Austin and San Antonio, with no other human soul in sight. There was only me and the vast October sky. No lover. No children. No friends. No traffic on the winding farm-to-market road a quarter mile down my rocky lane, the nearest neighbor acres away.

Warm yellow lamplight from open farmhouse windows at my back cast my silhouette across the pebbled road at my feet. I turned my head toward the heavens. "Mama? Where'd you go?"

The wind breathed the tall brown grass.

"I know you're there somewhere. How long before we connect?"

As I bathed in translucent moonbeams, my mother's mysterious and often repeated claim to magical powers played in my mind. "I'm a witch. A bit *fey*, you know. It's that dark, brooding Welsh blood. Don't think for one minute you can get away with anything without my knowing it." Recalling the many times she had proven her intuition, I laughed and murmured toward the stars. "Surely, after telling me what to do my whole life, you won't give up now just because you've taken up residence on the other side."

My mother wasn't, of course, a real black-hairs-on-your-chin, bubbling-cauldron sort of witch. Overt revelation of witchy ways would never do in my childhood hometown, deep in the Pineywoods of East Texas. Even in the twentieth century acrid whiffs of Salem Witch Trial condemnation still lingered in the air we breathed. No spooky stuff, no knowledge allowed except straight from the Good Book. If you knew what was good for you. Mother abided by these Christian rules even though the idea of a man hanging on a cross and bleeding to death scared her away from darkening the door of the First Presbyterian Church. Out of self-preservation she hid her aversion to church or any other way of thinking and believing which ran contrary to *Old Longview Society* – the country-club crowd which ruled who was in, who was out and whether a woman might marry up or down. Mother steered her life and the lives of my only sister, Jo, and me by this one inviolate commandment: "Not only can you not afford to do anything wrong, but you can't afford to do anything that *looks* wrong." Revelation of Mother's mind-reading, prophesying and devilishly accurate intuition was unthinkable in God-fearin' Longview, Texas.

Even if nobody else knew about Mother's spooky mind reading, I never doubted her when she claimed, "I have eyes in the back of my head." So what if I couldn't see those witchy eyes? When I merely thought wrong, Mother knew it. In glorious circumstances when I was sneaky enough to manage doing wrong, she busted me and swooped down with fury. "You are somebody, Sandy! And don't you ever forget it!" This drama played out times without number, often embellished with, "As God is my witness!" Mother had a thing for *Gone With the Wind*.

Following her signature Scarlett-esque tirade, a litany of impeccable family history would follow. This was scripted, predictable, varied in detail, but seldom in length. A good hour was to be expected, coupled with viewing the ancestral portraits on what I called — only to myself — *The Dead People's Wall*. Like water dripping on rock, Mother's metamorphic history-whipping for unacceptable behavior proved more effective than being made to stand in the corner, spanked with a slender switch from the Bridal Wreath hedge, or being sent to bed without dinner.

The Cliff Notes version of the Fine Old Family torture went like this (ad infinitum in original form): Because our industrious Longview ancestors counted a mayor in the Flewellen pioneer lineage, owned the lumber mills which built the town and also donated lumber for the construction of the First Presbyterian Church. And because the Flewellens built the railroad, ice house, electric company, emporium and oh, yeah...drilled those oil and natural-gas wells. And most of all, because Longview wouldn't exist unless our forefathers and other broken-hearted Confederates like them were forced to retreat from Sherman in "his Godforsaken march-to-the-sea," my sister and I were required to remember who we were...and act like it. Whatever that meant. I always seemed to zig when I was supposed to zag.

But I did get the message. "This family has a proud reputation to uphold!" I hasten to add, fragile as it was given the colorful lives my mother and grandmother led. Herein lay the precisely sharpened point. Membership in Old Longview Society, which Mother claimed as her unalienable birthright, required an impeccable code of conduct. Muted tones read well, and vivid moves of any sort were regarded as suspect. This presented a problem.

My mother Wilma and her mother Beth — Mamo to me and Jo — did not blend. These two generations of Flewellen women were backslidden, shamefully bright rainbow fish swimming in a pond stocked with sensible bream. "Plain as the nose on the end of your face," as Mamo liked to say to prove a point, all of Longview knew the truth. In this conservative land of the eternally-married, many husbands had come and gone from my mother and grandmother's lives. Responsibility for restoring honor to this family rested solely on Jo's immature shoulders and mine.

Where did all those husbands go, anyway? None of them lived with Mother, Jo and me, at Mamo's house. This was certain, yet puzzling. Throughout childhood I made it my Nancy Drew mission to discover their whereabouts, or at least a clue to their demise. Were the husband stories buried beneath the lumpy Aubusson carpet in Mamo's prissy Victorian sitting room? I snooped for signs of the lost husbands in every corner of her columned brick house, thick with musty antiques. But when I asked my excellent detective-work questions of Mamo, she silenced me with outrage. Crow-black eyes popped behind wire-rimmed glasses, and straggles of fugitive black hair escaped the mesh hairnet which in less troublesome circumstances squished her hair into place. Her ferocious face turned the same shade as scarlet lipstick which leaked into the creases around her lips. "You have foot-in-mouth disease, Sandy! Mind your own business. Do as I say do, not as I do! You hear me?"

Without help from grown-ups, understanding what actually happened with my father became an especially daunting assignment. Somehow, I erased memories of him as soon as we set foot in Mamo's front parlor when I was seven, Jo was two and Mother was twenty-six. Maybe I forgot because I finally felt safe. Or maybe I forgot because Mamo called my father bad names like honky-tonker. When she thought of him, Mamo could be cross for days, and this was no fun for anybody.

My grandmother's outbursts both puzzled and disappointed me. Modeling my behavior after Mamo or Mother couldn't be considered. The proud forefathers were the act to follow, so they said. But dead people are hard to get to. Besides, even if I could talk to the forefathers, I was a girl, not a boy. Shouldn't I figure out how the foremothers acted and copy them? It was altogether confusing.

Furthermore, I wasn't inclined to believe what seemed like fairy tales about our Fine Old Family. Never just *our family* like the kids at school talked about theirs. Mamo and Mother said Fine Old Family with capital letters like The Star Spangled Banner or The United States of America. Even though I tried, I couldn't figure out what all the fuss was about. I mainly paid attention to Mamo and Mother for premeditated purposes: to extract information...when I wanted...about what I wanted to know. To me they were both stupid and mean. They embarrassed me. Mother was either angry, sad or pretending she lived at Tara, so I couldn't trust a word she said. And Mamo made the Wicked Queen in *Snow White and the Seven Dwarfs* seem like a fairy princess.

Early on I developed a strategy for making sense of these forbidding women who ruled my life: Read a lot. Think a lot. Watch happy people to figure out how they got that way.

My attention span was limited, however, since feeling bad for Mother and wishing I could fix it took up a lot of my time. Seen through my bewitched and frightened young eyes, my mother was beautiful...and still a spook you'd better mind your manners around. Five-foot-two with tennis shoulders, a wasp waist, horses' mane of wild auburn curls, green eyes the color of new fern, Cherokee cheekbones, sparkly teeth like sunlight on the river and a glossy red-lipstick smile, she could have been a movie star in the magazines I wasn't supposed to touch, but did. Now I was losing her...my mother...my best enemy...my friend.

Jo and I and our five grown children — a.k.a, The Cousin Club; two girls and a boy for Jo, two girls for me — had been on death watch for a week, but on alert to the end for two years. Only last week my cell phone rang at midnight just as I turned out the light. I knew from the strained tone in Jo's voice that this was about Mother and it couldn't be good. "Mother's assisted living called...she's been hospitalized…not breathing well. They are starting tests in the morning. I think you should come."

Impending-ness hung in the empty space between us. The emotional ground beneath my feet shifted, and I felt myself tumbling headfirst off an inevitable cliff. "Oh...my God, Jo. We've seen this coming. I'll see how I can work this out. I know the girls will want to come, too."

My sister answered, "It's what you do, Sandy."

Here, for the sake of honesty, I ought to admit that I have always held my sister's manners in high regard. By this I mean: I'm jealous of her. By the time Jo — five years younger than me — came on the scene I still struggled with folding my hands in my lap, crossing my ankles so my panties wouldn't show, squeezing a lemon so it didn't squirt on anybody and never speaking to adults unless spoken to. Tasks which Jo achieved, no sweat, as soon as she could walk and talk.

Now, as our mother's life hung in the balance, here Jo and I were…like always. Me, a disorderly mass of protoplasm. Her, Grace Kelly. Across the miles between Houston and the Hill Country, years of restraint oozed out of the crevasse where all the real feelings were hidden. Furious to be lectured about social appropriateness when death knocked at the door, I shot back. "I know that, Jo. I was in the Junior League. Before you, if you'll remember. I've got clients. Sarah's a senior at UT. Lacie's married. She and John work. We don't have the leisure to pick up and leave on a seconds notice. Of course I'm coming. After all, she's my mother."

Immediately I felt angry with myself. Fighting — although I'm exceptionally good at it — went against my recently enlightened code of conduct. It had taken years, actually, tons of therapy and lots of money to realize I didn't get anywhere when I argued. And worse, I had a hangover after Jo and I fought. Stand up for my beliefs, yes. Respect myself to the best of my ability, definitely And at the same time, stop controlling her — as only big sisters can do — and simply allow my sister to be. Not speeding up when she criticizes, or slowing down when she praises, but just keeping steady. It was a plan, anyway.

Mother might not be long for this world, and our family drama still exploded. Most unacceptable…and pointless anyway due to irreconcilable differences. Marriage partners aren't the only ones who get divorced. Through the years I had drifted further and further from conservative family shorelines and drawn my own map, which was un-navigable in five-years-younger sister sight. We were continents apart.

"Have it your way. You usually do." My sister's words clinked out like ice cubes from the freezer to the glass.

With an equally hard edge, I replied. "Thank you. I'll call and let you know when we're coming." If I planned to avoid a volcanic eruption, I knew better than to say more. Sergeant Friday's words from the *Dragnet* detective show of our childhood popped into my head: Just the facts, ma'am. This situation required major constraint. Even good relationships are strained when a parent is close to death. Jo and I were a long way south of good.

Until this gray October morning as my girls, Lacie and Sarah, and I drove toward possibly the last days of Mother's life, we ritualized our pilgrimage to Houston by blasting Alabama's *Roll On* and singing our lungs out. Today, the air sagged heavy and silent as my red Jeep ate up Texas Interstate 10. Spent grasses, ashen and wasted stubble lined the road beneath leaden autumn skies. Feeling flattened and squashed as the lifeless insects splattering across the windshield, Mother's imminent death was the only thing on my mind. I couldn't shake the sadness or lifetime memories of this woman who was central to my being. Eventually, I quit struggling and gave myself to reminiscing, beginning with events which had drawn her from San Antonio to Houston.

For eight years — the last of my twenty-six year marriage — Mother had lived close by in a garden apartment in our San Antonio neighborhood, Alamo Heights. In Confederate style *sans* parasol, Mother held court from her front porch, attracted and fell in love with an aging World War II pilot. Mainly, it seems, because of Hank's pet name, the Great Wilma. Finally, in her sixties, Mother found a man who recognized her for who she believed herself to be. But Hank became ill, moved home to New Mexico and Mother's luster began to fade.

With Mother, mad always trumped sad. Soon after Hank's life-giving admiration emptied from her life, I commiserated with her over chicken salad at our favorite Alamo Heights sidewalk cafe. It was a setup. Doesn't everyone break up in a restaurant? Our waitress — a woman of size — clatteringly piled our plates as she cleared the table following Mother's disdainful declaration, with eyes pointedly sweeping the waitress' body, "Dessert is not an option for women with girlish figures." Having taken the waitress down a notch or two, a favorite defense mechanism Mother launched when she felt small and unsure of herself, she lit a cigarette and took a long drag. Fortified for battle, she leaned forward, braced her elbows on the table and lasered me through slitted eyes like a sniper sighting her prey. "I have something to say to you, Sandy. I don't know how you can stand living in Mexico! I'm moving back to *Texas*!" This meant Houston.

I never expected Mother would leave San Antonio. Now, as I drove toward Houston, my head completely absorbed with the potential deathbed confrontation which awaited us, I finally understood. Even those two years ago at the Alamo Heights cafe, Mother realized she was ill...and chose not to share it. Her fighting spirit was strong. Defined by war, from *Dubya Dubya Two* to Remember the Alamo to the Battle for the Confederacy, my mother was no pusillanimous Damn Yankee. If she had carried a personal battle flag it would read: Anger Will Get Me Through.

Evidence of repeated injury, "...damn dry heat that shrivels your skin...Mexicans incapable of speaking English...such Godforsaken soil the azaleas can't grow..." supported the notion that her move to Houston was San Antonio's fault. The city had gotten on Mother's bad side and was in deep trouble. A lovely lunch, balmy spring sunshine, kind breeze and my superb company had done nothing to diminish Mother's irritation. In a diatribe of discontent, unbridled disrespect for the Hispanic population (the enemy) and disgust for human frailty, she blew smoke. Literally, one cigarette after another and figuratively, point upon point.

She was good. Who could disagree with her rationally irrational logic? If Mother hated San Antonio, she hated it. Never mind she had just turned seventy; the lady was mad and she was leaving.

Wilma Foster went home to Houston and the watchful eye of my sister, who, innately more southern-mannered than

I, was therefore much less inclined to get in Mother's face. Given the opportunity I might have figured out Mother's game. After all, I was onto her habits during the last eight years of her San Antonio reign.

Most of all, understanding my mother trained me young to become a psychotherapist, with graduate school and state licensure merely an essential afterthought. Of course Mother disdained my actual credentials and elevated my achievements to a place of greater importance...much better for bragging. "Madame Psychologist," Mother would announce, "I need a little therapy."

To which I would futilely protest, "Mama, I'm not a psychologist! I wish you'd stop calling me that. Psychologists have a Ph.D. I have a M.A. I'm a psychotherapist and that's plenty good enough!"

Mother's pretentious "My daughter the *psychologist* says..." was predictable. More is more. She couldn't help herself, and neither could I; my bullshit meter was having none of it. How silly of me to encourage the truth. In the South, honesty is considered a character flaw. Scowling her disapproval of my conduct, Mother brushed me off as she would an irritating mosquito. "Oh! I know that, dum-dum! Just listen to me!"

But she quit talking — a sure clue that some scheme was in the wind. Only now did I grasp the scary situation which she faced solitarily, independently. No support required. None needed. Mother knew she was dying, and doctors were out of the question since they have the nasty habit of admitting sick people to hospitals. She was buying time. Elephants search for their graveyards. My mother sought hers.

Feeling lonely for her insults, aching to connect with her essence before she slipped away, my reverie was not near complete when the Houston exit loomed to the right off I-10. Nor was I ready to search for Mother down some colorless, inhospitable corridor. She would have preferred her garden.

Frail and spent like a baby bird plucked from its nest, Mother's shrunken self looked wretchedly out of place pressed between sterile white sheets. The doctors had warned that her cancer was so far advanced she wouldn't be able to speak. Still, I wasn't prepared for the tortured rasps which erupted from each wrenching breath. Her struggle filled the room. Holding back the tears, Sarah, Lacie and I gathered around the metal bed rails. Reaching to connect, my fingers grazed the scratchy covers and recoiled at the ultimate affront. These were not the sheets to which my mother was accustomed. Even as she gasped for life, I knew that somewhere inside herself, Mother shrank to escape dreaded 180 count polyester/cotton blend. She simply could not tolerate this situation.

Despite her heaving chest, Mother appeared to sleep while her family stood mute and helpless by her side, overwhelmed with the burden she carried. But she must have sensed our presence, because her eyes flew open. Stark terror glittered in her gaze, then quickly clouded over. In that instant I realized there was nothing wrong with my mother's mind. She knew what she knew. Lacie, Sarah and I had driven over from the Hill Country. "I deplore a death watch! I won't have it!" She had often said this. Vehemently. Absolutely. So that even imbeciles such as we might translate her wishes. If she could speak she would say it now.

So this was it. The truth was out. Such finality was unbearable. Mother lifted her fingers as if she intended to touch my hand, then a look of determined resignation flashed through her eyes. She had changed her mind. She would not connect. With deliberate resolve, her eyelids closed. Drawing the drapes on this whole distasteful scene, silently she slipped into a coma…or so it seemed.

IN THE ARCTIC HOSPITAL ROOM flooded with harsh corridor lights as nurses checked Mother's vital signs every fifteen minutes, the dark night swelled with a lifetime of memories. Deep sleep still shrouded Mother, with every ounce of her strength spent on the next breath. I purred over her, stroked her hair, murmured how much I loved her.

Realizing the futility of hovering to catch one last word, a look, a final goodbye, I wrestled with slippery sheets on the roll-away bed pulled alongside hers. The crackle of my plastic mattress loud as gunfire, I sensed the caustic sound must drive Mother batty. Even if she seemed unconscious I knew better than to assume she was unaware. The effects of Mother's witchy intuition — experienced up close and personal throughout my life — converted me to belief in mind-reading and gritty clairvoyance. My mother was way bigger than this small woman struggling through the last hours of her earthly life.

Bone-weary but giving up on sleep, I plopped my feet on the floor and paced, skirting around and beside Mother like a shadow, trying not to but counting each breath. By the time the repellent smell of bacon and eggs seeped along the hushed hospital corridor, I had reconciled the highs and lows of our lives. I hoped Mother had heard me throughout the night and knew how much I loved her deep down with respect for who she was, what she had to deal with, her shortcomings and mine.

Staring from the hospital window as the sky turned from pitch black to velvet blue and a bold golden glow cracked the darkness, it dawned on me that Mother would never give up her body while someone watched. Above all else, she was a woman of strength who wouldn't tolerate an unattractive death scene. Hadn't she told her family as much, many times? What was I thinking? She would die in my arms? Not my mother. The intuitive realization that Mother waited for a solitary moment to slip away with her dignity intact set me free from the ache I felt. I emptied my heart of hope for one last heart-to-heart connection and released my mother to do what she must, when she must. It was over. This was the ultimate endgame...and good enough.

The hospital awakened, buzzing with muffled voices up and down the corridors, clattering carts, the morning shift nurse poking her head into the room — "Just checking" — and then a *whoosh* as the heavy door slid back into place. Having spent the night at Jo's, Lacie and Sarah crept into the room as lemony sunbeams pierced the industrial-strength plate-glass windows. Sarah didn't get far before she stopped dead and stood still, listening. Her smooth olive complexion paled and angular features drooped beneath the reality of Mother's agonized breaths which lengthened as if each would be her last. Sarah cupped her hand and wailed a whispered protest in my ear, as her distressed small-self used to do in grown-up church when she ached for an end to the long ordeal. "Poor Bebe. How can she keep on like this?"

The sight of my girls was an oasis of relief. I nodded with tears in my eyes. "I know. For her sake, I hope not long."

Sarah was the contemplative one, always taking stock before she voiced an opinion and then bold in her comment. Even as a baby she stared unblinkingly, evaluating strangers until they squirmed: "What's that baby looking at?" Lacie came into the world grinning. Strangers itched to get their hands on her, and eased up to me for the chance, asking, "What is that baby smiling at?" But Lacie wasn't smiling now.

Her pixie face was drawn into square-jawed acceptance. With no nonsense, my eldest looked me up and down, surveying the damage of the night and offering support. "Go get a shower, Mom. Bebe will know we're here."

I escaped to the bathroom and turned the water lever to scald. Seconds later, with shampoo in my hair and my eyes closed, the metallic screech of the shower door grinding open sent me ballistic. "Mom!" Lacie spoke in a tense rush. "Bebe just stopped breathing for a long time. We thought she died. Then she opened her eyes. She looks scared. I think she wants you."

Hair tangled and dripping wet, I wrestled into jeans. With my heart thumping, barefoot and still pulling on a shirt, I rushed to Mother's bedside. Bending over her frail form, I squeezed her hand and held on. "Mama? I'm here, Mama. Can you let me know you hear me?"

Her eyes were closed, her body unmoving except for the irregular rise and fall of her chest. Did I imagine it, or did the second finger of her right hand lift almost imperceptibly? My throat felt strangled as I forced words through my mouth. "Oh. I'm here." Tears splashed down my cheeks. "I didn't leave, Mama. I'm sorry I'm crying. I know you don't like tears, Mama. I'm here."

Mother lay motionless and deathly still. The only sound was sniffling on the other side of the forbidding steel rails as Lacie and Sarah passed Kleenex from hand to hand.

Like it or not, Mother would have to endure this full-out death watch. No way could I leave. My legs had turned to mush. There was nothing to do but wait. I settled in, lowered the bed rail with a grating screech and hunkered down, draping my wobbly body close to Mother, her limp hand cupped in my sweaty palms. Not trusting my strength, I sent out an emergency prayer. Making sure I covered all bases, I silently prayed to God, Goddess, Buddha and any available angels who might be willing to help us get through this: *Help me be here. Really be here.*

Behind me, the thick hospital door whooshed open and silently closed. Jo and her girls — Jennifer, petite and Cover Girl brunette, and Mary, blond, tall and lean like a Ralph Lauren model — tiptoed into the room. A day earlier, after Sarah, Lacie and I arrived at the hospital, Jo and I connected superficially...icily. The girls and I showed up at Mother's bedside two days — maybe three — later than Jo expected us to come. It was what it was. Today Jo and I had nothing left to say to each other. Nor was I capable of carrying on a sensible conversation with anyone. I couldn't even manage "Hello."

All I wanted to do was crawl in beside Mother, hold and comfort her. But I knew better. We were not a touchy-feely family and this was a poor time to start. Was this the end? Was Mother going to die in my arms after all? I focused on making sure I breathed so I wouldn't faint, continued to hold Mother's hand in my clammy palm...and waited.

Little did I know. Within moments my belief in separation between this world, the world that was, and the world to come, would be shattered.

Without warning, an electric bolt of energy sizzled through me. Top to bottom, my body buzzed and my hair stood on end. I knew this feeling. When the girls were small a lightning bolt struck a hardwood tree in our front yard. A blazing blue ball of fire smashed a window and blasted through the house with tremendous force. This shockwave felt the same. I gasped and cut my eyes around the small, tight room, searching the faces of Lacie and Sarah, Jo, Jennifer and Mary, for a sign they felt it, too. They stared blankly back at me. Lacie and Sarah through puffy red eyes, and Jo — it seemed to me — with a lidded-lizard gaze that dared me to wiggle. Which of course I was clearly doing. Our family system seamlessly rotated in orbit, while my poles wobbled, blown off center by the equivalent of a super-galactic fireball.

Feeling possessed, I muttered in Mother's ear. "Mama, did you feel that? Did you do that?" As if in answer, magical images scrolled across my minds' eye. Fast-forward, high def scenes from the East Texas of Mother's childhood leapt through my head. Alongside the images, my emotions wailed with distress sirens and bells.

What is this? Not like the spiritual epiphanies I've experienced through meditation and contemplation, a conscious seeker opening my heart and mind to the transcendent. I didn't open this door. The door blew open without my conscious agreement. The Mother Ship has landed, taken my thoughts hostage and swallowed me whole. Somehow, though...this feels every bit as sacred and filled with beauty as meditation ever has. I breathed belly-deep and said "Yes" to this love-field which led who knew where.

"Mama?" Crouching low, I whispered in her ear. "Are you doin' that life-passing-before-your-eyes thing?"

No response.

Fearing I might break the spell now that I understood this electric energy as benevolent, I whispered as quietly as I could given the orgasmic explosion of bliss which vaporized my grief of moments before and riveted me with expectation. "Mama? What do we do now?"

Nothing. No movement. No sound except the now rhythmic cadence of Mother's breath, which replaced the irregular stops and starts of only minutes before. I leaned close and whispered, "How about if I share the pictures I'm seeing?"

I hesitated, took another deep breath and vaulted into translation of vivid images which raced through my imagination, so real I could almost touch them. "Mama, I'm seeing a handsome man dressed in khaki riding britches and a funny-looking bowler hat. He's pulling two little girls in a small wagon that's hitched to a huge brown horse. Oh! That's you. Isn't it? And this must be Louise...your big sister, so little and cute. And Angus? Is this Angus, your daddy? I think so…." I couldn't stop myself from asking questions although I had begun to realize Mother was probably incapable of answering. Her body was on pause, but certainly not her mind. This life review seemed propelled by rocket thrusters making it almost impossible to keep up. "…you and Louise are so cute. You're screaming and giggling. I get it. Your daddy is teasing you. The louder you squeal the faster he goes. He's throwing his head back and roaring with laughter."

"Now here you are at the Old Home Place….an adorable blond-headed little thing with a Buster Brown haircut…maybe four years old. Green lattice skirting is pulled away from the high front steps and set aside. I'm seeing the playhouse you've talked about…hidden beneath the steps of the Old Home Place where all the cousins played in the summertime. And Little Black Mandy is with you. 'She was my best friend,' I remember you telling me. And now I see her! Mama, this is unbelievable."

The scene shifted. "It's night…hot and damp…children are giggling and shouting. You're older now…maybe five or six. All the Flewellen cousins are chasing lightning bugs in the front yard of the Old Home Place. The grown-ups are watching and rocking in metal gliders on the porch." *Squeak. Squeak.* The strain of rusty metal grated in my ear. "Do you hear that, Mama? The squeak? It's so real."

"And now you're at Aunt Bodie and Brother Charles's Wil-Lou Lakes Farm in Kountze…swimming in the rocky artesian swimming pool under tall magnolia trees. The water is so cold you have goose bumps on your skin. You're screaming and trying to swim away from the slimy black tadpoles…but they're everywhere!"

I hesitated for a second and attempted to process the images through my own understanding. "You spent a lot of time with Aunt Bodie when you were little, didn't you,

Mama?" There was no answer. The DVD of Mother's childhood flooded my awareness, speeding ahead on fast-forward with no pause button, filling me with transcendent feelings of elation, ecstasy and irrepressible joy. I stumbled to keep up. "Now you're at Aunt Bodie's home in Beaumont, all piled up in bed like a princess. You're sick and Bodie is bringing you lunch on a bed tray...lime-green fish-shaped Jell-O and tiny olive tea sandwiches. Oh, I get it. You caught a cold from that freezing water, didn't you?"

"And now it's another day...still in Beaumont at Bodie's house. Your cold is better. Aunt Bodie is letting you fish in the goldfish pond, out back in the garden. But you don't have a hook. The cane pole is strung with kitchen string and a big piece of suet for bait. 'This way the fish don't get hurt,' Bodie says."

High-voltage scenes, sounds and sensations shifted lightning-fast, faster than my tongue could shape words to share. "I hear children running and shouting. There you are...a whole bunch of kids are chasing each other. Of course...hide and seek! It's the cousins...the Flewellen cousins. You're in a park....'Daingerfield Park,' the sign reads. It's a big family picnic in the summertime. You're maybe seven or eight. The grown-ups are spreading long pine picnic tables with blue checkered cloths and bowls of fried chicken, corn on the cob and potato salad...and a platter of deviled eggs sprinkled with paprika...and then pickles...gherkins. Gherkins! I can't believe I know the name of those tiny pickles. You're blowing my mind, Mother. Now Mamo's hollering for you. It must be her, but look at her...so young and pretty...amazing, completely amazing. Mamo cups her hands to her mouth and shouts, 'Wilma! Wilma! Come eat before the ants carry your food away!' You giggle...run away...hide...because you don't want to stop playing."

Transported completely into the ecstatic freedom of

Mother's childhood, I wanted to laugh out loud. But I stifled my maniacal expression of joy, suddenly aware of how insane I must already appear, disheveled and partially dressed, crouched over Mother, intensely muttering in her ear. Self-awareness was only a momentary blip on my radar. Nothing in me wanted to say no to the supernatural force holding me captive. I plunged ahead, reporting who, what, when, where and how — I had no clue why — like a contemporary journalist who stumbled through the wardrobe into Narnia.

"Okay. We're still in about the same period in your life, Mama. The sun is at high noon and we're back at the Old Home Place. How precious! You're swinging from the tall rope tied high in the oak trees...higher and higher with your cousins reaching out to grab you as you swing past. From the front porch Mamo shouts, 'Wilma! You're gonna break your neck! That's high enough! You hear me?'"

Layer upon layer, year after year of childhood experiences transferred from Mother's mind and imprinted mine. I felt it all, grasping as each scene unfolded that this was a sequential remembrance, through youth to young womanhood, where the innocence of childhood transformed into the smoldering longings of a woman in love.

"Now you're all grown up...like a little doll with that eighteen inch waist you've told me about. You weren't kidding. And this must be George...oh my God...George...my father. He has his arm around you. Look at him. He's a hunk! It's night...so cold your breath looks like puffs of smoke." I struggled to retrieve stories Mother had shared, hoping I could make sense of what I was seeing. "Maybe this is Colorado...snowy mountain peaks all around. Soldiers are everywhere...and he's in uniform. I get it. It's *The War*. You're wearing a plain gold band. He must be on leave. '*Sonofabitch!*' He's swearing as he grabs the car door and slides behind the wheel. You're in the car waiting and looking worried. No wonder. Hotel after hotel is turning you away. You look at him with smoky eyes, 'I don't care...we've got each other,' you say and kiss him. I don't feel like I should be seeing this! But oh well...he's driving and your head is on his shoulder. The car roars up steep, snowy mountain roads. Oh...you're gonna have to spend the night in the Pontiac. Mama! This is so real I can almost touch the amber-colored Indian Chief hood ornament. Truly...you loved him so very much...."

After what must have been a long time, even though it was impossible to measure this journey in minutes or hours, I saw a gentle bridge which arched gracefully over a small, tranquil stream. The whole sky was painted in shades of pink and purple, with puffy clouds floating overhead like an Impressionist painting. The numinous beauty took my breath away. On the other side of the stream a crowd gathered... laughing, shouting. "They see you Mama, and are waving their arms to get your attention." I recognized some of the faces, although most of these people were younger than I ever knew them, if I knew them at all.

Trembles of awareness rippled through Mother...and me. "Mama, look who's here: There's Mamo and Angus, Trey, Bodie and lots more, a huge crowd of joyful, happy people. This is so beautiful." Hot tears rolled down my cheeks. "They've all come to see you across. They're waiting on the other side." I stole a quick glance around the room to get my bearings and make sure I was still here in Mother's hospital room and hadn't lifted off to this eternal place that charged my mind. Jo and her girls were gone. Lacie and Sarah still stood on the other side of Mother's bed, weeping full-out.

Mother and I had reached a stopping point. "It's time, Mama. I know how scared you've been. How much you've dreaded the Grim Reaper. But it's not like that at all, is it?" I stroked her arm and felt immense peace — whether my own or Mother's, I couldn't tell. There was no separation between us. "When you're ready Mama, all you have to do is walk across this beautiful bridge. We all love you so much...in this world and the next...we're all here with you. Just cross over...whenever you're ready...you can go anytime you want."

Rays of Indian Summer sunshine slanted low on the horizon as Sarah, Lacie and I kissed Mother goodbye, wound our way through the antiseptic maze of hospital corridors and climbed into the Jeep. I navigated toward San Antonio, bundled in a contradiction of feelings; both wrenched emotionally from leaving Mother's side and, at the same time, filled with deep peace. I felt only halfway present in my own body. A part of me, the emotional part, stayed behind with Mother, feeling her more than I felt myself. Primeval faces and places drifted through my consciousness, ghosts unbidden, building a nest in my head:

The Old Home Place: The Flewellen family home; raised Victorian-style house set caddywampus on a corner lot in downtown Longview, in shambles and abandoned by the time I saw it. The haven grown children and grandchildren returned to when life was cruel and too much to handle alone.

Mamuvah and Papaw Flewellen: Philada "Ada" Virginia and Junius Jefferson, the matriarch and patriarch of the clan, the ancestors Mother worshipped. Together they created a culture of safety and security constructed on a foundation of hard work and sorrow. "Mamuvah lost a child every spring," Mamo had once shared.

Mamo: Elizabeth "Beth" Virginia Flewellen Miller Eddins (last infamous husband's name omitted as unclaimed). My grandmother, young again as I imagined her at Mother's bedside, a breathtaking Welsh beauty with intense black eyes and hair.

Angus Pitser Miller: Mamo's first husband, Mother's father; the grandfather I never knew.

Aunt Bodie: Mamo's sister. Of the five surviving Flewellen children, the older sister most adored and honored; wife of Brother Charles, a Beaumont attorney. As I remembered him, stiff and preening like a peacock.

George Porter Foster: My father, a glowering monster dressed in khaki; the man my mother loved beyond all reason.

Trey: My son, Lacie's older brother, Mother's first grandchild and the author of her grandmother name, "Bebe." Mother called him "Trey Baby," and he called her "Baby" right back.

All of them gone, a whole generation passed away, so bright in Mother's recollection yet dark in mine. After years of therapy I had laid the past to rest, reinvented myself, moved on into the present vitality of my own life and dreamed different dreams for future generations to build upon. But grief had come to call and the presence of the ancestors crowded around me as if they were flesh and blood, and not merely dead-and-gone family members whose stories had seemed like myth until now.

All the Flewellen ancestors had passed on, but not George, my father, not yet. At least I didn't think so. Thanks to Mother's life review, I had just seen him as young and handsome, but I didn't remember him this way. I didn't want to remember him at all. Almost all my life — from seven years on — he was father in name only. Aside from his deposit of DNA I never claimed him as "Father" — certainly never as "Daddy." He was just George to me: George Foster. I shivered at the thought of him and calculated the numbers in my head: forty-seven years. It had been a lifetime since I last saw him. Where was he now? Was he even alive, and did it matter? He was dead to me and my children.

Lacie and Sarah had curled up in the back seat, all of us

silent with our own emotions and thoughts as the Jeep settled into an easy seventy miles per hour, heading west beyond Houston and Texas's flat coastal plain. The terrain of the raw countryside rolled into gentle slopes and valleys. Barbed-wire fences marched around patchwork fields plowed for winter rest. Mammoth cylinders of hay scattered across open pastures where brown and white cattle grazed around clusters of rangy scrub oak, brier-y mesquite and huisache. Mahogany-tipped grasses bent beneath the wind. A flock of wild geese banked in formation. Salty, blistering tears stung my eyes and melted into the beauty of life. Mine to live; Mother's to leave for an eternal world that had never felt more certain; mine to glimpse through the veil of limited human awareness; hers to embrace.

The Jeep glided along the interstate, dangerously akin to an unmanned boat adrift on emotional seas. I desperately needed to focus and glanced in the rearview mirror, the sight of Lacie and Sarah calling me back to the land of the living. They were restless, not asleep, and like me, they appeared emotionally drained. Not only their faces but even their hazel eyes were bleached of color. Speaking to their mirrored reflections, I said with as much energy as I could coax into my voice, "Hey, you two. I don't know what I'd do without you. Are you okay?"

They smiled anemically and nodded their heads up and down like a bobblehead Jesus perched on the dash. Lacie spoke first, "I'm sad, but I'm glad we were there. I think Bebe was glad we came."

"Me, too," I nodded with relieved agreement.

Sarah's forehead wrinkled into a frown. She pulled herself upright and leaned forward, resting her chin on her folded arms. "What was going on, Mom, all that time when you were so close to Bebe? I've never seen you so focused on someone for that long."

My voice sounded strange to my ears, lapping onshore

from another ocean, far, far away. "I know. I wanted to tell you what was going on, but I got so caught up in it I couldn't stop." I swiveled to make eye contact, and purred. "I'm so sorry I left you in a lurch."

"No, it's okay, Mom! I just want to know what was happening."

"Well....I'm still sorting it out. Near as I can tell, Mother's life passed before her eyes and I tuned into her movie. Clairvoyant telepathy...I suppose...but nothing like I've ever experienced before. Way bigger than a hunch. Beautiful experiences from Mother's life landed in my head, beginning with her childhood. I don't know if she was sending and I was receiving or what. I can't explain it." I took another deep breath, feeling surreal and lightheaded even talking about it. "Does this make any sense?"

Lacie brightened and bolted to the front of her seat, leaning into the open space between the front and back seats, side-by-side with Sarah. "Yes! I thought that's what was happening!"

"You did?"

"Yes! Trey came to me, Mom. He told me to tell Bebe it would be okay."

My heart skipped a beat and thumped against my chest. "What? Trey did? Truly?" A liquid sensation of warmth coursed throughout my body.

In a rush, Lacie explained. "It was wonderful. I had a sort of vision of Trey. He stood in a field, dancing and waving bright colored streamers like gymnasts do. He told me to tell Bebe that it was okay. That she didn't have anything to be afraid of. That he would be waiting for her."

"Oh my God, Lace!" I gasped, feeling astounded at Lacie's simultaneous visions and yet at some level not feeling surprised in the least. From the time she could talk Lacie startled us with knowings which made no rational sense. I found this especially helpful when her toddler self warned from her car seat that a policeman hid around the bend and I'd better slow down, or when she unerringly intuited the location of my misplaced car keys. If anyone in this family seemed to have a leg up on being *a bit fey* — as Mother referred to intuition — it was Lacie. "I saw him, too...on the other side of a bridge which separates this world from the next," I said. As I spoke, I turned to look straight-on into my daughters' eyes, feeling tremendous love and warmth for them and timeless connection to the son — and brother — who was once ours. "It's beautiful that Trey appeared to you, Lace. And gave you such hope."

Sarah squirmed on the edge of her seat and vaulted into the conversation. "It's so weird when you two talk about the brother I never knew and never will know. It's like you were a whole family before I ever got here and I can't ever be a part of it."

Immediately, I felt regret. Lacie and I often shared spontaneous *woo-woo* awareness, but I never wanted to exclude Sarah, or make it seem as if my relationship with Lacie was in any way more special than my relationship with her. It just came first and we'd been at it longer, that's all. Under normal circumstances I created boundaries around Lacie's and my insider conversations about the brother who was gone before Sarah was born. Forget normal. I wasn't sure we would ever visit normal again. "Oh, honey," I sighed. "That sounds hard. But he's still your brother whether you knew him or not...and you're here now. That's what matters. I can't imagine life without you in it."

Enough said. I was tempted to argue that Sarah's soul was headed into this family long before Trey left us...but I didn't have it in me. She was right anyway. A whole lifetime had been lived before she ever showed up. I wish she had known him. But life didn't ask me what I wanted. It seldom does. I just knew that my youngest was experiencing her first real grief. And the separation of death magnifies every other separation which came before.

Lacie wisely let Sarah be and stuck with processing her impressions about Mother. "I don't think we're done with Bebe yet, Mom."

Venting her displaced feelings seemed to satisfy Sarah and she picked up the conversation. "I think that's right. Bebe looked so scared. I don't think she was ready to go."

"She's sort of with us already." Lacie opened her eyes wide and shrugged her shoulders as if to say, "Duh. Isn't this what we'd expect?"

"I agree," I said. "I do feel her. And when Mother's soul actually does cross over and her eternal spirit shows up — like I expect it will — I'm placing my order for sweetness and light. Bebe will make a lovely guardian angel. Don't ya think?"

MOTHER HAD PASSED AWAY a mere twenty-four hours ago, and transcendent feelings of peace and harmony passed right along with her. Already my sister and I argued over funeral details. Of course we did. Heaven forbid we should throw arms around each other's neck and sob in grief because our mother has died. How distasteful. Why not fight over Mother's burial? "Anger will get me through," is after all, the family creed. The fact that I no longer read from this script was little known. I had discovered that in disagreements with my sister, the most excellent defensive posture was withdrawal of energy. No argument. No reasoning. Just a solitary return to the neutral stance which encompassed the possible. This tactic seemed very Zen to me — what you resist persists — and worked remarkably well when I was capable.

Should our mother be buried three days after her death? Four? Five?

"We can do five." I said.

"Not right to wait," she said.

"Five," I said.

"Not proper," she said.

Three days was more than Lacie and her husband John or Sarah and I could arrange. And anyway, I didn't know whether Mother had specifically requested burial three days after death, or not. Since I had returned to San Antonio following the last tender, living hours at Mother's beside — only a day ago — and Jo lived in Houston, she could get her hands on Mother's hard-copy funeral arrangements. Arrangements which Mother had reminded us "...are kept in the small inside left-hand drawer of my Henredon double-bonnet secretary." I wasn't certain about Mother's time-sensitive burial request if there were any, but I did recall the most critical specifics of her wishes, often repeated: "I will be buried in Longview beside Mother." Upon stating her request, Mother would frown and give me the skunk-eye before continuing. "Elizabeth Flewellen Eddins. Don't forget. That's how her gravestone reads." She would pause. I would nod to convey immaculate attention, and only then would she cock her head to one side and grin like a little girl as she impeccably delivered the punch line. "There's not much room in the cemetery plot. But I'm not very big. Maybe they can scooch me in if they fold me over."

Arranging transfer and final destination of cargo, Jo assured me that Longview's Rader Funeral Home had attended to Mother's correct positioning in Grace Hill Cemetery. Duty bound to do my part, I volunteered to call the *Longview News-Journal* and file a brief obituary, but the story got away from me. The more factual details I shared with the eager reporter, the more questions she asked. Having stumbled upon a historic relic, she couldn't get enough. "I so wish I'd known your mother," the reporter cooed. "She sounds like such an interesting person. I'd like to ask her questions. She's the real thing. There aren't any more of her around."

The paper ran a half-page story on Thursday, October 31, 1996, page one of Section B, East Texas, titled "Funeral Set for Pioneer Descendant," with the remainder of the article found on 3B. This was more than even Mother could have asked. When my Grandmother Mamo died — at Christmastime when Sarah was two months old — she had spent her last five, sadly demented years in a nursing home. *The Longview News-Journal* gave Mamo's passing only a polite nod with an anemic six inches of copy. This aggrieved Mother. Now the Great Wilma's final exit, stage left, would be accompanied by ardent applause.

After our un-sisterly hassle exhausted its nuclear charge, Jo and I scheduled Mother's long-anticipated, and remarkably specific, interment for five days following her death. Even though my scheduling option prevailed, I still felt uncomfortable with this sham of a death ritual. In life, Mother's morbid fear of the "blood of Jesus" led her as far away from the church as she could run. Clearly, I needed to overcome my own cringe level which elevated remarkably when I thought of plasticized corpses and expensive caskets. Why not a reverent cremation and sacramental dusting of her beloved East Texas? This would be my way, but Flewellen tradition held fast — confines I ruefully respected and from which I had finally broken free. Or so I liked to assure myself.

Although Jo and I put our heads together to arrange the details of Mother's burial, negotiating a peace agreement was too much to expect. We were well into a serious pout that should carry us right up through the funeral and probably for a good year beyond. If history held, during this time we wouldn't speak. We would send sanitized birthday cards signifying nothing. Perhaps Christmas cards as well. I hated that. Ever since divorce from the girls' father six years ago, I had no photograph of the family dynasty to glue to the front of a card. There would be no family newsletter. Now I sent images of lone trees, or frolicking wee mice singing *falalalalalala-la-la.*

From the time our family — Lacie in seventh grade and Sarah in third — bailed out of Houston and relocated to San Antonio in search of greener pastures during the oil-bust days of the Eighties, my marriage hit one pot hole after another. Signage for steering clear of financial hardship didn't exist on our way-finding road map. Both dreamers, my husband and I were Dulcinea and Don Quixote. But love seldom counts the cost, and often overlooks reality: *The Impossible Dream* is a fantasy unsuited for mortals.

I fell madly in love with the girls' father on our first date. With a crowd of his fraternity brothers and their dates we hooked up on a steamy September night at Charlie's Playhouse, our sophomore year at the University of Texas in Austin. The music of Bo Diddley, James Brown, and Ray Charles wailed from sax and guitars as we Shagged, Shrugged, and Boogalooed across the tight, sweaty dance floor, bod-to-bod with the all-black crowd who felt like my brothers and sisters. After several hip-grinding hours, we collapsed at our table and sank into a dripping pitcher of cold beer. Heads together. Heat rising.

By Christmas break when I took my boyfriend home to Mother's tidy Longview bungalow where we had lived since I was in junior school, his fraternity shield pendant dangled from my neck. Since being dropped signified I had landed this guy, I assumed Mother would be thrilled. After all, her highest aspiration for me was attainment of a MRS degree: Well-pedigreed husband equals social sanction and security. I felt smugly satisfied imagining Mother's grateful smile of relief when she heard I was almost engaged and she wouldn't have to take care of me anymore. But I soon realized the complexity of this issue. "He's a Damn Yankee," Mother hissed, cornering me in the bathroom as I brushed my teeth, preparing for bed on Christmas Eve. "Have you lost your mind? What are you thinking!" My boyfriend had grown up in Washington, D.C. and his Yankee accent turned me on. What was I thinking? *Marriage*.

It was love at first sight because our families were equally dysfunctional and because he played his guitar and sang "Moriah," each strum of the strings causing shivers as I imagined those hands touching my skin. I understood him, he understood me, deep down where no other guy had touched me before. Together we would create a better world. He battled windmills. I felt safe and secure. For many years this pattern served us well, until financial hardship reared its dragon head.

Twenty years into marriage, we evacuated from Houston and the country club, society church, high-hot-and-a-helluva-lot business climate which turned us into people I no longer recognized. And frankly, demanded more edge than my husband possessed. For this I was grateful. Sandy to the rescue, I charged into San Antonio with the bit in my teeth, determined to carve out a career of my own and end the financial-dependency nonsense which led to painful yeses when my instincts said, no. I enrolled in graduate school and dumped my Junior League, trophy-wife mannequin. My husband hardly felt shocked. From the get-go — even though I tried to look the part — my rebellious tendencies made me a poor candidate for Stepford Wife.

Our church denomination — Episcopal, *God's Frozen Chosen* — where once upon another lifetime, I tried to save myself by teaching Bible study, now seemed hypocritical, intolerant and oppressive in its insistence on rigid dogma. Study did save me after all, but not in the way the conservative church understands salvation. Reading between biblical lines led me to a personal faith which was my own, no longer dependent on church definition. Spiritually promiscuous and shamelessly satisfied, I slept around in dangerous metaphysical practices and studies: Buddhist meditation, Black Elk's Lakota Sioux earth wisdom, teaching from Ancient Mystery Schools, Joseph's Campbell's, *The Power of Myth,* Carl Jung's *Man and His Symbols.* I couldn't get enough, and in my insatiable appetite imagined myself like Vishnu, the Hindu sacred being with many arms, every part of me reaching to grasp the transformative love central to all religious faiths. No amount of caution for sure excommunication from the Bible Belt — and a number of my friends — could make me stop. To quote Campbell, I had "...moved out of the society that would have protected...and into the dark forest, into the world of fire, of original experience. Original experience has not been interpreted for you, and so you've got to work out your life for yourself. Either you can take it or you can't. You don't have to go far off the interpreted path to find yourself in very difficult situations."

There was no end to my fall from grace, even though it took my husband years to identify my changed beliefs and attitudes as seismic shifts exposing personality traits long buried, rather than as annoying opinions provoked by PMS. Eventually, the futility of hanging on to our so-Sixties, trophy-wife/three-piece-suit/three-martini-lunch/kids-in-private-school marriage got through to him, and he gave up insisting we patch the cracks in the sidewalk when I was hellbent on re-landscaping the entire yard.

After grad school and catching fire with imagined potential, I barely resembled the white-gloved child bride who said "I do," in a pink-and-white wedding deep in the hidebound Piney Woods of East Texas. Grief over President Kennedy's assassination on my twenty-first birthday catapulted me straight into the arms of picket-fence comfort. Now twenty years later, one Alamo City morning with purple Mountain Laurel in bloom and decent grades to my credit, I took a sobering look at myself and saw a wild-woman wannabe rather than wistful Dulcinea. Thanks to the inspiration of Jungian analyst, Clarissa Pinkola Estes and her mystical *Women Who Run With the Wolves,* for the first time in my life I grasped the beauty of being a woman, solitary and empowered in myself, not second best to men. Loving men — my man in particular — you bet. Longing for partnership with my equally loving man? Absolutely. In Houston I was still a girl, but San Antonio made me a woman anxious to step forward and own my half of adult responsibility for our family. Not walking ahead of my husband (I might not lead) or straggling behind (I might not follow) but settling into an easy gait alongside his wide stride.

At the end we had been together for twenty-nine years, a long time to remain coupled in unyielding roles. But the shift to an egalitarian partnership which might have saved us was simply a leap we couldn't take. Especially since my conservative marriage could only understand such concepts as equivalent to Devil worship. In the end I still loved him, but I could no longer love us.

My sister stayed very married to an attorney who practiced his litigious skills in the banking world. From the beginning of their relationship, Jo's husband and I seldom connected heart-to-heart as I wanted. Doubtless this was due to my free-thinking attitude which cut both ways. It seemed to me that my brother-in-law clearly, if reticently with guarded legal appropriateness, condemned the heresy of divorce: mine in particular. And why wouldn't he? After all, the break-up of a long-standing marriage is completely unthinkable in a Tammy Wynette, stand-by-your-man culture. What if some of my free-and-single vibe rubbed off and infected his wife with the wild-woman virus?

Only days following my freedom walk through courthouse doors, I realized a stray female threatens married women. Especially if said stray is the one who decided, "Enough!" This divorcee-aversion appeared equally true for relative strangers as well as for-real relatives. And forget about being invited to dinner parties of your former — also very married — friends. Does a woman instantly morph into a *femme fatale* simply because she is divorced? Well...maybe...as soon as I bought fuck-me pumps and made a trip to Victoria's Secret to get my single-woman game on. Come on. Did I really ache for Wedgwood and Francis the First? Hardly. I was done pouring wine into Waterford.

Predictably, these past six divorced years, Jo and I had

less in common, a shift in worldview which Mother's traditional burial ceremony magnified. Wherever she was, Mother undoubtedly felt pleased that her uber-funeral requirements proceeded unflawed. Most likely, she also felt proud of the newspaper article: public acknowledgment of her Fine Old Family. Unfortunately, my transcendent connection with the exquisite beauty of Mother's ephemeral soul was now gone, gone with the wind.

The perfect irony of my mother's departure from planet earth during this eerie holiday season didn't escape me as Lacie and John, Sarah and I shuffled luggage into the back of the Jeep and prepared to hit the road for Longview and Mother's funeral. After all, yesterday was Halloween and today was All Saints' Day, a Catholic holiday for honoring the dead. Catholic or not, Mother was among them, with her funeral-home visitation tonight at 7:00 PM. And there was more. She would be buried tomorrow on the Christian holiday of All Souls' Day, celebrated by San Antonio natives as *Dia de los Muertos*, The Day of the Dead. Spiritual folks somehow agree that the souls of the departed are loosed this time of year when the veil is apparently thin between this world and the next. If there was ever a good time to die, Mother chose the very best.

These next few days promised to be long and emotionally challenging. But fortunately, Lacie's husband — a substantial six-foot-one, blond hunk of a guy with a round face and crinkly eyes — volunteered to drive. Except for considerable difference in height, John and Lacie could have been twins, they looked so much alike. From the first night we met, Lacie's then-boyfriend felt like one of us. I didn't have to evaluate his offer to chauffeur, but snatched the mindless opportunity to stare out on the Andrew Wyeth countryside, sepia-toned with autumn fading into winter — a perfect match for my brooding mood.

Glancing over my shoulder for reassurance, I felt grateful for these daughters curled up in back seat as they had only days before, to and from Mother's bedside in Houston, and countless times when they were children. Would I forever picture them as young and innocent? This wasn't difficult since both barely grazed five feet. Not that height ever held them down when it came to being mouthy or stubborn, should the need arise. At five-foot-two, I would forever be taller than my daughters. Even so, Lacie was twenty-six and Sarah twenty-two; I considered them grown. And yet, knowing that confrontation with mortality is the absolute death of innocence, my heart hurt for them. What was going on in their heads? Did they feel at peace about Mother's death, or were they unsettled? Their relationships with Grandmother Bebe enjoyed a plethora of interesting moments.

Since the tyranny of conformity ruled my childhood, freedom of expression seemed the greatest gift a parent could offer a child. Above all else, I wanted my girls to discover who they were for themselves. I didn't want them to be like me, or their dad, or anyone, but who they were naturally, from their own creative impulse. As long as their freedom wouldn't land them in jail or make me a grandmother prematurely.

Working this out day to day with *please*, *thank you* and learning responsibility for their actions proved challenging, especially in Lacie and Sarah's relationships with Mother. Once the girls became teenagers and their personalities seemed pretty well set, I took a breath, backed off and prayed for a minimum of bloodshed. Lacie had her way of dealing with Mother, and Sarah had hers. When *Bebe* was difficult and overbearing (when was she not?) Lacie made a joke and slid away with a giggle. But then, Mother never instructed Lacie's boyfriend — as she did Sarah's — that he should wear boxers, not briefs which were tighty-whities and would make him impotent.

Not long after Sarah explained the meaning of *impotent* to her boyfriend, she and Mother chatted on the phone one afternoon. Standing at a distance and not paying attention to their conversation, I swiveled to attention when I heard Sarah scream, "Fuck you, Bebe!" My delicate daughter hurled the receiver and stomped away, slamming doors as she went. Probably, Mother shared further birds-and-bees wisdom, although I'm not sure what was said because I considered the content of their conversation private and ab-so-lute-ly had no interest in taking it on.

Sarah and Mother were actually closer after that: a line drawn, a boundary established and respected. And Lacie and Mother were kindred spirits from the beginning somehow. Thinking through their relationships, I smiled inwardly. The girls had little to regret, nothing left unsaid, no dangling ends. No irreparable damage had been done by allowing my daughters to be themselves.

In this car I would be the only one who felt costumed for a Halloween party. The only one wondering if I could survive immersion in *Old Longview Society* without tearing my clothes and running down the street like my hair was on fire. Maybe a better person wouldn't overreact as I was doing. Better person I was not. I had moved beyond Flewellen pretense and dreaded returning to the scene of la-di-dah crimes of self-importance.

Our solitary funeral procession from San Antonio to Longview would take at least eight hours of bumping north through a succession of minuscule East Texas towns which the twentieth century had forsaken. I let the window down a little way, hoping the autumn chill might cool my irreverent attitude. It didn't help. I couldn't locate a transcendent bone in my body. My one-note brain could only obsess about whether my wardrobe would represent Mother as she would wish, and did I remember to pack the pearls?

Satisfied I had reworked as much family history as any human could tolerate, with still six hours to go until we reached Longview, I slumped against the door, closed my eyes and prayed for unconsciousness, or at least a nap. This wasn't to be. Out of the blue a voice shouted, "Sandy!" Startled out of my self-imposed stupor, I jerked around and scanned the back seat. Sarah and Lacie were asleep. Clearly, no warm-blooded creature in this car had called my name. "Sandy! Listen to me!" the frighteningly familiar voice said. "I have something to say to you."

An electric shiver vibrated my scalp and bolted down my spine. I knew *what* this was. I knew *who* this was. I didn't want to believe it. I stole a sideways glance at John to see if he heard the voice. Eyes front, John purposefully steered this car of grieving women toward two marathon days that couldn't be fun. No clue evident that anyone was aware of the disembodied voice which demanded my attention.

In shock, I swiveled toward the open window and feigned rapt adoration of the landscape, while inside my head I screamed: *Oh my God! It's Mother! Angelic spirits aren't pushy. She's an effing ghost!* I shuddered, afraid even to breathe. Then sat deathly still, pretending I was invisible so she might overlook me after all and float away somewhere.

No such luck. Mother's throaty *Texas Tawk* shouted in my ear, directionally located at my left elbow as if her ghost was straddling the cup holder on the console beside my seat. "Sandy! Listen to me!"

I answered in my mind with as much self-control as I could manage. *What, Mother? You don't sound sweet. I expected sweet.*

Acknowledging her presence did at least tamp down the agitation in her voice. The next communiqué came through as if it were holy writ, minus incense and candles: "You are my lineage bearer. You can do what I could not. Take care of your sister."

Feeling stunned and furious I shot back, *What the hell are you talking about, Mother?* Such arrogance! Defining me based on who I am in relation to her: a retread of our earthly relationship. Giving me orders to take care of Jo, like she always did as I watched her breeze out the door of Mamo's house dressed fit-to-kill for her day of who knew what with whom. *Mother! Don't you know you're dead? Oh my God! I can't believe you! You didn't cross that bridge. You have seriously messed up. What do you mean: lineage bearer? Take care of Jo? Are you nuts? If you're a ghost, then can't you spy on people? Don't you know Jo and I aren't even speaking? She doesn't need — or want! — me to take care of her. And what lineage? I have to say, your request sounds loaded with pretense.*

Silence.

Long silence.

My adrenalin pumped; my synapses snapped; I felt so frustrated I wanted to cry. Until this wretched moment, I believed my earthly struggles with Mother were a wrap; a now-you're-gone-and-we-all-love-each-other fade with only her funeral left to endure. Not so. This was nothing like the love-and-light hospital room experience. This was the Mother I loved to hate.

Mother! Listen to me! Don't do this. Ghosts are miserable creatures. It's unnatural. It's wrong. Go to God, Mother! Go to God!

Silence.

Mother! Talk to me!

Silence.

Unwholesome silence.

I can't do this, Mother. I love you. I knew you'd be back, but I didn't expect you'd be pushy. I expected a guardian angel who would come when I asked for help. Let's talk. Come on! Don't do this hit-

and-run thing. It's bad. Very bad. You're making me crazy. You started this! Now talk to me, dammit!

Silence.

Inside of me something crumpled and folded into existential angst. So this is the way it was going to be. Nothing had changed. We were back at the beginning, or maybe at the near-distant ending when she left San Antonio in a blaze of haughty contempt. She was queen. She proffered declarations. Her subjects hastened to respond.

My funk deepened. Lifting the window and curling against the seat back, I pretended to sleep. I was far from it. Measuring my options, I hunkered down inside myself and mapped out a battle plan:

No, I won't do it her way. I'm actually holding the stronger hand. I'm a walking-around, flesh-and-blood mortal. Mother is far from grounded. She's a restless spirit, a ghost on a mission. Not returning to me as an emissary from the Great Mother as I'd imagined, parting the Red Sea and lighting the path I tread. My good-fairy fantasy has no relation whatsoever to the present, horrendously tedious fact: My mother is still my mother.

I felt desperate to alter the tenor of her demands...and make her go away. Clearly I needed to employ every bit of diplomacy I could muster. *Mama. It's me again. I'm sorry I got angry. How about we start over? I'm giving you benefit of the doubt. I get how this might work in ghost world. Maybe you're not saying anything more because you've spent all the* Ghost *strength you've got. I saw the movie. So here's the deal: I'll listen if you'll act nice. Why not try a little kindness on me? It works much better.*

You want something from me? To be your lineage bearer? Is that like carry your banner, or what? Honestly, right now you make me tired. Please consider the cruel and unusual circumstance: We're on the way to your funeral. Did it occur to you that your family might need something from you, too? How about this: Help us get through the next few days and I'll get back to you later...

OVERCAST SKIES ROLLED ACROSS East Texas while a Roto-Rooter snaked through my head. One hairpin curve after another I attempted to make sense of Mother's ghostly visitation… *hum…*visitation. *Like the way that sounds: ghostly visitation. How about lose ghostly…just plain old visitation? No need to designate Mother as an official ghost…even if she is. Visitation sounds better…feels less apocalyptic. Admitting the truth — my mother is a ghost — is beyond weird. An ordinary life suits me just fine. I'm actually missing it quite a lot. Instead of normal I'm looking at the world from this sinkhole I've fallen into. Questioning my reality. Not trusting myself.*

Am I going crazy? Talking to myself? Like that lock-up ward patient, a two hundred fifty pound, over six-foot guy I talked down from his no bigger-than-spit bedside table where he perched on all fours like a frog on a toadstool — so terrified the whites of his eyes filled his entire face. THEY were coming to get him, so he said. I get it. Feels like Mother is after me. But visitor *instead of* ghost *is good, like Mother just dropped by for a Coke and then would be on her way, driving her Buick LeSabre with the Native Texan sticker on the back bumper.*

My vomitous brain was relentless. All the way to Kilgore I Roto-Rooted and chewed on my cud like brown and white Herefords meandering across ashen fields, grazing on hay bales tossed at random intervals behind barbed wire. Chomping on indigestible flotsam, swallowing and regurgitating *ad nauseam,* gagging on Mother's visitation message: "You are my lineage bearer. You can do what I cannot. Take care of your sister."

How could this be happening to me? It just isn't right. I can't feel any way but pissed at her for hanging around telling me what to do when respectable people go ahead and depart for the Great Unknown. She ought to know better. Amy Vanderbilt would never approve of crashing a party uninvited. HER party, for God's sake! Her fricking funeral. This is so wrong it can never be right. And what am I going to do about it? I am so clueless about how to proceed.

Unable to swallow Mother's lineage-y, Fine-Old-Family-ish bullcorn, I chewed on the delivery: Wilma Foster's uniquely throaty, mashed-potatoes-in-the-mouth Texas Tawk. *All right. So I've got a Texas accent too…and I'm sort of fond of it. But do I push it, exaggerate it? Use it to emphasize my Texicality which is only slightly lower than the angel's? So annoying to have a mother whose elevated self-worth makes God seem like a wimp. So wrong. So impossible to change. Even now when she's supposed to be dead. No matter how I cut it, I heard Mother. Not the suggestion of a voice as I've been fortunate enough to experience once I sit still long enough to listen for the still quiet voice that mystics talk about. No. There is no hint of Holy here. This is flesh-and-blood Mother with the ego in, not deboned, easily digestible, angelic fodder. She even shouted to get my attention…like always:* "Sandy! Listen to me! I have something to say to you!" *We had played this scene time after time, rebellious reluctant daughter to conniving coercive parent, in-your-face hollering which must have entertained the neighbors.*

OK, so consider the possibility that I am *nuts. Then what? As soon as this funeral is over and I'm back in San Antonio I call a shrink. Tell them Mother died and I'm so crazy with grief I'm hearing voices. A little Prozac. A lot of Xanax. Done. Nice tidy little bottle of cures and it's over.*

Nope. Not gonna fly. I heard her. I know I did. I need to trust it, figure out what she's saying and fix it if I can.

Are you there, Mother? Would you be willing to share your specific expectations? Please, flesh out what it is you want from me in contemporary terms I can understand. I'll be delighted to do your bidding if this satisfies your last wishes before you roll on into the Hereafter. Come. Let us reason together. Sound like a plan?

With Longview's Rader Funeral Home only fifteen minutes away, I felt like an overused fingernail file that has lost its grit. I rummaged in my purse for lip gloss and lowered the mirrored visor, putting on my face, cleaning up my act.

Without thunder or lightning as warning, tumbling gray clouds dumped buckets of Texas-sized wet, smearing the windshield with flat, broad blobs of chilly rain, instantly dropping the temperature. The Jeep came alive as Lacie and Sarah in the back seat and John behind the wheel wriggled in their seats, making ready, chit-chatting about what to expect when we arrived for the *visitation. There was that word again. But at least at the funeral home there should be a silent viewing. One can hope.* I sighed and focused on the rhythmic thump of the windshield wipers which sounded like a metronome and might potentially lull me into a sense of harmony... as long as I stayed in the here and now, and forgot that my mother still roamed the earth.

John slowed the Jeep and eased through the slippery four-lane boulevard on the outskirts of Kilgore. Glancing toward the intersecting crossroads before I bronzed my pale and pasty cheeks, I noticed a prehistoric blue Ford sedan rolling to a stop. But fate had other plans. Like a bad dream, the blue Ford shot across the boulevard and clipped the left front fender of the Jeep. We spun across two lanes. The Jeep mounted the curb and shuddered to a stop facing in the opposite direction from the traffic flow.

The blue Ford guy pulled up on the side street, got out and walked towards us, staggering as he went. Quickly a sheriff's car showed up, red lights rotating, while a stream of rubberneckers slowed down for their Friday afternoon thrill. The driver — a toothless old guy with skin lined like dried tobacco leaves — flapped his mouth with explanations for the wreck, claiming to have been "a Kilgore native all my life" — as if this gave him license. John traded my laminated State Farm insurance card for the old guy's lop-eared Allstate and discussed the wreck with the officer while the old dude kept at it. He apologized for darting into the intersection. "Thought I could make it," he said. He had only "gone out for a quick run to the 7-Eleven, you see."

I didn't have to be a Phi Beta Kappa — which I'm not — to realize this guy's old buddy, Lone Star, rode shotgun. But there would be no Breathalyzer test, no DWI issued. Not that I really cared. My insurance would cover the loss and I honestly felt sorry for the crippled and toothless old man. But why did the county mounty look the other way?

The answer was stated plainly for strangers who read Texas, or for expats whose memory is more calculated than mine. In the past few hours, as we drove deeper into the thick of the Pineywoods, the more I had noticed roadside signs which warned the wary, "This is God's country. Don't drive like hell through it." John got the point and didn't speed. Soon, we would also get the drift.

In wrapping up his accident report, after Lacie, John, Sarah and I remounted the Jeep, our homeboy deputy appealed to a sense of reason which made no sense except in these here parts. "Sorry about this, folks. He does it all the time," he explained. Offering additional pertinent information, the deputy draped an elbow on the driver's-side window just as the sun erupted from behind a cloud and blindingly glinted off his wire-rimmed sunshades. Toothily, he boasted that the son of this Kilgore relic was his "law-enforcement *compadre*. Like a brother to me." But there was more. "East Texas takes care of its own," the officer declared with a sickly sweet smirk that said, "We don't tolerate a ruckus around here. And if you don't like it you had best get on…if you know what I mean."

We were shiftless drifters and he was John Wayne running us out of town. Clearly — and hadn't I said so myself? — I no longer belonged. I wasn't mad, really, maybe a tad amused that the Old West was alive and well. But more, I wished to hell it was tomorrow at this time and I was sitting behind the wheel, steering us home the long way around Kilgore and these here parts.

As John righted our unattractively creased vehicle and we headed on towards Longview, vastly late, totally bent, I felt more powerless and out of control than I had all day. Not only because of the accident but because I began to wonder how hard it would be for a ghost to manipulate a boozy old guy with a history of accidents. Whether she had a hand in this or not, I got the message: If I thought I could dictate to my mother — the Queen of Mean — without blowback, I was wrong.

At the funeral parlor we found Jo and her husband in the casket showroom with a shiny pewter number, the patina of heirloom silver, chosen as Mother's final resting place. Or, more specifically, the repository for her earthly remains. Jo proceeded with signing the moneyed contract for the hovering funeral director as I explained the reason we were late. Clearly, my sister wasn't buying the wreck I was selling. I don't know what she was thinking, but her actions screamed displeasure. Her single raised eyebrow and saccharin smile reminded me of Bette Davis…or maybe it was Joan Crawford…in one of those grainy black-and-white midnight TV movies I succumbed to when I was a boy-crazy teenager and couldn't sleep. I could almost hear the thrumming of strident violins as the leading lady poured tea and fingered the vial of arsenic hidden beneath the white lace napkin in her lap.

I was onto my sister. I knew where she was: mad instead of sad. I suppose your only sister not being there when you need her is as good a justification for anger as any. I couldn't blame her, but shouldn't the Anger Will Get Me Through, family battle flag expire with Mother, or at least retire? How were we ever going to get through this if we didn't find a way to love each other? We were all the family we had left.

My loving-family myth be damned, it soon became clear that I wouldn't feel warm and fuzzy anytime soon. The segueway from the casket room to the frigid funeral-home chapel — good for bodies, not so great for people — hardly facilitated a friendly mood. Like a church altar, Mother's closed casket perched front and center at the end of the oblong room, with rows of chairs arranged on each side facing, and an aisle down the middle. Church. It was laid out just like church. I exercised restraint and didn't explode into gallows humor with an Episcopal minister's bellow, "Let us pray." Rather, as an alternate plan for dealing with what seemed to me, a macabre Halloween scene, I scavenged my personality for a scrap of civility.

A more reasonable person than I might acknowledge that some people actually *like* funerals: the noble marble marker, the ritual of commemorating birthdays and Christmas, flowers on the grave, a place to remember and mourn. *Remember and mourn, that's where things get iffy. Would Emily Post recommend mannerly remembering and mourning when a spirit has abandoned the body and meanders hither and yon?* I was at it again. Driving myself crazy trying to find an unmovable standpoint where I could plant my feet and make sense of this theater of the absurd.

How I wished I could tell someone what was going on. There was no one. I racked my brain trying to remember when a friend ever shared her mother's refusal to go quietly into that good night. *Like never. Nobody can get this. Not my friends.*

Definitely not Jo unless and until she tells me Mother is chatting with her, too. Nope. Not happening. Too much of a stretch. Dead people talking to you is too New Orleans-y. Too Black Magic-y. Magic equals witches, equals hellfire-and-damnation to good Sunday churchgoers. Errant spirits might as well be the Devil.

At least Mother hadn't shown up since I told her to buzz off a few hours ago — however immature and ill-advised my lashing out at her might have been. But her body was laid out in that coffin. *We're not talking Easter here. This is Halloween.* My creep level increased, a brown haze of anxiety coloring everything my eyes could see.

To deal with my agita, I arranged yellowing family photographs on the lectern beside the pewter casket, making the room appear welcoming and as if we expected mourners. If anyone read the obituary and article in yesterday's Longview paper and was brave enough, they should arrive soon. It takes courage to attend funeral services since burial weekends are bound to remind us we are mortal and might be next. This was especially true for the aging Longview populace, the only ones I expected might make the effort and come tonight, or maybe tomorrow for the actual cemetery interment.

I doubted any of my high-school friends would show. I was here for our last class reunion, but few of us resembled the senior photo nametags pinned to our chests and this puts a crimp in conversation. Sure, resurrecting our *Seventeen* years and denying that *Gidget* could use a lift was entertaining. But truthfully, relationships with the rest of my old crowd and come down to, "Great to see you again, and don't you look great!"

My two soul-sister friends, Ann and Cheri, were another story. Through the years, weddings, babies, highs and lows, and living in different parts of the country, we were never far apart in spirit. Cheri — shorter and blonder — and I had been friends since we took our first walks together, at a distance and out of sight within our mother's tummies. But she lived in Chicago, and the trip to Longview for the funeral was a stretch. My other close friend, Ann — tall and lanky with almost black curly hair — was the new girl in Mrs. Bowles's fourth-grade class at First Ward. Cheri, Ann and I remember how we became BFFs — best friends forever — beginning with the first recess. In high school I escaped to Ann's for sleepovers almost every weekend. Sneaking out was a workable option. The weekend Ann's sister got married and her daddy smuggled two bottles of pink champagne to the greater girl group proved exceptionally memorable…especially Cheri's midnight moon bath on the broad hood of a chromed-up Chevy. Ann and her husband were out of pocket this weekend, but I never doubted the faithfulness of these two true friends. Without spaces in our togetherness we would connect later, after the crisis passed and I needed them the most.

An empty room wouldn't be surprising really, since none of us — Mother, Jo or I — had lived in Longview for twenty years. But solid memories of the good times filled up the empty spaces well enough. At least a respectful number of flower arrangements flanked Mother's casket, indicating that several someones cared enough to send their very best and might even come tonight.

Curious to see who still felt connected with Mother, I held my anxiety together by reading the enclosure cards. An impressive spray of white lilies was signed "Edwin Booth." If I remembered correctly, Edwin represented the only remaining Flewellen kith and kin. In confirmation, beneath his name Edwin had signed: "For the Family." So that was promising, and good to know that there were people out there. Feeling encouraged, I hurried along to read the gift card on a gargantuan spray of roses, lilies and gladiolus. Among the names, I recognized "Dorthea, Eloise…," but I couldn't picture the faces of the remainder of Mother's eight girlhood friends.

Beside the showy arrangements, a cellophane-wrapped pot of yellow mums looked sadly out of place. This card simply read: "George Foster." I gasped, and staggered as if an earthquake had shaken the floor. My hands tingled. My face felt numb and spots floated before my eyes. *So he knows Mother died...knows about her funeral. Dear God. I can't do this. George Foster...my mean, horrible, scary father!* With my heart pounding in my ears, I whirled to face the double doors, my head spinning with memories. Memories forgiven, forgotten and so long past, even his name — George Foster — echoed like a malevolent character in a Faulkner novel. I never intended to lift this book again.

I don't know if I looked as panicked as I felt, but Sarah slipped beside me and wrapped an arm around my waist. "Aren't they adorable?" She gestured toward the clatter of refined older women who swept through the doorway like a gently spirited gust of wind. "They must be Bebe's old friends, all dressed up for a party. What you bet they went out for dinner and a glass of wine beforehand? I can picture Bebe right there with them." Arriving at seven o'clock sharp and clicking along on two-inch heels, more than any of the gentle souls in a crowd which eventually numbered close to fifty, Mother's friends helped us get through the night.

Even as I carried on my own conversations, I couldn't take my eyes off Sarah and Lacie. My girls were enchanted: giggling, tossing their heads back with infectious laughter, completely captivated by Mother's long lost sisterhood. While Edwin Booth, the husband of one of Mother's favorite cousins — startlingly thin and white-haired since we last saw each other so many years ago we couldn't remember when — and I shared stories about "those crazy Flewellens." And while I chatted with storekeepers, neighbors and acquaintances of Mother's, my eyes kept roving towards Lacie and Sarah. As I worked through the crowd and finally joined this sisterhood, their shared stories about Willy — their pet name for Mother — the parties, shopping, "cutting a rug at the Reo Palm Isle and having a helluva good time," made me realize that these soul-sisters were better than family.

Now I understood, now I saw their faces. In Mother's last years she shared that the worst thing about getting old is losing your friends. Much as she must have wanted and needed to be close to me and my girls, and then with Jo and her family in Houston, we were a poor substitute for these Longview women who still hung out together and fiercely loved each other.

The girlfriend memories were mostly about the War Years. "When we were young and gay," Mother would say. Or was she saying? Who cared, anyway? For this enchanted moment of spellbinding sharing, analyzing the origin of my thoughts seemed almost sacrilegious. No matter how — or if — Mother edged her way into the conversations, I could only imagine the bliss she must feel re-living the high times before Pearl Harbor and America's fated agreement with FDR, "The only thing we have to fear is fear itself." The aching lovers' farewell kisses, honeymooning in the car, girlfriends gathering in front of the Philco to hear Edward R. Murrow report troop movements and casualties. Rosie the Riveter and the War Effort, personal comforts sacrificed so soldiers on the battlefront could be fully equipped. Cars painted only black because color demanded greater factory production needed for tanks and planes. And then V-Day with Boomer babies like me slung on their hips and G.I. Joes returning home in a ticker-tape shower of hope, renewal and vowed promises that this country would never again go to war.

With every memory shared, I fought back tears, feeling tender, touched by the love. I couldn't get enough of their animated expressions, their giggling interruptions, details tumbling around like kittens batting a ball of yarn. These gutsy gals had been through so much…together. Without each other, they wouldn't have made it. And there I had been…a tiny baby completely unaware. Window peeping into Mother's life, woman-to-woman for the first time, my impatience and pissiness seemed embarrassingly childish. I ached for this woman I had never known as these friends knew her.

Feeling wrung out, I sighed with relief as the echoing funeral parlor emptied at the close of two emotionally charged hours. In farewell, Dorthea — Cheri's mom — never one to shrink from saying exactly what she felt in spite of being Texas chic, with dramatic white hair and her waist cinched with a classy Judith Lieber belt, cornered me affectionately. "Get something to eat, Sandy, you've lost too much weight. And get some rest. You've got dark circles under your eyes." She squeezed my shoulder and smiled. "We'll see you in the morning."

Dot — as the girl gang called her — was real, a woman of independent means earned from years of hard work and smart investment, sure of herself, the mom of one of my two best friends and the woman who I just now realized had modeled permission for saying what was on my mind not with anger, but with love and concern. I hugged her feeling weepy. "Love you, Dot…always have…always will. You have no idea how healing you and all Mama's friends have been for us tonight."

As footsteps of the last visitor echoed up the hallway beyond the double doors, I was beyond ready for Vitabath and a pillow. Even though a Rader employee shutting the chapel doors seemed to end the visitation, the evening was far from over. For all the tender affection of the night, and monumental relief that my father hadn't appeared, I felt less than eager when the funeral director glided quietly to my side and whispered, "Would the family like to view the casket?" Maybe curiosity made me want to look — empirical evidence that Mother had indeed departed her body — and maybe wistful thinking. Following this endearing evening of recollection surely Mother could celebrate how well her lineage held up. Maybe she would feel motivated to claim her heavenly life, and I could sanely get on with the business of making peace with her death. Creeped-out or not, motivation for closure drew me towards that casket.

Jo's handsome son, Reagan, over six feet tall and essential for this job, assisted the funeral director in cracking the weighty pewter lid. Lacie, Sarah and I held onto each other as we stepped forward and peered over the beige velvet lining into the casket.

With only an appalled first glimpse I backed away and grabbed my mouth to smother a gasp. Mother never did this to herself, rouged her cheeks and painted her mouth pink. She was a natural sort of girl with an olive complexion and reddish brown hair; her skin glowed with warm oranges and rusts. This plasticized corpse reminded me of the Kewpie doll prize Mother won at a Dallas State Fair shooting gallery. And that beige wool suit — probably Ben Reig, her favorite designer — with fourteen-karat and pearl earrings at her ears made the overall image an excellent candidate for a Fifties wax museum. Yet ghastly as this likeness seemed, I was drawn, impelled to make Mother's death real, to begin the actual, physical goodbye. I wasn't thinking. I acted without consideration, stepped forward, leaned down and kissed her rigid, cold cheek. Waves of nausea rolled over me and I tasted bile. Abruptly I jolted backwards — horrified that I might heave in the casket — and retreated for those double doors, with fresh air my destination.

But no amount of distance could erase the image — or feel — of Mother in that casket. And as I would soon learn, I wasn't the only one feeling sick.

Settling in for a brief night at the homogenized Executive Inn, before Lacie joined John in the connecting room, she cozied up to me on the edge of the king-sized bed Sarah had already climbed into. I hugged Lacie and wrapped my arm around her shoulders as she pointedly asked, "Mom, did you get anything when you were looking at Bebe?"

Her question jolted me and I cringed. "Get anything? Yeah. That was an undertaker's fantasy. Mother wasn't there."

"I know." Lacie cocked her head to one side and riveted me with an unblinking gaze. "She was standing behind me, Mom."

"My God." I shivered and goose flesh popped up on my skin. "Lacie…tell me."

"Well…" Lacie shrugged her shoulders. "Bebe was just there behind me, like she was looking over my shoulder. I didn't really see her, but she talked to me."

"What did she say?" I whispered, feeling my body go numb.

Lacie sighed and with sadness in her eyes continued. "Bebe said, 'I'm sorry I did it this way. I had no idea. Please forgive me for putting you through this.'"

This was one of those nights that wouldn't let go. Sleep was no friend of mine. All night long I stole the covers from Sarah as I thrashed my way towards morning. My head kept spinning and spinning, like a washing machine wringing out wet clothes: *Of course Mother can get through to Lacie. Of course Lacie would hear her. I suffer from terminally unique thinking. This is a family affair. Me. Lacie. Can Sarah be far behind? But how do I handle this? Draw a line and say, "Everybody who talks to dead people please step forward." No. Not even funny.*

So where am I? If anywhere? I have decided not to demonize Mother. That's something. She isn't the Devil. This isn't Salem, Massachusetts. It's Texas. And in Texas people are friendly. We visit. So, she's not a ghost. Mother is a visitor. I have made progress. But this situation requires a lot of Hail Marys.

Maybe I could co-opt Lacie and Mother's relationship style. They're agreeable…even pleasant. But then Lacie always had me for backup whenever Bebe's fur stood on end. I protected Lacie. And I know how. Maybe I should trust myself to do and say the right things. Truth is: I'm pleased with my catfighting skills. Depending on Me, Myself and I was my only protection from Mother's meltdowns. Developing self-reliance has done me a world of good.

But still…I'd like to hear, "Please forgive me for putting you through this." That's nice. Feels good. Nothing I've ever heard from Mother's mouth. We fight. We argue. We disagree. Nobody backs down or admits fault. Maybe in part that's what this is about. Taking our relationship to the next level. Establishing rules of decency. Repairing what's broken. But how?

Toward dawn I dozed off, and as sunlight seeped around the edges of the blackout drapes, I woke with a disturbing dream: *I'm dressed in a long white gown, apprehensively walking along a narrow basement hallway lined with antique doors arched at the top. My arm is stretched high, holding a flickering candle, the only illumination. I suspect what I'm looking for is behind one of these doors but I can't decide which one and freeze, clutching the burning candle, knowing I need to take a step before the light goes out. But uncertain which door to open…*

A CHILLING AUTUMN WIND stirred the almost naked sycamore, elm and oak branches. In stiletto pumps I picked my way down the cemetery lane, careful to avoid spraining an ankle on the hard nuts dropped by summer-weary sycamore trees. ("I hate those spiny little balls!") Mother's narrative voiceover, a running commentary detailing the back story, rattled in my ear. Her spirit was with me this morning; I heard and felt her, in step, walking beside me.

And even though my eyes felt gritty and my jaws ached from teeth grinding, evidently something shifted in me during the sheet-wrestling night. This morning, instead of feeling irritated and angry, I felt a surge of admiration for Mother's passionate aversion to these silly sycamore nuts. She loved and hated hard, no wiggle room, just devilish determination to have her way with you. Like that one Christmas I remember when Mother and the sycamore balls had an intimate relationship. ("The white, silver and gold Christmas..." Mother explained.) With Jo and me as backup, Mother scouted Longview and scavenged a basket full of sycamore nuts wherever they fell, in whoever's yard. Then sprayed the spiny nuts gold and dangled them — along with silver and gold glass balls — from our perfect white-flocked tree. At the moment I felt fairly gilded myself.

I shivered in my thin silk suit as cascades of yellow, gold, red and rust leaves ("Caught in a devil wind...") plummeted to earth and swirled around my feet. The smell of fresh creosote from Highway 80 running alongside Grace Hill Cemetery, and bacon-y, waffle-y aromas from the Waffle Shoppe just up the road, wafted over me. My stomach felt like I'd swallowed broken glass. Fortunately, I hadn't eaten breakfast, so there was nothing to throw up.

Jo and I — and the Great Wilma's five grandchildren — arranged ourselves in an informal receiving line as Mercedes, Buicks, Cadillacs and a solitary Rolls-Royce maneuvered into place along the graveyard's bumpy macadam lane. As they had promised, several of Mother's closest girlfriends had come and now parked beneath a grove of trees. They waved and nodded at a distance, allowing space for another group of less familiar faces to offer their regrets. The consistent stream of Longview gentry, women elegantly suited in muted fall shades of silk and wool, men starched and pressed in bankers' suits and wing-tipped shoes, flowed before us in a memory-provoking wave.

Among them, a genteel older woman approached with a satisfied smile wrapping her face. White-gray hair swirled in a twist and pearls clasped at her ears, she daintily clapped her manicured hands and cooed, "I'm Evelyn Cloninger. You won't remember me, but I surely remember your mother…and your Foster family as well. I talked with your aunt yesterday morning after I read the obituary. I see she's here this morning, as she should be." I had no idea who she was talking about, and didn't want to know. Whoever they were, I hoped they kept their distance. Mrs. Cloninger cradled first my hands and then Jo's between her soft palms as she effervesced. "Oh, my. Look at you two girls! Lady Di and Jackie O! Wilma would be so proud!"

Jackie O. She must mean me, I realized with shock. Since nothing in me claimed *Fine Old Family*, this lovely woman's observation felt mildly horrifying. But at the same time, it was gratifying to realize my disguise worked. Cloaking my true self behind a coffee-colored Chanel-style suit, my hair stained an Aveda shade of brown, traditional brown suede pumps on my feet — even if the heel was slightly slut puppy — and of course wearing essential pearls that I had remembered to pack, no one would suspect this heartland conservative had morphed into a touchy-feely wild woman who runs with the wolves.

I glanced at Jo, five feet seven, reed thin, dressed in an understated taupe suit, blond and elegant whether she tried to be or not...the once and forever Lady Di. With agreement rarely reached over the past few years, Jo and I smiled at each other in mutual understanding of a job well done: *Mrs. Cloninger got it right. Mother would be pleased.*

And yet, it occurred to me we had both chosen not to wear black. Hard as it was to admit, this telling choice hinted at the truth. I felt relieved Mother's tsunami personality could no longer inundate my life, and suspected Jo felt the same.

Never mind the teensy detail that Mother walked beside us, invisible to the eye, without a white sheet or gauzy apparition — so far — but freely offering commentary as she chose. No way would I share Mother's ghostly decree of a few hours ago: "You are my lineage bearer. You can do what I could not. Take care of your sister." As far as I knew, Jo was not a true believer in things that go bump in the night. Yes, we agreed that Mother had eyes in the back of her head, but only as our joke, not as acknowledgment of Mother's Morgaine le Fey-ish ability to see, hear and perceive things beyond what ordinary human sight, smell, taste, touch and hearing reveal. My sister would hardly welcome this information — assuming of course that Mother wasn't getting through to her, too — and things were going too well at the moment to self-destruct.

But even without lobbing thorny information in Jo's direction and cringing in anticipation of the certain fallout, things weren't going as well as I hoped. With each carefully coiffed and suitably suited expression of sympathy, I felt tighter. We didn't have to rend our clothes and pour ashes on our sackcloth, but a tear or two would have helped. A quiet moan would have been nice.

Who was I kidding? We weren't set up this way. Civilized people don't *do* that. Public displays of emotion are right up there with swear words and cleavage. Passion is best expressed in private, behind closed doors where all the secrets are stashed. I was onto myself. Much as I wanted to believe the real Sandy didn't live here anymore and had become immune to textbook etiquette, not only did I look the part, but I obviously remembered my high-tea manners. Pleasantries slid from my mouth like marmalade on a muffin. With every "It's so kind of you to come," I felt more stunned. I performed flawlessly, choreographing cordial euphemisms, captured in the voodoo of my childhood. I was so mired in phony I couldn't manage one heartfelt response to these faithful souls who loyally honored Mother's passing.

If I hadn't been depressingly preoccupied with observing my Fine Old Family mask slipping into place, I might have felt sorry for the Presbyterian minister, ill-equipped to offer his prayerful presentation beneath the green undertaker's tent. He had no idea who my mother was. But he had agreed to do the job. One would think, he would also have done his homework, perhaps read the article in the *Longview News-Journal,* or looked up the Flewellen page in the commemorative *Longview Texas Centennial,* and could therefore speak well of the Flewellen family from whence Mother came. (Narrative voiceover from Mother: "This is your family, too, you know!")

Focused only on the enormous relief I would feel when this ordeal was over, I was thoroughly unprepared for the shock delivered by a small woman in blue. The minister wasn't the only one who had done his homework. A long-abandoned past was coming home to roost.

At this graveside moment, since I was five years older than Jo and present for the interminable dramas before her birth, I was the lone executrix for the dissemination of sordid family history should I care to go there…which I did not. Jo and I hardly grew up in a traditional *Father Knows Best* family like the other Longview kids. None of my classmates came from a *broken home*: the euphemism for *divorce,* a concept so foreign the word itself was unspeakable. Avoiding our swampy past was easy though, since there were no childhood photos to pore over and wonder about. Not a single one.

With no father or recorded past, and a shadowy present, throughout our childhood Jo and I were isolated from the rest of Longview society. Why? Because — or so Mother and Mamo said — our family was *better* than most of the people in our speck of a town. When I was little, I speculated that those other people might have leprosy, the disease Mamo told me about, which killed lots of people back in the old days.

But by the time I was in high school, I realized Mother spent Jo's and my childhood years crafting our coming-of-age wardrobes from Tara's green velvet curtains. She introduced us to the holy grail of Longview society through membership at the Pinecrest Country Club, where we sunbathed in Catalina and lunched in Lily Pulitzer, rubbing elbows with Pineywoods' elite. Teas and luncheons followed, given in honor of our Longview High School graduation and then our weddings — the motivating reason for all the fuss — captured for all eternity in Who's Who-signed guest registers displaying matching Kodachrome smiles alongside our hostesses, established behind white linen, Waterford and Royal Doulton.

Because of this stellar upbringing, Jo and I recognized the names and faces of Longview gentry who had come to pay their respects. But I had no clue about the identity of the small, gentle woman dressed in blue, who approached with a soft step but determined gleam in her eye. I shot Jo a questioning look, hoping she could identify the blue lady, but Jo frowned and subtly shrugged.

With no time to solve this mystery, the stranger with the kind smile was upon us, a plastic Piggly Wiggly grocery sack in her outstretched hands, as if this explained her arrival. "I read the paper this morning and knew I had to come," she said with a thick East Texas drawl. "Wilma wouldn't approve, but she's gone now ("Ha! Little does she know..." Mother snorted), and I couldn't stay away. Here, I brought these for you." She pressed the grocery sack into our hands. "These are pictures of you girls when you were children."

I went mute while my mind bounced from corner to corner in search of memory. Jo must have looked as shocked as I felt, because the blue lady laughed and hurried on in a rush of words. "Oh, I'm sorry. It's been over forty years. You were just children. I'm Aunt Margaret. Your father's sister." She smiled and patted my arm. "You were the flower girl in my wedding, my little blond Sandy. Do you remember?"

She beamed at Jo. "And you were the cutest little baby ever."

Stunned, I opened the plastic bag, whose contents Jo and I pounced upon. Yellowed photographs spilled out. Posing in front of a round-hooded car, what appears to be a mother, father and grandparents disconcerted by a curly-headed girl who wriggles to be free of her father's grasp. ("Wasn't George handsome?" Mother chortled.) A beautiful young woman is perched on high porch steps with a tiny baby in her arms. ("See, I told you I was pretty then!") In matching dresses, an older girl grins and grasps a smaller girl's hand.

Never before had I seen these images. My heart thumped as I leafed through one emotionally jarring photograph after another. Then my eyes fixed on the picture of a grinning girl wearing a party dress. Tightly she clutched a bridal bouquet.

I gasped as a rush of recognition pulsated through me.

Incredulous, hardly capable of taking in the information, I blurted out, "Margaret? That's me! Isn't it? I remember the blue dress with flowers in my hair!" I looked up from the photographs. "And you're her, aren't you? The pretty girl who got married?"

Margaret laughed. "That would be me." Just then the funeral director approached and indicated with a nod of his head that the service should now begin. As quickly as this stunning revelation had begun, it ended with so much left unsaid.

Shaded beneath the canopy that billowed in blustery November wind, chairs were arranged four across in neatly ordered rows. The funeral home representative gestured, and murmured softly that the immediate family should sit in the front two rows.

I took my seat, third chair on the right; first my sister's husband, then Jo, then me. The chair beside me was empty. In a coupled, linear world, these four chairs made perfect sense. The funeral home didn't know whether Wilma Foster's two daughters were both married or not. But the unoccupied chair beside me hardly felt vacant. It was taken. Mother's spirit was there, quietly observing, perhaps daunted by the finality of her burial...as I was. At least for the moment she wasn't buzzing in my ear. I wished for a second that my girls' father occupied the empty chair. After all, Mother had the nerve to die on his birthday. He certainly deserved a final complaint. And there was a sunlit boy who made me laugh. Crowded, much too crowded, this empty chair beside me.

Mother's casket swayed on brass fittings and creaked above the crudely disguised hole in the earth, the only sound as an expectant hush fell around us. Futilely attempting to mask the truth, ashes to ashes and dust to dust, a carpet of garish green Astroturf rimmed the burial site. In the stillness, I took a deep breath and then another, imagining I was steady and strong like an oak. Only my best therapeutic visualization wasn't working. The branches of my oak tree wouldn't stop trembling.

Twisting around in my chair, I glanced behind me. Reassured that Sarah, Lacie and John sat within reach, I patted their knees, offering motherly support. When really, I felt like a small child incapable of supporting anyone. Anxiously, I surveyed the sea of gentle faces, searching for Aunt Margaret, but I couldn't find her.

After the young Presbyterian minister's brief but thoughtful sermon, I stood on weak knees and faced the kind faces. As the clergyman and I arranged in a phone conversation the day before, I added my voice in honor of Mother, "I'm reading a poem from Kahlil Gibran's *The Prophet,* about death. This is for Mama." I raised the book heavenward, then lowered the thin volume and read the whole poem, which closed with: "For what is it to die but to stand naked in the wind and to melt into the sun? And what is it to cease breathing, but to free the breath from its restless tides that it may rise and expand and seek God unencumbered? Only when you drink from the river of silence shall you indeed sing. And when you have reached the mountain top, then you shall begin to climb. And when the earth shall claim your limbs, then shall you truly dance."

Several people made eye contact and smiled with tenderness in their eyes, seeming to understand the choice of this prose, given the desperate, breathy illness that had claimed their friend's life.

As I slid back into the chair, the squeaky metal no longer felt cold and forbidding. Images of Mother sliding down moonbeams, free at last, bathed me with airy tranquility. She wouldn't always be a disembodied voice popping in and out of our lives here on earth. Eventually Mother would achieve whatever it was she had returned to earth to accomplish. One day she would literally see the light and begin to live her greater spiritual life.

As I bathed in the warm glow of forgiveness and understanding, Jo touched my arm. She inclined her head toward mine, and hissed, "Why wasn't it enough to allow the minister to perform the service?"

If she had slapped me, I wouldn't have felt any more shocked. With a thud, my energy deflated. I felt like Icarus who soared so high he almost touched the sun, only to melt his wings in a blast of solar heat and crash back towards earth.

What is wrong with her? My mind raced to make sense of my sister's contempt. *Doesn't she know the time-honored tradition of family members rising to acknowledge their departed loved ones? The Baptists do it. Even the Episcopalians do it!* It hadn't occurred to me beforehand that the words of a Lebanese prophet — no matter how profound or meaningful — are ill-received by followers of John Calvin and his ideological ancestors who defined this Presbyterian soil on which I trespassed.

Stifling a gasp, I commanded myself not to move, not to respond; not to twitch an eyelash. I wanted to smack my sister. Something I had never achieved…but recently been inclined towards. Figuratively, I stuffed a sock in my mouth and groped toward an internal, hoped for, peaceful center. The tranquil, still God-place where nothing said externally disturbs the cool waters.

Knowing the Gandhi-esque thing to do is one thing. Doing it is another. And for an opinionated woman like me, excessive self-talk is required: *Stop the karma. Just walk on. Take no hostage. Inflict no wound. Let there be peace on earth. Let it begin with me…*

REACHING FOR NOON, the sun arced high in the cloudless November sky. The goodbyes and thank-yous had all been said and the cemetery deserted except for my sister, her family and mine. Sarah, Lacie and I stood in the hot sun, pinched by high-heeled pumps and funeral suits, while John stood vigil at a respectful distance. We waited.

A short stretch of marble gravestones away, Jo and her brood huddled around an open map pressed on the hood of her Acura. They pointed and gestured, naming streets and figuring out directions. I wished they'd hurry up. We couldn't wait much longer.

But instead of leaving, Jo cheerily breezed up to us as if we were peaches and cream and none of the nastiness of the past week had ever happened. *How does she do that?* I asked myself. *Pretend nice. When I'm schlumpy I can still pull off nice…with nice people. But my sister has pissed off Precious. The best I can manage is to say very little and resist a phony smile that makes my teeth itch.* "Before we head out for Houston, we're going to take a tour of Longview," Jo said with a *Vogue* smile guaranteed to sell copy. "Maybe go to Mamo's house and see if we can get inside. Everyone's curious. I want to show them where we lived. Y'all wanna come?"

I managed an ironic grimace and said, "Maybe we'll catch up to you later. I want to make sure things are finalized here. Thanks, anyway."

"Okay. We'll miss you," she said and hurried off on a sightseeing sweep.

Satisfied that Jo was out of sight, I approached the two

gravediggers — gnarled and bent like ancient oaks. Awkwardly they leaned on their shovels beside the mound of freshly dug red clay soil, a trace of impatience on their faces. In preparation for burial they had removed the tarp that disguised the naked mound of earth during the service. I made my request, decided upon during the restless night, "If you don't mind, we'd like to shovel the dirt on the casket."

I could almost read their thoughts: *What ize wroooooong wid 'dis woman? 'Dis ain't 'de way 'de white folk does it.* I wanted to hug them and say, "Your being here means the world to me." But they could hardly understand my burst of gratitude for their black skin, or the cascade of memories their presence evoked. Seeing their faces, I came home to the best part of my childhood.

It wasn't only the musical lilt in their voices that had seeped into my East Texas blood. By osmosis if not by birthright, I felt part black and as if this was the better part of me. What did I know of the hardship that African-Americans faced in the segregated south? Nothing at all. As a sensitive adult, I realize it's an insult to claim "I feel part black" without having lived through the ridicule, humiliation, abuse and contempt they suffered because of the color of their skin. But for a child growing up in a household of uptight, neurotic and depressed southern white women, Annie, *the maid,* and Anderson, *the yard man,* were the sanest people in my life. Their lowly titles hurt my feelings, as if they weren't human beings but only human *doings.* When to me, these two kind and tolerant souls represented human warmth and salvation.

"Annie is high yeller," and Anderson, "black as the ace of spades," my grandmother said. This led to the conclusion that shades of black determined who you were. The closer to white...the better, smarter and more reliable. The closer to deep black...not good. I didn't see their color. Mamo had no clue who Annie was to me, *my other mother,* just as Anderson was *my best daddy.* She would have had a fit and fallen in it if she understood I adopted her *colored help* as my make-believe parents.

Annie and Anderson treated me like I was a real girl, not a Madame Alexander doll to show off in public. Their manner of expressing themselves was so true, to the point and without pretense that I mimicked their style. Under their wings, I could act like a child instead of pretending — with little success given my temperament — that I was the little lady my mother and grandmother expected me to be.

Annie and Anderson's pet name for me was Little Chitlin, although they never let Mamo hear them refer to me this way. I understood that because I frequently got it wrong just like them, they wanted to protect me. Often, Annie warned me, "Yo' betta watch yo' mouth chile." And shared Annie wisdom I would remember all my life: "Now yo' listen to Annie. Who yo' is, is who yo' is. Yo' don' needs to fight about it. Yo' mama and yo' grandmama is et up wi'd sorrow. 'Dey can't he'p 'demselves. 'Dey don' mean no harm. Best yo' can do is jes be yo'self. God don' 'spect no mo' from any of us." Annie saved me from many a switchin'…until things got so dreadful I had to fight, no matter the consequences.

Since grumpy Mamo drove me to First Ward every morning during the school year and parked her Buick at the curb every afternoon, waiting to bring me home, there wasn't much daytime left for Annie. From September through May, Annie went home after spreading supper on the metal kitchen table. But in summertime, silly school didn't interrupt my real life lessons.

In the wintertime when frost was on the ground, I couldn't see much of Anderson since he pruned, hoed, raked and swept daytime weekdays. But before and after school I trailed after Annie, making beds, cleaning toilets and oiling the mahogany, safely shielded behind her broad bottom. With white flour flying in Annie's kitchen sanctuary I learned to cook biscuits and dumplings, scale and fry bigmouth bass Mamo caught on Lake Cherokee, and truss a chicken for baking. Annie even looked the other way when she discovered my box of kitchen matches and pack of Viceroy cigarettes that I hid beneath the large stone step-up to the lean-to colored bathroom without a door, out back, tucked into one corner of the detached garage.

In contrast to Annie's kitchen wisdom and good-natured grumblings, Anderson silently tolerated my shadowing him as he gardened, shuffling along unhurried like a big old bear from the Uncle Remus stories. Summer heat, spaded earth, fresh grass clippings and man-sweat blended into a strong scent that smelled just as safe as Annie's kitchen.

Anderson was as kind to me as Annie. Although he was particular about keeping the St. Augustine lawn and azalea beds manicured, Anderson permitted my untidy animal burial grounds, which I dug into the front side yard beneath a canopy of crepe myrtle and bridal wreath.

I glorified my burial grounds as animal, when the small graves were actually the final resting place for earthworms fried on summer sidewalks, crickets, grasshoppers, doodlebugs and an occasional lizard whose destiny had been determined by the cat next door. Beneath miniature twig crosses strapped together with ivy vines, you couldn't really tell what sort of body was buried there, anyway. And besides, the effect of row upon row of crosses was quite noble. Sort of like the final resting place of fallen soldiers in Arlington Cemetery. Anderson said he believed in the Hereafter even for my bugs, and he conspired with me to keep the graveyard secret.

Anderson betrayed me only once, and first warned me he must. One late summer afternoon, while raking my splendid play house secluded behind bushes and vines spanning the length of the two-story garage and tool shed, Anderson discovered petrified poop. These scandalous remains had collected undisturbed all summer long. Deposited secretly and efficiently into the well of a low, concrete birdbath whose lid set aside made a perfect potty. Quite clever of me, I thought, impatient with the foolish idea of going inside when necessities could be tended to right then and there. Yet this pile of evidence represented an intolerable affront to Anderson's gardening sensibilities, and demonstrated such grave disrespect that he "tole' Miz' Elizabeth," just as he said he would.

"Nudin' ain't wrong wid' me," I wanted to answer the gravedigger's stares, and sob with appreciation for their blackness that was so full of light. They were not Anderson. They were not Annie. These rugged souls only appeared worn and tired, and rightly so with a job to complete and be done with it. But their supportive presence seemed like angels in disguise: a gentle gift from God. A gift I needed.

Still haunted by the specter of Mother's grotesque Kewpie doll death-mask, it was past time to put it to rest. I wasn't alone in this. The looks that Lacie, Sarah and I had exchanged beside Mother's open casket last night spoke chapters of distaste. Remembering, my throat felt tight and choked with disgust, finding release only as I pierced the earth with a spade.

The wooden shaft felt solid in my hand. Hefting the dirt was absolute, substantive grief I could get my heart and mind around. *Scrunch...s*hovel points penetrated the loose soil. Twist, turn...*whoosh.* In benediction and prayer, clumps of red clay soil rained on my mother's gleaming pewter casket. *Scrunch...whoosh...scrunch...whoosh....*

My daughters and I shoveled in silence. Before long I sweated like a field hand, sopping wet, filthy dirty, but feeling alive for the first time in days. I didn't want to stop until the casket was completely covered, the red clay heap flattened, my mother's body entrusted to the forgiving earth.

The six-foot gouge was filled halfway when Lacie gently grasped my arm and pointedly looked into my eyes. We held the gaze. Sarah stopped shoveling and leaned on the wooden shank. The moment froze. I took a breath, stepped back and measured my daughters, the feminine line between us unbroken: The Great Mother...to the Great Wilma...to me...to Lacie...to Sarah. Separate and unique but of one blood, a tender sense of unity brought tears to my eyes. The tightness around my heart let go. Collapsing into finality, I nodded and said, "It's over." Then turned and handed the shovel to the black man with the outstretched hand.

Hurrying sundown, the sun dipped in the sky as the ancient black men bent their backs in rhythmic cadence, completing the task that Sarah, Lacie and I had begun. The double shot of adrenalin zinging me these past six days emptied into a puddle around the bumpy, red-clay-clumped soles of my shoes. Suddenly depleted, I stared as the men shoveled, feeling rooted to the spot and unable to move. *Now what?* I asked myself. *Mother's body is in the ground. Nothing left to do. Just empty. No. That's not totally true. There's still family…living family...the girls…and John, who honestly feels like a son. Jo, not so much. At least not now. Later. We always have a second act even if it's next year. I might not be ready before then. But we're still sisters. Nothing changes that.*

And then I remembered: *Margaret, now there's Aunt Margaret after forty-seven years, family, close family, loving family if I can trust the warmth of her smile, which I do. It's almost unbelievable. How do we do this? Pick up where we left off when I was seven? That's awkward.* With a sigh of relief, the Sandy who Margaret seemed to remember flashed before my eyes:

Pollyanna before I became Dorothy trapped in Oz. *Those photographs. I put them in the car. Little girl with starchy ruffled dresses, long blond curls, dancing eyes…innocent eyes. This is a definite improvement from Jane of the Jungle (Tarzan's girlfriend, climbing forbidden trees, swinging from branches, scraping a hefty rock on the concrete until it resembled a knife) who I became when I was thirteen and life changed forever.*

I opened my purse, and checked to make sure I had Margaret's phone number. As we parted in a jumble of feelings when Mother's graveside service began, I had almost forgotten to ask how to contact her. Hastily on a Post-It note I scribbled her number with the familiar 903 East Texas area code. When we would see each other, I didn't know, only that we must.

But to know Margaret was to know my father again…an unhappy thought. Clearly, he lurked somewhere in the Pineywoods.

"Mom!" Sarah startled me out of my journey to Mordor. "Let's go! I'm starved, and I've gotta get out of these clothes. Is there somewhere we can change?"

I threw my arm around Sarah's shoulder and squeezed. The relationship with my youngest always felt like a comfy pair of jeans. "*Awww…Pobrecita.* You must be exhausted and starved. Me, too. I know a great little Colorado-ish cafe downtown where we can eat. It won't be too weird to change in the bathroom." I grabbed my keys. Arms around each other, Sarah and I headed towards the Jeep where Lacie and John waited.

"Hey, you two. Are you hangin' in?"

"Just barely," Lacie said, her face the color of newsprint. "I'm hittin' the wall." Coming from an Energizer Bunny who dreams of some day climbing Mt. Everest, this was *sirus* — Lacie's toddler pronunciation of serious that stuck.

"No wonder, honey! Look what we've been through.

Let's go! Hey, how about I drive for a while and give you a break?" John shrugged, smiled and ambled toward the other side of the Jeep. He's not a talker, that one, but in his silence, the soul of support.

The *bumpity-bump* of familiar brick streets laid a century before sent me whizzing through a time warp. "I'm taking a teensy detour here, you guys. Hang in for a minute. The cafe is only a few blocks away."

"Just so it's quick," Lacie piped up from the back seat.

The Arlene Movie Theater where in seventh grade I first held hands with a boy was closed. I tried to locate the radio station where my high-school boyfriend and I, along with our crowd of "going steady" friends, broadcast the "Teen Time" radio show. I pictured his lanky gait, black-rimmed glasses and earnest brown eyes, crop of dark hair I liked to run my fingers through. As always when I thought of him — my first love — I smiled inside.

The broadcast building had lost its Fifties façade and been stripped to reveal the original brick architecture. An important-looking brass plaque with the name of a prominent Longview law firm was fixed to the brick wall by the front door. Bustling Longview of the Fifties — streets lined with wide storefronts, neon signs, broad plate-glass windows and women's shop mannequins — was no more. Viable commerce had migrated to far-flung suburbs, deserting the courthouse square and brick streets, now eerily quiet. I pulled up in front of Martins — the only women's dress shop still standing. Several well-dressed customers entered through the same double plate-glass doors I had breezed through countless times. "Wow, I can't believe it. Martins is still here. If you guys are up to it, I'd love to check it out after we've eaten and changed clothes."

"Sure, Mom." Sarah placed her hand on my back, and gently steered me across the street toward the cafe while I rattled on about fall, winter, spring and summer shopping trips, miserably tugging my blossoming teenage body into too-tight dresses. Certain the sun would go down before I met with her approval, I modeled for Mother where she perched on the couch in the oversized oval fitting room with ghastly, revealing, ceiling-to-floor mirrors. "How awful, Mom," Sarah said. "Bebe couldn't have made me do that." I laughed in agreement, remembering that Mother didn't do too well when she tried to make Sarah conform. But I couldn't let it go at that and said, "Trust me, honey. If you had been her daughter, it would have been a whole 'nother thing."

Scrunched down in a cozy leather booth and satiated after chugging several cups of coffee and inhaling a turkey panini, I almost felt human again. Soon we would be home, and my laid-back Hill Country front porch would restore me — body, mind and spirit. Bare feet propped on a hand-hewn column and sunrise shouting, "Hallelujah!" to a gloriously uncomplicated day.

But in reality, eight hours stood in the way. And there was one more thing I simply *had* to do. As we angled toward the Jeep, I negotiated. "How about this, you guys? I'll trade you Martins for something more important. It won't take long. It's on the way out of town."

Threading irregular downtown streets, I found my way to the turn-of-the-century Nugget Hill neighborhood, took a left on Charlotte Drive and pulled up in front of my Grandmother Mamo's house. Commanding a rise on the hill, in my mind and in my dreams this was the home of my childhood. As I remembered it, the house was a substantial brick colonial with square columns, large central door and four symmetrical windows across the wide front porch framed by dark green shutters. I cut the engine and gaped at the modern incarnation. The shutters were gone. Ochre paint wrapped the once white, painted-brick exterior. The whole structure seemed smaller than I remembered, and the front door panels had been replaced with beveled, leaded glass panes.

The collective sigh from the back seat was audible. "Don't worry," I reassured my family. "It'll only be a minute; five max." I didn't want to go inside. Frankly, the idea felt overwhelming. I only wanted to breathe in the smell and feel of this place from a safe distance, absorb the past and lie it down. Shovel dirt on memories within my mind and say, "Amen."

Within seconds my emotions spiraled downward into entangling muck. *Maybe this wasn't such a great idea,* I thought. Rather than closing a door, taking in the home of my childhood opened a cavern that echoed with Mother's ghostly declarations: "You are my lineage bearer. You can do what I could not. Take care of your sister."

For the first time since Mother dumped this on me yesterday, I took a look at what she might mean. *To bear: to hold, to carry. It's possible Mother was just stating the obvious: I carry family memories. Well, don't I? Isn't that what I'm doing here? Remembering.*

This was an altogether depressing thought. If Mother stated fact — like maybe she knew things I didn't yet know — then would I fulfill what was beginning to feel like her prophesies? I got it. This thing wasn't going away. Right now not only Mother's visitation but what she had to say felt bigger than I wanted to know.

I started the engine and eased the Jeep away from the curb, heading home. Nightfall would wrap around me in a few hours, drawing me into myself. But even without darkness I had crawled into the cave of remembering. I was here...at the beginning...the day Mother, Jo and I arrived back home. I didn't know it then, but we would live with Mamo for six long years…

A mirage of heat vapors radiate from the red-stained concrete walk. My twenty-six-year-old mother leads the way while my two-year-old sister and I — seven years old and convinced I am grown — trail in her wake.

Mamo apparently heard the horn honk. Uncle Gene, Mamo's brother and Mother's uncle, picked us up from the airport. When he saw Mamo standing in her front door, Gene honked a second time, waved and noisily drove away. We are trapped. Instead of rushing down the sidewalk and hugging us hello, my grandmother steps no further than the front porch. Puffing on a cigarette and blowing smoke in our direction, she stands beside the massive front door. At least she has opened the door wide, but I know she's not happy to see us. The angry look on her face flashes like a caution light. I feel nervous.

With every step I'm thinking this is a really bad idea. About halfway up the walk, I can't stand it another minute. Grabbing Mother's skirt, I jerk. "Mother!" Jerk. Jerk. "Listen! I need to ask you something." Mother turns her head, glares at me and frowns in disapproval. I keep on. "Why does Mamo look so mad? She's scaring me."

"Shhhhhh." Mother stomps her tiny high-heeled foot, places a finger to her lips. "Shhhhhh. Be quiet, Sandy. Just go on." She pushes me forward, waves over my head toward Mamo and in her most cheerful voice shouts, "Hi, Mother! Aren't you glad to see us?"

I can't be put off this easily. "Wait!" I pull on Mother's arm. "Stop walking! I think this is a bad mistake. You said Mamo would be glad…our coming home to live…like you did at the Old Home Place when your daddy was murdered. She doesn't look…."

Mother gasps, grabs my shoulders and shakes me. I have said too much. Now I've messed up for sure. Mother shoots an anxious glance in Mamo's direction to see if she heard me. Satisfied that no damage has been done, Mother rasps in my ear, "Shut your mouth, Sandy. What happened to my daddy is none of your business!" She punches my chest with the flat, stiff fingers of her right hand. "Don't ever mention that again. Now march up those steps, young lady." She turns me around and pushes me toward the front steps. "Go...go...go..." Over my head she sails a peace offering. "I'm sorry, Mother. Sandy is just a little tired." Push...push... "We're worn out. Can we come in?"

Mamo smiles, but I can see she isn't pleased. She drags another puff off her cigarette. Mother is acting cheerful, but I don't have happy thoughts: Mamo is mean! How am I going to stand living here? I don't know the answer, but I do know what to do next. Pretend pretty like Mother is doing.

In a sing-song voice, I say, "We're home, Mamo. I love you, Mamo." Smiling my best make-believe grin, I tiptoe to kiss her wrinkled cheek, which is all but hidden beneath bright pink rouge.

Mamo stiffens. "No need for that," she says. Then glares over my head to the spot on the sidewalk where Mother and Jo have come to rest. "You're not fooling anyone. No love lost here. Even a simpleton could tell that. Come in, Your Highness." Bowing low, Mamo gestures with a sweep of her arm. "I knew you and these children would come back sooner or later. It might as well be now."

II

PINEYWOODS OF EAST TEXAS

Sandy and Jo on Grandmother Mamo's front porch

MAMO MADE HER HOUSE RULES clear on that terrible day in the Fifties when Mother, Jo and I flew home to Texas and walked up her red-stained and every-which-way, marked-up sidewalk. The walk was supposed to look like big stones, I guess. To me, it only looked fake. "My house was brand spanking new when Lacey and I built it in the Thirties!" Mamo hollered at Jo and me before we put one foot past her icky Victorian front parlor. "And I intend to keep it that way! You hear me?" This was gonna be awful because Mother says we are "home to stay."

"Yes, ma'am," I say, feeling insulted. I didn't intend to mess up her pretty house. I never had before in the many times Jo and I spent weeks at Mamo's while Mother went away to be with our Army father. I didn't make a mess at my Grandmother and Grandfather Foster's house in Marshall, either, all those other weeks when Jo and I stayed with them. It was all a blur, really, the moving, staying here and then there. But for sure, packing and moving into the several houses that Jo and I shared with Mother and our father during the past seven years, Mother had taught me to pick up my clothes, put up my toothbrush and comb my hair. I was completely tidy.

Besides, I liked Mamo's pretty house. Except maybe the front two rooms, all stuffy with mauve velvet settees, fussy chandelier lamps, and marble-top tables that tilted when I played underneath and grabbed a tippy corner. And maybe not the stiff dining room with long mahogany trestle table where Jo pack-ratted her secret supply of cookies. But the wide hall with the huge mirror at the end was excellent for dancing up and down, and playing monster. And Jo's and my bedroom — off the hall with Mother's bedroom behind and a bath in between — had a cedar closet that smelled like outdoors and a high four-poster bed that Jo and I shared. Both places perfect for making tents and hideouts.

The sound of children playing was not one of Mamo's favorite things. Play had to be done very carefully. Attracting Mamo's attention was sure to bring a list of complaints: "Don't spill on the Aubusson! Stay off the Belter! Get away from the Duncan Phyfe! My poor, poor things!" Rugs weren't just rugs. Sofas weren't just sofas. Tables weren't just tables. Everything had a name. Everyone had a place.

Annie's kitchen was the best room in the house, white and wondrous with glass-paned cabinets and a tin-topped table in the middle of the room. Sweet Annie allowed me to sit on a stool beside the cook table and watch her bread fish, chicken, okra and eggplant for frying. "Now you jes' sit still and I'll lets you watch. But don' you be thinkin' I'ze gonna lets you worry my cookin'." Annie's round face crinkled into a grin and she winked one huge, twinkling brown eye.

Annie didn't really mean it when she sounded gruff. This was our game. I felt really bad for her, grumpy-sounding but soft and kind underneath…and maybe sad. I knew because I asked Annie once if she had her own children. She exploded like Coke spurting out of the bottle when it was opened too fast. "Sho' I have chi'ren!" I might have thought she was mad except I saw tears in her eyes. I didn't like that. It made me sad to think of Annie working here all day and missing her children. Annie didn't want to talk about it either. She turned her back on me and rustled in cabinets, mumbling about what we were cooking for lunch.

Even if she hadn't missed her own children, Annie had reason to be grouchy. All day long, she worked hard doing mother things, which somehow Mother and Mamo didn't seem capable of. Mamo's house would have been horrible without Annie. But even Annie's kitchen was dangerous sometimes. One day she was electrocuted.

We had just finished rolling and cutting dough into biscuits. Annie opened the oven door to slide in a baking sheet. At the same time, she grabbed the door of the refrigerator with her other hand to collect ingredients for our next cooking project. Annie froze to the spot, turned as white as the kitchen, hollered and shook. Not until Mamo went outside and flipped the breaker switch did Annie let go of the refrigerator and oven handle, stumble backward across the kitchen and land in a heap against the sink. Mamo slammed through the back door, rattling the jalousie blinds. She looked Annie up and down and then threw her head back and bellowed like a donkey hee-hawing, "Pshaw, Annie! Nothing wrong with you! It did you a world of good."

Annie didn't look all right to me, but she only mumbled, "Yes'um." No matter what you felt, this was the best way to answer Mamo.

Lucky for me, Mamo had two brothers, Gene and Junie, who lived in Longview, and two sisters, Nana and Bodie who lived in Beaumont. They were lively and entertaining. All four of Mamo's brothers and sisters were small, cute little old people with straight noses, long chins and wide-spaced eyes beneath straight strong eyebrows. I liked their mouths the best, generous with straight teeth and big smiles. Mamo looked pretty much the same, only she was wider and puffier. My great-aunts and great-uncles were all married, except Nana, because her husband, Nunca Nimma, had died. But it was okay because Nana lived in Beaumont on Calder Avenue next door to Bodie and her husband, Brother Charles. Mamo wasn't married either, of course. At least not right now.

Aunt Bodie was pink and flowery with honest-to-goodness rose colored glasses. Bodie loved practical jokes, like filling iced tea glasses with fake plastic ice cubes with dead flies inside. Bodie made me laugh but her husband, Brother Charles, was tall, scrawny and quite nasty.

Every holiday Bodie and Brother Charles' chauffeur, Spain — always wearing a black uniform with gold buttons and a gold front tooth to match — drove my great-aunt and great-uncle to Mamo's from their home in Beaumont. Bodie didn't drive because she had never learned how. Brother Charles could drive but he didn't have to, and so he didn't. They had Spain instead.

When they arrived for a visit, Bodie and Brother Charles stayed at least two weeks. Maybe more sometimes, like for the whole "holiday season" from Thanksgiving to Christmas and New Year's. They slept in Mother's room and shared the adjoining bath with Jo and me. Only when Brother Charles went into the bathroom he always made a mistake and forgot to lock the door. More than once I busted in on him. There he was, stark naked with a big thing sticking out in front that looked like the handle on an old-fashioned water pump I saw once beside a well in the country.

I was mortified! Brother Charles — in all his wrinkly nakedness — would smile at me and ask, "Sandy, don't you want to touch it?" Certainly, I did not! I always slammed the bathroom door so hard I was afraid someone might hear and come running…but they did not. I felt dirty and nasty because I saw Brother Charles, and so embarrassed I didn't even tell anybody about it.

After a while I learned to knock before I entered the bathroom. Even if Brother Charles said, "Come in, Sandra," I did not. Thank goodness Bodie and Brother Charles came to visit only in the wintertime and for Easter.

Sometimes, funny Junie and Gene would come to call on Mamo. They were quite interesting. Mamo entertained them on her comfy sun porch with wide chairs and slouchy sofas. Mamo's sun porch was situated off her bedroom toward the back of the house, with three walls of jalousie windows overlooking the St. Augustine terraces. Terraced rock walls separated the lower yard and goldfish pond from the upper yard where my playhouse hid — far, far away from Mamo's sight. When my great-uncles came to call, if I said nothing and sat so still a fly could land on my nose and I wouldn't move, I was allowed to stay and eavesdrop on their conversations. Mamo had warned me in "no uncertain terms" that I was "a bane to her existence." Besides that, I was "vaccinated with a phonograph needle." Near as I could tell, these were almost fatal conditions.

Junie and Mamo talked about gardening. Sometimes we all walked outside so Mamo could brag about her prize azalea and camellia bushes, or show off fat goldfish swimming in the rocky pond.

Gene and Mamo talked about the *all bidness* and put their heads together over bound, black-and-red ledger books. Mamo stored her books in the mahogany claw-foot secretary in her bedroom. The slant-front top made an awful *whack* when it was opened. I sort of liked the sound, though. It sounded important and businesslike.

During their visits, Junie, Gene and Mamo usually got around to telling stories about their mother and daddy, Mamuvah and Papaw — Philada Virginia and Junius Jefferson Flewellen. I liked the stories, but it made me sad that my great-grandmother and great-grandfather died before I was born. Junie, Gene and Mamo were really good at bragging about their pioneering stock, which as I learned from Mamo was different from the *stock* in chicken soup.

Papaw's daddy, my great-great-grandfather Thomas A. Flewellen, was a captain in the Confederacy and the first Flewellen to arrive in Longview after the War Between the States.

Captain Flewellen was even Mayor of Longview when our town was only ten years old. Maybe, they speculated, Thomas Flewellen stood on a piney hill that overlooked the wide Sabine River Valley, and he probably said, "It sure is a long view from here." And so our town was named, the town that Mamo's daddy, my great-grandfather, Papaw Flewellen, helped to build.

I couldn't keep all these people straight, but I liked seeing Mamo smiling and happy when she talked about the Flewellens. Actually, Mamo wasn't happy *unless* she talked about the hard-working ancestors. But it seemed to me something was wrong with these stories. If work was so good, then why didn't Mamo work? Or Mother? Really, I couldn't tell for certain if Mother worked or not. She left the house every day "dressed fit to kill," as Mamo described her outfits. I didn't know where Mother went or what she did when she got there. Wherever she went, Mamo didn't approve.

Junie and Gene didn't work either, even though they bragged about the Puritan Work Ethic and how hard Papaw worked all his life in the lumber business. What did Papaw's grown-up children do with themselves all day, anyway? They talked about how Papaw believed it was his "God-given duty to offer one son to God, one to the law and one to medicine." Then they would laugh and say, "He failed on all accounts." This didn't sound funny to me. It made me sad.

But asking questions was dangerous business. I learned to measure my curiosity, depending on the number of times I heard Mamo's empty Budweiser cans clink into the trash receptacle just outside of Annie's kitchen. When Mamo had drunk a lot of beers, Mother said she was "in her cups." That was a stupid thing to say. I never saw a cup. Mamo was in her cans. And that meant I was in trouble. If she was unhappy with me on many-beer-can days — and she usually was — Mamo had an ugly way of teaching me a lesson, much meaner than switching.

"Sandy! Sandy! I need you! Come here!" She would shout, sounding like she had marbles in her mouth. This was an ugly-day routine that happened often. Cleaning toilets was not nearly so gruesome. Mamo smiled a crooked smile when I finally made my feet walk through the doorway to her sun porch. Like always, she sat in the green chair surrounded by a circle of cigarette holes in the blue, red, green and white braid rug. Mamo wasn't really smiling, though. Her eyes narrowed to little slits, like dogs' eyes do right before they chew your leg off. Then she would point to the navy blue center circle in the braid carpet and make me stand in this exact spot. It was always the same.

"Did you know you look just like your daddy?" Mamo squinted at me through puffy eyes, wire-rimmed glasses crooked on her nose and a cigarette stuck between her stubby fingers. This is how it always started. "*Little Georganna*. That's who you are. The spitting image of your godforsaken-honky-tonking-sonofabitch father!"

Whew! I didn't think I was supposed to hear these words. They blistered my ears. For sure, Papaw wouldn't like hearing her talk this way if he was still alive to hear her. But I knew better than to say so. Mamo wasn't done with me yet. "Now, Sandy, recite *Georgy Porgy Puddin' and Pie* for me."

"I don't want to." I always protested — not begging, because that just made it worse, but hoping that maybe just once I could say "no" and Mamo would stop. It never happened. By this time I felt so twitchy I couldn't stand still, and was afraid I might wet my panties.

"Come on, Little Georganna. Make your grandmother laugh. I have precious little to laugh at anymore."

Before she finished with me, I always recited the whole nursery rhyme, usually several times. Mamo laughed so hard tears ran down her cheeks, causing the front buttons on her housedress to pop over her big stomach. Then afterward —

maybe for a whole week — I was cured of talking back or asking questions.

When we got to Mamo's, Jo hadn't been walking and talking all that long, so she got by without doing much wrong except hanging around on Mamo's sun porch. I guess Jo wanted Mamo to read to her or talk to her. But Mamo shouted at her if she got too close. "Leave me alone! Children are to be seen and not heard. You hear me?" Jo didn't fight or talk back like I did but just wandered off to our room, where we had books and toys.

I felt really sad for my baby sister. She looked so lonely. But she had me. It was my job to make her happy. I did, too. When I wasn't busy cooking and making beds with Annie or asking Mamo questions, I played dolls and school and read books to Jo. I felt really proud of how smart she was. In no time she knew her alphabet from the funny faces I made from each letter. And she could draw the ABC's in her Big Chief tablet, too, all the way to X,Y and Z.

Having Annie made me feel important and strong. In between my *Little Georganna* punishments, if I acted "civil for a change," brushed Mamo's hair before she took naps and rubbed Jergens lotion on her feet, I got brave enough to snoop again for answers that might explain all the "spite and malice." Good words for meanness, which I learned from Mamo. I collected lots of questions during those days when Mamo was mad at me.

This work business was at the top of my questions list. I itched for answers like I itched from chiggers when Mamo made me drive with her to collect rent from the "poor white-trash tenants" who lived in her "shotgun houses." Mamo said that walking to their front porches through the tall grass caused the chigger bites. I never saw those chiggers or a shotgun. But I felt nervous knowing they were there.

In the time before we moved in with Mamo I had seen

white people work. It was hard to remember, but I did…sort of…kind of fuzzy, though…not exactly like I saw things in front of my nose right now. But I did remember my Granddaddy Foster working every day at the Foster Butane business in Marshall. He usually wore striped overalls with a red bandana stuck in the left pants pocket or khaki britches and shirt. Sometimes I saw lots of men standing around in the dirt driveway at the back of the house. Not one of them was black. Maybe they didn't have black people there in Marshall and that's why the white people worked. The big garages where the trucks parked were right behind the high hedge at the edge of the driveway. I wasn't ever supposed to go back there. But I peeked, and so I knew what it looked like.

My Grandmother Foster worked hard too, cleaning the big old two-story white house and cooking breakfast, lunch and dinner. In between she hoed in her garden and canned fruits and vegetables. We picked wild blackberries on the sides of country roads and Grandmother made pies out of those. It seemed that almost every day Grandmother Foster washed clothes and hand-wrung them with the washer tub roller. At night she practiced piano because she played on Sundays for the church choir. Sometimes she took me with her. Grandmother Foster did lots and lots. So much work she sometimes had tiny beads of sweat on her top lip. When I stayed with them — before Jo was even born — I learned that laziness was a bad thing. I wondered why these Flewellens never learned that important lesson. They just collected money from other people's work.

"Why don't you work, Mamo?" I asked one afternoon right after she rose from her nap, before she had time to drink another Budweiser.

"Oh. So you've figured out that money doesn't grow on trees, have you?"

"Yes! That's why I'm asking!"

"Now don't you get all uppity, Miss Smarty Pants! If you must know, it was the oil boom and Papaw. There was never a better man on the face of the earth."

This sounded alarming, and I wanted to know why, so I asked, "What oil explosion, Mamo?"

"Oil boom, you *idgit*!" This meant ignoramus or idiot. I wasn't sure which. Probably both, and it wasn't good. "Didn't your mother teach you anything?"

"No, ma'am."

Mamo hurried to correct my ignorance. As the story went, in the Thirties while the rest of the country was almost buried by the Great Depression, Papaw Flewellen and his friends in the Longview Chamber of Commerce raised the excellent sum of $10,000 and talked oil-drilling companies into coming to East Texas. Wildcatters struck it rich in the thousand-acre Flewellen Big Woods and all over the East Texas Salt Basin.

No telling what they looked like! I got all excited thinking about those wild cats. *They were fierce, for sure…maybe like lions and tigers or a cheetah.*

Looking puffed up like a bullfrog, Mamo explained, "It only took three years. More than twelve thousand wells sucked *black gold* out of the ground." *I knew a few things, like about Fort Knox and all those gold bricks. But black gold? How hard was it to pull those big black bricks up that tiny little hole those wildcatters dug?* "When it was discovered in the Thirties, our East Texas Field was the largest in the world. The whole world! Can you imagine that, Sandy?"

"No, ma'am," I answered truthfully. "I'm having trouble figuring this all out."

"Well, just listen to me! You haven't got the sense God gave little green apples! Where was I? Oh, supply and demand. Here's the problem: Demand was low." Mamo frowned and went on to explain "supply and demand." I tried but couldn't keep up. When Mamo remembered how clever Papaw made the family rich, she kept talking about the *all bidness* like she was on skates, rolling so fast downhill she couldn't stop.

Even if I didn't get it all, it was probably important to understand that way back then only a few, fancy new Ford V8's roared around — one for every sixteen people. The thing was: the smart businessmen in the Industrial Age were only beginning to get excited about fossil fuel being terrific to add to Yankee coal and the steam engine for energy, and Yankee coal and steam business people got jealous. I couldn't blame them. It was like somebody doing long division better and faster than me. Truth is: I'm not very good at it and I get jealous of kids who whip out those long-division problems so fast at the chalkboard it makes me want to cry. Those coal and steam-engine people must have been good at energy and didn't like Texas oil and gas butting into their business and maybe being better than they were. So, the price of a barrel of sweet crude fell from its high of $1.30 a barrel to a stingy three cents. But "mineral rights would be Flewellen-owned *in perpetuity*. And that's a long time," Mamo said. The thought of *perpetuity* made her happy. But she never could stay that way for long.

Maybe I had trouble getting Mamo going, but there was no stopping her once she was wound up. "The oil ruined your mother, just ruined her!" Mamo hollered. "She's the black sheep of the family, you know."

"How, Mamo?" I felt excited to learn something juicy that I might be able to understand.

Mamo roared at me, her eyes burning red like a house on fire. "Well, hellfire! I'll tell you, so you leave me alone about it! Papaw had a stroke not long before he died and it made him sentimental. When it came time to deed the oil royalties among us, he gave your mother a child portion instead of a grandchild's share as was her due."

"Why did he do that, Mamo?"

Mamo smirked at me like I was one of those simpletons she accused people of being. "Don't you know anything, Sandy?"

"No, ma'am, I don't. Tell me."

Mamo wagged her head back and forth, and grunted. "*Uh...uh...uh*," talking more to herself than she was to me. "Never should have named her *Wilma*, after *Wilber*."

I could tell Mamo was winding down because she had started staring into the back yard, so I poked at her. "Who's Wilber, Mamo?"

"My brother!" Mamo shouted. "Caught spinal meningitis and died when he was in medical school at John Sealy in Galveston. At the end Papaw was so sick...couldn't bear hearing Wilma's name without thinking of Wilber. To make himself happy, Daddy gave Wilber's child portion of the oil royalties to your mother. Now, that's enough, Sandy!"

"Well, I think that's nice," I said, meaning Papaw was nice. I felt bad for Papaw, losing his son and being so old, sick and lonely for him. I was starting to get the picture. Somewhere down the line Mamo messed up. How else did she get so mean when her Daddy Papaw was sweet and kind? Right there on Mamo's sun porch I decided I wanted to be like Papaw. Definitely not like Mamo or any of my living family members...Mother included. They were a little batty.

While I was making plans about how I wanted to be, Mamo stared, lost in outside. She was a little slow sometimes. But then all of a sudden she realized I said the *nice* word and that set her off again. She whipped her head around, glowered like a Jack-o-Lantern and shook her finger at me. "You'd be the only one in the family to think there was anything nice about your mother, Sandy. When she got the oil money, Wilma thought she was rich. Miss Gotrocks! Got her inheritance at fourteen and bought a car. Chased all over East Texas like Lady Astor and she's still doing it to this day! Are you satisfied, now, Sandy? Shut your mouth and leave me the hell alone!"

Unlikely, I thought. *Highly unlikely....*

EVERY YEAR WE LIVED with Mamo, I felt older, smarter, and stronger and could tell that Jo was, too. Mamo seemed to notice. I don't know if I made it up because I wanted so much to have Mamo feel better — and treat us better — or because something changed with Mamo. But it seemed to me that as we went along she drank fewer cans of Budweiser.

Sometimes when night fell and Mamo dialed the Zenith to her radio programs, she even invited Jo and me to sit with her on the sun porch. Mamo had two favorite programs: *Gunsmoke* with Marshal Dillon, Miss Kitty, Doc and Festus, and the *Inner Sanctum Mysteries* with that scary squeaking door. It was even okay to talk during the radio programs. Mamo would repeat something like, "...the whole shovel full Miss Kitty" — which Festus said in his whiny country voice. Then she would laugh and mimic Festus over and over again, and so would we. Afterwards, on some especially funny nights, all three of us would act out the whole show with voices and everything.

Other nighttimes when a Blue Norther blew in and the jalousie windows rattled from the north wind, Mamo reached for books by Mark Twain, and read aloud as long as Jo and I could listen without wiggling. Mamo called her Mark Twain books "these treasured Flewellen volumes from the Old Home Place." And explained, "These are the same books Papaw read to us when we were little like you girls are." The soft and gentle way Mamo held the wine-colored books with gold writing, I sometimes felt like we were in church. In fact, Mark

Twain's words made me feel better than the preacher's sermon in the First Presbyterian Church at Eastertime:

"The frost was working out of the ground, and out of the air, too, and it was getting closer and closer onto barefoot time every day…and then right away it would be summer and going in a-swimming. It just makes a boy homesick to look ahead like that and see how far off summer is. Yes, and it sets him to sighing and saddening around, and there's something the matter with him, he don't know what. But anyway, he gets out by himself and mopes and thinks; and mostly he hunts for a lonesome place high up on the hill in the edge of the woods, and sets there and looks away off…and everything's so solemn it seems like everybody you've loved is dead and gone, and you 'most wish you was dead and gone too, and done with it all.

Do you know what it is? It's spring fever. That is what the name of it is. And when you've got it, you want — oh, you don't quite know what it is you do want but it just fairly makes your heart ache you want it so!"

Listening to Mamo read, I sort of wondered if she was telling about herself somehow, and not Tom Sawyer. She never said so, and I never asked. But knowing what I knew about Mamo's lonely stares out onto her back yard, Tom's ache without a name seemed to be Mamo's ache, too. And besides, Mamo's sharing these stories she loved, and Papaw loved, and the whole Flewellen family loved, somehow made me feel closer to her…and yes, I guess you could say I loved her when she read Mark Twain's stories. Not for always. Not every day. Not hard and true with never any doubt, but good enough for a granddaughter to love her grandmother, I suppose. And anyway, loving Mamo was selfish, really. Stopping my own meanness made me feel much better whether Mamo ever knew what I had decided about her or not.

In the summertime, after I grew tall enough to look at

Mamo almost eye to eye, she invited me to go fishing in her beat-up, green rowboat which she kept tied to a tree at her piney lot on Lake Cherokee. All by ourselves, Mamo and I dragged the boat into and out of the muddy lake, sort of like Huck Finn and Tom Sawyer on an adventure. On fishing trips, Mamo didn't drink beer at all. There was only the *zzzzzzt* of dragonflies lighting on our cane fishing poles, the drumming of woodpeckers searching for insects, muddy water lapping against the sides of our wooden boat when another fisherman rowed by, crows cawing in the dead pine trees flooded by lake waters, and the sunshine, baking all my worries out of me. I felt proud and special knowing that Mamo and I were the only fisherwomen I ever saw on the lake. And sometimes my proudness and specialness made me believe Mamo might even like me a little.

On warm Sunday afternoons — probably you're not supposed to drink beer on the Lord's Day even if you never go to church — Mamo might sometimes invite me to come along for a drive through the Flewellen Big Woods. "The family doesn't own the land anymore, but only the mineral rights *under* the land," Mamo explained, looking as pleased as she might have been if all this land still belonged to her. I didn't understand, but I did know that talking about mineral rights usually led to telling stories about the oil-boom days, especially when we had to stop and wait for cows to poke across the road.

There were no fences around the open pastures where oil jacks bucked up and down like ponies. But in downtown Kilgore — "which is quite a sight to see," Mamo said — those oil ponies pumped up and down all over town, even in people's front yards. Every single oil well was surrounded by a chain-link fence with signs that read: Keep out! This means you! I asked Mamo, "Are these people with oil wells in their front yards afraid their pump jacks will gallop away?" Mamo threw her head back and hooted and hee-hawed. She liked it when I was funny so I tried as hard as I could to think up funny things to say.

Mamo and I laughed a lot about silly stuff when we took drives together. And if nothing was especially funny she asked me riddles like "Why did the chicken cross the road?" Mamo could make a joke about anything, mostly at other people's expense. Laughing felt good anyway, though. I even felt glad Mamo was my grandmother...until we went home.

At 815 Charlotte Drive, even when there had been sunshine the day before, a cloud of Mamo's sadness and anger was just around the corner. Mamo was the boss who couldn't boss my mother around. Nothing seemed to satisfy Mamo when she was mad at Mother for running around like Miss Gotrocks Lady Astor. If nobody in her house just this minute was angry at anybody else and nobody here had done anything wrong, it seemed like Mamo couldn't stand it until she picked a fight with someone.

Talking about how horrible Mother was seemed to make Mamo feel better, but not me. Even though I didn't like hearing bad things about Mother, I couldn't argue. First, because I could see that Mamo might be right in some of the things she said. And second, because I had already figured out that if Mamo was going on about how awful someone was and they weren't there, but I was, then she would fuss at me like I was the one who made her mad. At least I knew how Mamo was, and how best to stay out of her way. That is, if I wanted to.

Mamo did have a point about Mother being Miss Gotrocks Lady Astor. Much as I listened to Mamo complain, I sure didn't know what to do about it. From the first day we arrived at Mamo's, the black telephone which sat on the hall shelf started ringing off the wall. It was always for Mother with friends calling...and that man Tom. I supposed Mother had fun with Tom, but I didn't like him at all. His fingers were greasy from running them through his black hair, and they felt slippery and nasty even if he did look like Gregory Peck, as Mother said. Besides, he reeked of booze, not beery like Mamo smelled. I tried not to get too close to either one of them when they had been drinking because I didn't like their dead-rat breaths blowing on me.

To Mamo, Tom was a whole lot more than icky. She downright hated him, or so she said. Apparently, I wasn't the only one to know this. One Saturday at noon, when we sat down for lunch in Mamo's sunny breakfast room just off Annie's kitchen, I learned why Mother stayed away from Mamo's most of the time.

Annie and I had cooked chicken and dumplings and peach cobbler. My mouth already watered as Annie spooned juicy bowls for Mother, Mamo, Jo and me. With dumplings rolling around in my mouth, I didn't notice when the argument began. Before I knew what happened, or what had been said, Mother's face turned red and she shouted, "And I suppose you think you did any better with men, Mother!"

Mother's mad words felt like a swarm of bees had landed on my head and were stinging the life out of me. At my back, I heard the swinging kitchen door creak on its hinges. I looked around to see Annie peering in. We rolled our eyes at each other. Then the door slapped shut with a *whomp*. Mamo had that mean-dog look in her eyes. "You started this, Wilma, and now I'm going to finish it." As she spoke, Mamo slowly raised her tall glass of iced tea and tossed the whole sticky mess in Mother's face.

Sputtering and throwing her arms around like a bird trying to land, Mother screamed, "How could you, Mother!" With a screech Mother shoved her chair back, knocking it over. Face in hands, my mother ran crying from the room like a bad little girl being punished.

With a half-smile and satisfied expression, Mamo slowly placed her empty iced tea glass on the white lace tablecloth. Then she looked at me and Jo and smiled like a crocodile "You can finish your lunch now," she said.

I could not….

If daytime fights weren't bad enough, under Mamo's roof, nightmares were a way of life. Many nights I jerked awake and sat up, listening for what startled me. Sweet, musty dampness clung to metal screens through open windows. Moonlight traced spider webs of silver across the downy quilt on my sister's and my high poster bed, wondrously fresh and clean-smelling. But Mamo's rooms were shrouded in shadow. Stale cigarette smoke from the day before still choked the air.

"*Uh....Uh....Uh....Uh...*" Mamo's scary moans rose and fell like screeches in a horror movie. And then her screams began, "*No....No....No.....No....*," growing louder with each sound until the walls rattled.

I waited to hear Mother's bare feet hit the floor and *thump, thump, thump* the twenty giant steps which took her to Mamo's side. Slipping from bed, I crept down the hall and hid behind the door to see what would happen next.

In the dark, Mother crouched over Mamo's moaning shadow, placed her hands on her shoulders and gave her a shake. "Mother! Mother!" Shake. Shake. "Mother! It's Wilma! You're having a bad dream. Wake up! Wake up!"

Mamo muttered, sleep clogging her voice, "Huh? Huh? Wilma? Oh. Wilma. It's all right. I'm all right. Go back to bed! Go back to bed!"

In the morning we never spoke of it. After a nightmare night I was up before dawn, tiptoeing onto Mamo's sun porch. There she would be, calmly sitting and smoking as if nothing had happened during the night. With her black hair — not a dab of gray — smashed under a fine hairnet and slicked behind her ears, Mamo was fully dressed and ready to attack another disappointing sunrise.

While Mother slept and Annie arrived to begin cleaning and cooking, Mamo drove me to school and then picked me up in the afternoon. In a few years Jo would be old enough for school too, and Mamo would grouchily drive us both, destroying Mother's character the whole way.

When I complained to Mother that taking us to school made Mamo mad, Mother explained it away, saying, "Sandy, don't be silly. Mother wants to take you to school. And besides, it's easier for her than it is for me. She gets up at dawn. It's good for her to get out of the house."

Something needed to be good for Mamo, so if taking me to school was, then I wouldn't fuss about it. But still, I wasn't sure Mother was right about Mamo *wanting* to take me to school. Did Mother really know what she was talking about? She was in trouble just as much as me, maybe more. After all, Mother wasn't the boss around here. She was more like my big sister who was old enough to drive and go play with her friends. And no wonder. Mother had me when she was nineteen. She wasn't very old, and so she still liked to play. Most nights Mother didn't come home until the moon was high and Jo and I were supposed to be sleeping. I know because I listened for the tailpipe on her cute little convertible to scrape real loud as it roared up the hilly concrete driveway to Mamo's house.

As I figured it I didn't know if what I did or didn't do, helped or hurt Mamo. I only knew that her sadness and anger had become a part of me, like an enormous anaconda snake — which I learned about studying science at school — slithering around every corner, waiting to swallow me whole. I wanted it to stop. In the afternoon when Mamo took a nap, I snooped in her closet for clues that might explain her unhappiness. Another Mamo lived in the muffled gloom, quiet as a mossy Louisiana swamp.

My Annie has gone home for the day. It is naptime for genteel women and girls, only not for me. I am already sure that genteel is nothing I ever want to be. With my hand around the crystal knob of Mamo's clothes closet, I hesitate to make certain she sleeps before I make my move.

Mamo lies sprawled out on her back with her housedress hiked so high I can see her twisted hose rolled down below her knees. In pudgy hands folded across her chest, Mamo has a death grip on her wire-rimmed glasses. Blowing about her face, straggly black hair loosed from a hairnet distracts buzzing flies threatening to land in her open mouth. She snores, then snorts, mutters in her sleep and turns over. The house becomes still once more, with only the sound of the ceiling fan whirring overhead.

I watch every twitch until Mamo's breathing settles into a rolling rhythm. Slowly turning the crystal knob, I creep into her clothes closet. In the pitch black, the cool smell of cedar surrounds me. Feeling for the overhead chain and giving a tug, in the dim light of the swaying bulb I see rows of dresses and beneath, on racks lining the walls, fancy shoes decorated with bows and ties. On tiptoe I slide the hangers along the wooden racks, smelling and feeling each soft dress.

Toward the front of the closet hang the clothes I know. "Housedresses," Mamo calls them — two blue, two beige, two brown. Beneath them, side by side on the bare wood floor, sit two pairs of lace-up leather shoes. Mamo says they are "Bally pumps imported from Switzerland." They look more like army boots to me. Certainly nothing a lady should ever wear.

I open the dresser drawer and poke around in cool, silky

underwear. Rummaging in another drawer I discover pearl necklaces, ear screws and a round cameo of a lady's face. In the bottom drawer are leather gloves, and tucked beneath them, lace scarves...and a carton of Viceroy cigarettes. Not giving it a second thought I slide a pack into my bloomer playsuit pocket, certain that Mamo will never miss them.

I consider slipping into the pale green party dress and twirling in front of the wide hall mirror. I know better. If caught I will surely have another whipping. I'm stingy about my whippings, saving them up like money in my piggy bank, breaking the rules only for something truly exciting and new like teaching my baby sister to smoke and play movie star.

Pressing my ear against the thick mahogany door, the sound of Mamo's snoring comes through loud and clear. Turning the knob and pulling the paneled door behind me, I silently creep from the closet.

What happened? When did Mamo fold up these pretty clothes and quit being happy? She never goes out with friends. A taxicab even delivers groceries. Drives in the country and fishing on Lake Cherokee are the only places Mamo goes. And I'm with her then, not friends. How sad. But it's best not to ask her, directly, I thought. *Then I might start having Mamo's nightmares. Asking Mother would be better, safer. When I could corner her and trick her into telling me the whole story about Mamo giving up on people.*

Until then, I tried to figure my family out from what I read about people in books. Stupid old Brother Charles sent me one each month. "The classics," he said, "to build your library." He always signed the front page in fussy, scrolly handwriting, "To My Dearest Sandra. For the love of reading which we share." Never would he call me by the name I liked better, "Sandy." Stupid old Brother Charles.

Brother Charles's classics — written by people so important their faces showed up on cards in our deck of Authors — were actually interesting. But *Little Women* and

Pollyanna were my favorite books because they told about kids like Jo and me. Pollyanna still managed to be sunny and bright when she could have been mean and ugly because so many hard things had happened to her. In *Little Women,* Mrs. March explained to her four daughters that they should marry for love, not money.

This seemed quite reasonable, since as near as I could tell, after my family struck it rich with oil they quit work and just sat around owning things. Maybe they even owned the people who did the work that brought the money. Just so they didn't own me. I wouldn't let that happen EVER. Less money and more good work seemed to make people happiest. And that's what I would do as soon as I grew up!

From Charles Dickens and Emily Bronte, I realized that some things can't be fixed when you want even though they hurt like the dickens. When things are bad you have to keep doing your best and wait for the good to come. Making certain, of course, that you stay good inside and don't let other people provoke you into ruin. Mean people always go bad, eventually. Sort of like the Christmas turkey left out so long it spoils. Reading these smart books, I realized that Mamo and Mother couldn't possibly drive me crazy for the rest of my days. After all, Dorothy found her somewhere over the rainbow...and so would I.

In the meantime, summer vacation was a huge relief. That's when my Aunt Louise, Uncle Dale and my twin cousins, Gail and Buddy, a year older than me, and Dianne, their little sister who was younger than Jo, came to Texas from their home in Illinois...but only every other year. Those other years we rode on the train from Longview to Chicago. Uncle Dale picked us up at the train station and drove us "like a bat out of hell," Mother said, all the way to their home in Rochelle. They had a big two-story house with a basement and as near as I could tell, no rules about what kids could and couldn't do, except we were expected to play long and hard so we slept upstairs all night. And didn't giggle, sneak around with flashlights and spy on the grown-ups through the stair railings.

My Uncle Dale was like a tornado with muscles bulging and Brillo-pad hair shooting in every direction, even when he stood perfectly still. The minute their station wagon pulled up in Mamo's driveway, Uncle Dale leapt from the car laughing and hollering as loud as he could, "Well, hi, y'all." They all piled out with arms and legs everywhere, wearing any old color of shorts and shirts — not necessarily going together — and carrying mismatched luggage. Mother drew her shoulders into her head, made a face and cringed when she looked at them like she had sucked on a lemon. She embarrased me. I hoped my aunt and uncle and cousins didn't notice how prissy mother was. It was disgusting.

With my Illinois family, everything was a joke and a game. They especially liked to make fun of the way we talked. "Have you got mashed potatoes in your mouth?" was Uncle Dale's favorite line. This caused Mamo to rise up like a cobra and strike up a fight. "You're a Damn Yankee, Dale! How would you know the first thing about elocution?"

Damn Yankee seemed the best way to be. When our cousins came to visit, Jo and I could run in the house which was against Mamo's rules any other time. They were such fun I hardly minded Gail beating me at jacks. She could bounce the rubber ball higher than anybody else and take her sweet time picking up tensies. We even practiced handstands and somersaults up and down the hallway after Mamo rudely shooed us off her sun porch.

I loved my Aunt Louise a lot. She was tall and bony with big feet and hands, instead of being short, tiny and curvy like my mother. Louise hugged me, when nobody hugged in Mamo's house. Because of Aunt Louise I decided bigger might be better.

It was sort of spooky how one of Aunt Louise's dark green eyes looked straight and one looked sideways. I tried to concentrate on the straight eye when we talked, but I couldn't help wondering what the wandering eye saw. After a while I forgot about the crooked eye altogether. Forgetting how Aunt Louise looked wasn't really too hard since she was good to me, asked me questions about myself and made me feel safe and happy...by really listening to what I said like I mattered to her.

In fact, Louise liked me a lot more than I even suspected. One especially rowdy afternoon, Mother had screamed at me, "I've had enough!" and sent me to bed before the sun went down. But Louise sneaked into the bedroom and sat on my bed. She smoothed hair from my forehead and whispered, "I'm sorry you and Wilma go at it so much." This already felt pretty good, but she wasn't done. With sad eyes, even the one that wandered, she said, "We love you, honey. Dale and I tried to adopt you and Jo after your mother and George married and then divorced the second time, but Wilma wouldn't let us. We wanted you, honey." She stroked my shoulder and kissed me on the cheek. "Your mother truly loves you, Sandy. I want you to know that. Do you believe me? Just remember that for Aunt Louise, will you?"

Grrrrrrrr...I didn't believe her. I was too angry to believe anything! Being Louise and Dale's little girl would have been so much better! After that I even told Mother that when I grew up I was going to marry Buddy, figuring that maybe I could find a way to live with them after all. But Mother told me I couldn't marry Buddy because we would have deformed children like the Hunchback of Notre Dame.

I did decide, though — cross my heart and hope to die — that I would marry a man for love someday. My husband would be just like Uncle Dale. We would be poor at first like

Mrs. March said in *Little Women*. But because we were so good, we would have wonderful children and everything we ever needed to make us happy.

This was nothing like the plan Mother had in mind for me, or Jo. And not at all like the stories about the fancy people staring down from fussy gold frames that hung on Mamo's bedroom wall. Those days when Mother felt especially lonely and sad were her favorite times for telling the pretty people's stories. I could tell how she felt by looking in her droopy eyes. But her face looked different once she was talking about the dead people. "Aren't they beautiful?" she would say and make me stand and listen as she went on about "our Fine Old Family."

I never needed to say anything but "*Um, huh.*" Mother wasn't really talking to me anyway. She was only making herself feel better. I paid attention, hoping she might eventually get around to telling me about Mamo's husbands. Then I might find out what made Mamo so miserable and what I could do to make things better around here. But Mother didn't enjoy talking about Mamo nearly so much as she did telling those moldy family stories. In fact Mother wouldn't talk about Mamo's husbands at all until she made me promise to act nice. Mother would always say, "You mind Mother, Sandy. She's had a hard life."

As nicely as I could, I would smile and say, "Yes, Mother. I promise." When what I really wanted to do was strangle her, or Mamo, or somebody for expecting me to behave so perfectly all the time. But I didn't choke anybody and so I learned about Mamo's husbands.

MOTHER'S PRISSY BEDROOM at Mamo's house was furnished with a four-poster bed, dainty bedside table with a doily on top and tall chest with a tilted glass mirror. If I sat on Mother's bed watching her "make pretty" before she left for the day, I could ask her questions about movie stars and make-up and maybe slip in more important questions, too. Really, Mother liked to talk so much, I shouldn't have worried. One way or another, I heard these stories about Mamo's husbands over and over, and over again....

Mamo's first husband was Angus Pitser Miller, Mother and Louise's daddy. They lived in a big house in Henderson that was sort of like a plantation as Mother told it, with lots of land, cotton fields and many men working for my Grandfather Angus. Only one day, when Mother was two and Louise was five, a tenant who lived and worked on their property in Tatum — "that Godforsaken Tatum" — asked my Grandfather Angus to meet him downtown so he could pay him what he was due. "But instead of paying my daddy the money he was owed, that horrible, horrible man shot my daddy dead! Right there in the middle of the street. And nothing ever happened to that lying murderer! Not a thing! Daddy's killer got off Scot-free."

The next husband, Lacey Eddins, was "...a good honorable man, well-respected in Longview, a businessman and widower. Lacey and Mother were married only a year. One year! And then he died of strep throat, right there in the bed where Mother sleeps every night. Can you imagine?"

The third husband was "...a good-for-nothing drunk. A

Fort Worth socialite, rich but mean. Every night, he locked the door to their bedroom. Yes, this same bedroom where Lacey died! He beat Mother, night after night. She screamed! How she screamed!"

Sometimes Mother got wound up at this point. Puffing, panting and waving her arms she showed me exactly how it happened. "I was fourteen. But I had my oil royalties. I had my car. I was grown. I wasn't going to take it anymore! One night I couldn't stand it another minute. I grabbed my riding crop." Eyes popping like a goldfish, Mother grabbed a fly swatter from the open window sill and swung it back and forth like an elephant trunk. "I threw my shoulder against the locked bedroom door and broke through! You should have seen that scoundrel's face, Sandy!"

I could picture it all happening and my heart galloped like wild horses. Mother jerked the swatter over her head and with fury she attacked her mattress. "I beat the living hell out of the rotten bastard. Until he cried and begged for mercy like the sniveling coward that he was!"

I realized that Mother was spookily sounding like *Gone With the Wind.* But she was doing such a good job I hated to stop her. It would be mean to call her a copycat when she was having such a good time. And besides, I enjoyed the show. Right in front of my eyes, Mother quit being my mother and become Scarlett O'Hara. She should have been a movie star.

After Mother beat up Mamo's playlike husband lying there on the mattress, she threw the swatter across the room, collapsed on her bed and sprawled out on her back with her feet dangling in air. With a huge sigh, she finished her story. "Mother kicked him out the next day. And that was the end of Mother and men."

After hearing those stories I realized it was no wonder Mamo screamed at night. I felt really, really sorry for Mamo. And Mother, too. As I sort of remembered him, my own father reminded me of Mamo's Fort Worth socialite husband. I knew what meaner-than-mean felt and looked like. Only my father wasn't rich, even though he was handsome and rough sort of like Rhett Butler.

Learning all this horrible stuff felt scary but good. Choosing the right husband was tricky business. I only hoped that one day I would know the good ones from the bad ones. And then when I found him, make sure I protected him so nobody could kill him.

After finding out about Mamo's husbands, nasty Brother Charles didn't seem so bad after all. At least he was alive. He didn't drink beer or whiskey. He didn't beat my Aunt Bodie. And so in the summertime — the year I turned thirteen and had such a growth spurt Mother said I needed to wear a camisole — I felt excited about taking a car trip with Mamo, Mother and Jo to visit Aunt Bodie and Brother Charles for two weeks in Kountze. This wasn't my great-aunt and uncle's town house. They had a city house in Beaumont where Brother Charles "practiced law," whatever that meant. Bodie and Brother Charles's Kountze, old log-cabin, country house — with two other houses hooked-up and added on — hid from the main highway down a bumpy, one-lane dirt path deep in the spooky Big Thicket of Southeast Texas. Bodie and Brother Charles named their many acres with split rail fences, two lakes and an artesian swimming pool, *Wil-Lou Lakes Farm*, after my Mother Wilma and my Aunt Louise.

Usually, we just called it *The Farm*. Even though farming was hardly anything that ever took place there. What happened at The Farm was more than I expected....and more than I ever wanted to know.

Low hanging tree limbs scratched against Mamo's green Buick sedan, bony fingers reaching out to grab me through thick, smoky green brambles and underbrush. Faint pinpricks of sunlight filtered through the tangle of trees and flitted like dancing fairies through the towering pines. Muffled and distant, deep in the forest crows cawed, jaybirds squawked. The clock on the dash registered early afternoon, but the deep wood was shrouded in secrecy, hushed and mysterious as bottomless night.

Finally! I said to myself as we jostled down the last stretch of winding, rocky dirt road that led through The Big Thicket to Bodie and Brother Charles's farm. Mother and Mamo had fought the whole six hours from Longview to the tip of Southeast Texas. Mamo complained about, "riding in the death seat," and fussed, "You're taking my life in your hands, Wilma! For God's sake slow down! You're driving like a bat out of hell!"

Mother argued that Mamo was "blinder than a *bat*." She couldn't drive this whole way, and if she didn't like her driving, she should get out.

Then Mamo shouted, "This is my car, Wilma! Who the hell do you think you are?" They would never stop. They were too good at fighting by now.

Kidnapped in the back seat, Jo and I rolled our windows down as far as they would go, to make as much noise as we could to keep from paying attention to Mamo and Mother. For awhile, we stuck our heads almost outside the windows, and hummed *OOOOOOOO* sounds with our mouths opened wide, wind puffing our cheeks until they tingled.

Then Jo grew bored and curled up on the seat like a kitten asleep in the sun. It had been a long time since I could do that. I was big now. Almost as tall as Mother, my head grazed her chin.

What did Mamo and Mother matter, anyway? It was summertime in Texas and blossoming circles of yellow, pink, white and red popped everywhere, watercolors tossed in parakeet green fields, hugging Highway 69 heading south. The sky was robin's egg blue, with puffy white clouds painting pictures of snowy mountains, angel wings and animal shapes of every kind. I felt happy. We would be at The Farm soon.

Two weeks! My thoughts sang. *Two scrumptious weeks of clever Bertie's country cooking...learning from Bertie's smart husband Eddie, the do-everything-man, how to string wire fences, fix the plumbing when the sink overflowed, light a charcoal fire in the rock barbecue pit, and make the house and land behave in every way just as he said it should. Aunt Bodie will take Jo and me fishing at Lake Wilma and for swims in the tadpole-y artesian swimming pool under the magnolia trees rustling with thick, glossy green leaves. At night when we snuggle under quilts on the screened-in porch, Bodie will tell ghost stories. Bloodcurdling screeches of night birds and animals howling in the deep forest making me promise that absolutely, I would not put my foot on the floor until morning. And there will be endless games of draw poker with Brother Charles and his four look-alike brothers, all smart-acting with white hair and lawyer-ish horn-rimmed glasses. I'm so excited I might wet my panties before we get there!*

Bump...bump....bump...bump. The Buick rattled over the cattle guard and burst into the wide clearing. Sounding like hundreds of galloping horses' hooves, crushed seashells scrunched beneath our tires. Naturally I would think about horses. When Bodie couldn't make me go where she was leading, she said I was "bucky, just like a pony." And when Mother wrestled to tame my unruly hair, she said it was "thick as a horses' mane." I didn't mind being horse-y. The description fit me rather well.

Our racket on the broad caliche driveway propelled Aunt

Bodie and Bertie from the log-cabin kitchen, both talking at once. "My precious! My precious!" With spirals of gray hair flying as she crossed the yard, Bodie clapped her hands together, threw her arms wide and wrapped Jo and me in her arms.

Energetic as a cricket, Bertie was at my side in a blink. "Miz Sandy! Look at yo' chile'! Yo'z all grown up!" Usually I didn't hug Bertie. To do so broke some stupid black/white, help/boss rule. But I did today. Grabbed Bertie around her aproned waist, buried my head in the kitchen smells of her flour sack dress, and hugged hard. "Lawd, Lawd, Lawd!" Bertie backed away and shook her head looking embarrassed, and giving Bodie a nervous sideways glance to see if she noticed. "Yo' is somethin' else, Miz Sandy! Always was...."

Sturdy as aged cedar logs that wrapped The Farm's log-cabin, Eddie balanced his weight in the flat bed of a blue pick-up truck. Carefully, he gathered Tungsten fruit from heavy tree branches and loaded the tough, lime green balls to take into town for sale. "A cash crop," Brother Charles had explained last year. Upon seeing us, Eddie's lined face — the color of dark molasses — crinkled into a smile. He hopped to the ground and headed in our direction. "Well'um. Good to seez yo' again. Fo' sho'!" Nodding his head up and down, Eddie shuffled dirt with the tip of a worn brown boot. Making certain he said "Hello," but also sure not to take up too much space.

Brother Charles appeared from behind the pump house, cautious as a hibernating lizard creeping from beneath a rock — pale hair, face and hands, poking from starchy creases of his white cotton shirt and trousers. As soon as he saw us he squared his shoulders, puffed out his chest and crossed the manicured lawn with giant strides. Before I knew it, he held my face in his trembling hands, planted a sloppy kiss on my check and murmured in my hair, "My precious, Sandra. I have anticipated your visit."

I pushed him away and frowned with sassy displeasure. "Sandra? I'm not Sandra! I'm Sandy!"

Mamo, Mother and Bodie were talk, talk, talking and not paying attention. I made a break for it and dashed up the porch steps to the kitchen. Coming out of my skin with anticipation, I cupped my hands and hollered from the screen door, "Bertie! Bertie! Come on! Show me! Whatcha got cookin'?"

I couldn't get enough, soon enough. I rattled lids on steaming pots of corn on the cob, mustard greens and potatoes that bubbled on the stove. The ancient house felt like a hug, warm and full, wrapped in an unsoiled jumble of smells: worn oak walls and floor, winter's fireplace ashes clinging to moist stones, earthy richness blowing in through dusty window screens.

Practically toothless, wiry Bertie hopped into the kitchen to rescue her dinner. "What else, you got cooking, Bertie? Biscuits? Cobbler?"

She swatted at me, pot lids rattling in her hands. "Chile. Get out of heah! Yo' knows it's gonna be good! Maybe tomorrow you can he'p me roll out the dough."

The whole house was waiting. I whizzed through the skinny dining room with a wall of open windows on both sides and endless pine table which Bodie called "the groaning board." The table was already set for dinner with white dishes, a blue-and-white checked cloth, and huge china rooster crowing over it all. I flew into the Great Room in search of wrapped surprises. Sure that Bodie had hidden them, to be unwrapped one day at a time — like always.

Stashed behind a sturdy cabinet, I found piles of bowed and boxed, pastel-papered presents. Impatient to wait another minute, I chased past the stone fireplace, which was so tall I could almost stand in it, and jumped down onto the screened-in sleeping porch. With rows of twin beds good enough for

Snow White and the Seven Dwarfs, the sleeping porch was my favorite room — a tree house, nestled in leafy, twisting branches.

Down below on the caliche drive, Mother — with Jo in tow — Mamo, Bodie and Brother Charles were still yakking. I cupped my hands on either side of my mouth and hollered, "Bodie! Come here! I found something!" With one hand, Bodie shaded her eyes from the sun, laughed and waved, "I'm coming, Precious! Hold your horses!"

The big wooden clock with a brass pendulum tick-tocking as it swung back and forth was the only clock at the Farm. Before long I even forgot what day of the week it was. Only the arc of the sun, breakfast, lunch, dinner and the thief threatening to steal my fun, "Nap time!" marked the summer of my thirteenth year.

"No! Mother, no! Let me stay up. I'll be real quiet," I protested when she insisted I lie down for a nap. Absolutely, I was not going to waste my time by getting my "beauty rest." *What nonsense. How pretty did you need to be, anyway?* Sitting at the round poker table and totally ignoring Mother, I fumed as I stacked cool, slick poker chips left over from the game last night. Hushed afternoon stillness settled over everything. Sunlight the color of warm butter filtered through the canopy of trees, creating liquid patterns across the length of the Great Room, melting everything it touched into pools of golden light. Bodie and Mamo had already disappeared into Bodie's bedroom for their nap. Jo was asleep on the screened-in porch. Not far from where I sat, Mother slouched in a worn chair and flipped the pages of a movie magazine.

Rescuing me from my predicament, Brother Charles's silhouette appeared in the doorway, sunlight from the dining room behind, casting his thin shadow across the green felt table where I played. "Sandra. The ewes have just birthed newborn lambs," he said with a soft and polite voice. "If you aren't napping, I thought you'd like to accompany me to Lake Louise and see them." Before I could answer, he spoke to Mother. "Wilma? Can she come?"

Mother glanced up from her magazine, disinterested. "I don't see why not." And then she glared at me and spoke with an edge in her voice. "She won't take a nap."

I felt offended. *Nothing new...Mother and Mamo are the queens of insult. Don't they realize how smart and grown-up I am now? Brother Charles understands. He treats me differently this summer, always appearing at my elbow, saying nice things and taking care of me. Like last night....*

As the brothers arrived for the poker game, and Mamo claimed her chair at the round gaming table, nighttime closed around us, murky and mysterious. I felt uneasy and silly for feeling this way. But then I remembered why. In her bedtime story the night before, Bodie had outdone herself. Her tale had been long and terrifying, about ravenous wolves prowling the forest in search of little girls to eat. At the end of the scary story, Bodie lunged, growled and scratched at Jo and me with her huge hairy wolf foot, hidden from us until just that minute. We screamed and screamed! Bodie laughed until she cried and then apologized, saying she meant to scare us with her fake wolf foot, but not this much.

The memory of Bodie's frightening story had stayed with me all day. I still felt spooked. Seated beside Brother Charles and ready for the first poker hand to be dealt, I glanced outside. Treetops were fading into shadow as daylight crept away. I shivered and pulled my white cotton sweater around my shoulders. Brother Charles touched my arm with his soft white hand and murmured in my ear, "No need to be afraid, my pet. Brother Charles is here to take care of you."

Beneath the hazy glow of the Tiffany lamp low over the gaming table, tiny golden hairs on my sunburned arm sparkled like Bertie's copper pots. Lamplight glinted off the glass of the six spectacled adults gathered around the table, every one of them with colorless hair, except Mamo. Her hair was black and forbidding, like her biting humor. Reassured by Brother Charles, I felt strong and confident again. It was my night. I drew winning hands, one right after another. Bidding was intense, each high-stakes round of ante making me twitch inside. But I knew how to bluff and felt proud of my tall stack of chips. Just as Brother Charles had taught, all night I kept my poker face straight and unmoving.

When I spread my first winning hand across the green felt cloth, the attorney brothers reared back in their chairs and whistled. One of them said, "Will you look at that? Drew to a royal flush! And got it! My oh my. Who taught this young lady, anyway? We have a little poker player here!"

Brother Charles blew up like a bullfrog sitting on a lily pad, bellowing a deep *ta-rump.* "Why, the best poker player at this table taught this young lady!" He went on to explain how he had taught me "all she knows about this game. And you must admit that is a considerable amount."

I didn't mind that he bragged. He was right. Without him, I wouldn't know how to play the game. We had been at the Farm for only a week, but with every tick of the mantel clock I felt more grown-up.

Still, today in watery afternoon light, even though I was full of myself after beating the smart grown-ups at cards, I felt uncomfortable about going all the way to the back woods. Night would fall soon, with wolves and wild animals on the prowl. *But,* I reasoned to myself, *they are probably asleep in the daytime heat like Jo, Bodie and Mamo. And no way would I be so babyish, boring or lazy as to sleep my life away!*

I jumped from my chair and shot Mother a defiant look as I said with a proud toss of my head, "Well, all right then, Brother Charles. Let's go!"

Fine dust sifted through my white leather sandals and powdered my toes as Brother Charles and I set out on our adventure. Close to the farmhouse we wandered past Lake Wilma — green and glistening in the sunlight — and admired lanky egrets perched at water's edge. In no hurry, we hopscotched across the cattle guard that led to the back pastures. On the left of the rutted path, fields of yellow flowers stretched to the horizon. On the other side of the dirt path, mysterious dense woods rose tall and dark. A sweet-smelling breeze tangled my hair and whooshed under my sun dress. I shouted with surprised delight and grabbed at my yellow skirt, pressing it down with my hands to keep it from flying over my head. I felt brave and special. No one else but Brother Charles…and I…walked to the back woods.

We took our time as if the afternoon would never end. Beneath towering cypress trees with strong roots holding onto the banks of Lake Louise, Brother Charles pointed out fresh deer tracks and, beside them, raccoon footprints. A sneeze away in a pasture grazed clean, we found the ewes and baby lambs. A newborn not yet on its legs lay in the fine soil and looked at me with enormous trusting eyes. My heart fluttered like butterfly wings. "Oh! How adorable! Can I pet it, Brother Charles?"

"Of course. Brother Charles will keep the mother from harming you."

I trembled touching the warm, newborn creature, so fragile, so innocent lying on the soft earth. "Oh! Is this okay?"

"Yes. Yes, my pet." Brother Charles kneeled beside me, wind blowing his white hair into his face, making him seem less stuffy and more human — like me. As he spoke, he stroked the lamb's soft coat, encouraging me not to be afraid. "Go slowly. Gently. Like this. Just stroke…gently."

We stayed a long while, until I felt full and happy. The sun had begun to sink on the horizon, but the afternoon was still warm and bright. Brother Charles shielded his eyes with a hand as he measured the height of the sun in the sky. "There is still time for another adventure, Sandy. Would you like to take a different path back to the house?" he asked. "We can walk through the woods where there are signs of wildlife."

Brother Charles held back a low pine branch as we stooped to enter the quiet stillness of the leafy canopy. Smells of damp earth, fresh pines and sweet, wild honeysuckle filled my senses to overflowing. Pine needles underfoot muffled the sound of our steps. The forest was alive. Squawking jaybirds set up a racket as we passed; two squirrels skittered overhead, barking and chasing through the branches. I stopped and craned my neck to search for the brown squirrel's high, leafy nest. Brother Charles walked on ahead and then hesitated, waiting for me to catch up.

As I caught up with him I realized he was staring at me...ferociously. I gasped, feeling alarmed. But before I could ask what was wrong, without asking Brother Charles shoved his hand inside my sundress. He fumbled with my skin beneath the camisole. I was horrified and gasped, "Oh! Stop it! Stop! What are you doing?" I grabbed at his hand and twisted away from him. As fast as my feet could carry me, I shot down the path, running ahead. Brother Charles stumbled and shouted only a few giant steps behind.

"Stop, Sandra! Stop! I'm sorry I scared you." He puffed and wheezed, "It's all right."

I wasn't fast enough. He caught me from behind, roughly grabbed my shoulders and twisted me around to face him. The fierceness was gone. He looked like he could cry and his voice sounded wobbly and scared. My heart hammered in my chest and thundered in my ears, so loud I could hardly hear myself think. "Now, now, now my pet," he begged. "Don't be scared of Brother Charles. You are such a high-spirited little thing!" I turned and twisted, trying to wrench away. "Now...now...now. Stop. Be still. It's only Brother Charles. There...there. There's no harm done. Let's not tell anyone about this. It will be our special secret...something that only you and I know about." He had tears in his eyes. "You're so...so beautiful...my darling girl...I couldn't stop myself."

I felt confused and madder than I could ever remember feeling. I twisted in his hands and kicked at him, screaming. "What are you talking about? Secret what? Of course I don't want to tell anybody. Tell them what?" Fury gave me power and I jerked away from him, screaming as I ran. "No! You stop! Stay away from me! Stay away from me! I'm going back to the house! "

I broke into a full gallop with Brother Charles running after me, grabbing at me, trying to catch me again. I kept screaming over my shoulder. "No! No! Go away! Leave me alone!" He thundered right behind, panting and shouting my name.

Breaking through the woods and rounding the bend, I leapt over the cattle guard. With the Farm now in sight, tears of relief spilled down my face. *This is horr-i-ble! Make it go away! Make it go away,* I thought. *I will! Erase it! Like in school...when I mess up in long division...or mop up spilled milk with Annie's dish towels. Clean it up. Get rid of it. Wash it all away. It's not my fault. I didn't do anything wrong. Forget about it...forget about it...forget about it....*

As I flew the rest of the way to the farmhouse, the smell of charcoal that smoldered in the square fieldstone pit flipped my world right side up. I wiped the tears away. *Steaks! We're having steaks! I'm starving!* The loppity screen door slapped shut behind me. "Bertie! Can I shake the salt and pepper on the steaks?"

At dinner I refused to look in Brother Charles's direction. It was over like it never even happened.

FORGETTING IS DANGEROUS. When Brother Charles asked Mother if I could stay on for another week with him and Bodie at their home in Beaumont, I shivered…halfway remembering the walk in the woods. But quickly, I shushed the memory. *No. That couldn't have happened, could it? Did it? Oh, no…just too strange. A mistake of some sort…a misunderstanding. It surely won't happen again. No way. I won't let it!*

Beaumont! My thoughts danced. *Bodie and Brother Charles's city house is excellent! I'll play-fish with Bodie in the pond out back. Suet tied to kitchen string and strung on a bamboo pole, fat goldfish nibbling for hours.*

I'll cruise down the street in the black Cadillac with Spain — tall and straight in his black uniform with gold trim. Helen, Bodie's town cook — wearing her gray uniform, cap and white ruffled apron — will cater to me like Wendy did for the lost boys in Peter Pan. *Maybe Helen and Spain don't act like Annie and Anderson or Bertie and Eddie. They are sort of stuck-up and don't talk to me. But everything they do for me is so fancy I can't get enough!*

And there are books! Rows and rows of books….

Endless volumes of "essential literary classics" lined the walls of Brother Charles's wood-paneled library. It was a puzzle how my great-uncle ever got the name Brother Charles. This had never occurred to me before. But this year, all of a sudden I seemed to want to know everything there was to know, and this question dawned on me when I had never wondered before. Maybe Brother Charles got his name from his four brothers, who looked like the white-haired and

spectacled men on the cherry-flavored Luden cough drops
box. He wasn't a brother to anyone in my family, but nobody
ever called him anything else. It did sound kinder and sweeter
and maybe smarter than just Charles, so maybe that's why he
liked it.

It didn't really matter to me. I would call him whatever
he liked as long as I could read these books. At thirteen I was
excited about the classics. Once I started I had trouble putting
a book down until the end where the good guys won, the boy
and girl kissed and everyone lived happily ever after...or at
least learned something about life. Steering the rickety ladder
along the stacks, I piled books so high I had to stop, or fall off.

Gathering as many books as I wanted from my "very own
private library" — or so Brother Charles said — I wriggled into
the swivel red leather chair beneath his "partner's desk." On
the green leather top, my great-uncle had stacked yellow legal
pads for taking notes and copying quotes that I liked. "This
study will make you a writer someday," he said.

Sunlight fizzed through emerald velvet curtains and
danced on jewel-toned book bindings, swirling dust particles
transporting me into lands of enchantment. What could go
wrong when Wordsworth opened my heart and made it sing?
"Our birth is but a sleep forgetting. The soul that rises with us,
our life's star, hath had elsewhere its setting, and cometh from
afar." Emerson made me believe I was set to accomplish great
things: "Do not go where the path may lead, go instead where
there is no path and leave a trail." Ideas so grand I felt dizzy
from the words, and imagined I could achieve anything
expressed within such great thoughts.

Brother Charles's ferociousness seemed a distant rumble,
replaced by a gentle breeze. Within a few days I began to feel
completely safe and at home. And no wonder. I had the run of
the house and the best of everything, with no one telling me,
"Be quiet!" Aunt Bodie pitty-patted around in lacy flower

dresses with a frilly white handkerchief tucked in her sleeve and a green bottle of smelling salts handy in case she had a spell of the vapors. I knew she was my Great-Aunt Bodie since she was my Grandmother Mamo's sister. But everybody in the family called her Aunt Bodie and so I did, too. Helen cooked up fancy meals, no detail overlooked. Even sandwiches were cut in animal shapes. And Spain! He was the regal coachman, steering my elegant Cinderella carriage. I even had my own quaint bedroom with a fluffy double bed, piles of pillows, silky down comforter and pressed sheets that smelled like outdoors. I felt like a princess.

Most every day, Spain chauffeured Bodie and me on afternoon shopping trips. Bodie dressed me, top to bottom, in prissy outfits and shiny Mary Janes like I was her live doll. "After all," Bodie said, "I don't have children of my own. But Beth's girls, Wilma and Louise, and you and Sister Jo are my own flesh and blood!" Mamo's children and grandchildren were as close as Bodie would come to having her own little girls because — as Mamo told me — "Bodie is barren."

Of all the things Bodie bought, she was especially thrilled with a silky "dressing gown" the color of strawberry ice cream with white lace at the collar and cuffs. The lace scratched but I couldn't bear to spoil Aunt Bodie's fun by saying how uncomfortable the robe felt against my skin. This time in Beaumont was my first separation from Mother and Mamo — the beginning of my independence. I didn't want to ruin a single minute.

In muggy early afternoon right after our lazy lunch with lots and lots of stories and conversations, Bodie tucked me into bed for a rest. Of course I protested — to which Bodie only tsk-tsk'ed, clicking her tongue like castanets. "You don't have to really sleep, precious girl! Read. Do whatever your little heart desires, while I go next door to visit with Nana." Nana was my other great-aunt, Mamo and Bodie's sister, whose husband had died. She lived through the hedge and across the stone footpath, in the drafty white house next door. "We'll take a drive with Spain when Bodie comes home!" Bodie promised. She stroked misbehaving hair from my face, kissed my forehead and was gone.

Helen went home after late lunch, leaving dinner prepared and waiting on the stove. This was Spain's time to run errands. Brother Charles and I were alone with the air conditioning purring, bubbles of moisture collecting on window panes and gliding down the glass. Smelling of Bay Rum and leather, Brother Charles stacked our reading for the afternoon on the fancy bedside table beside a plate of cookies and glass of bubbly milk. Pushing my comforter aside, he settled down beside me on the downy bed and propped both of us up with pillows behind our backs.

Brother Charles cleared his throat — *uh…uh…uh…hem* — like a smart lawyer in court. I especially liked how that sounded ever since he had explained about his important attorney work of fighting for justice and winning for good over evil. "Now my precious girl, we're going to read Tennyson." In his flowery attorney-voice he read of magical knights and ladies. "Under tower and balcony, by the garden wall and gallery, a gleaming shape she floated by, silent into Camelot….But Lancelot mused a little space. He said, 'She has a lovely face; God in his mercy lend her grace, The Lady of Shalott.'"

The poem made me feel sad, and I wasn't sure why. "What did she need mercy for? What happened to the lady, Brother Charles?"

"She died for love."

"What does that mean?"

"Do you want Brother Charles to show you?"

There was no time to answer his question. His fierce look had returned. Harshly, he grabbed at me, pressing me flat on my back, stripping me of white ruffled panties, flipping my body like a fish about to be scaled. He got on top of me and pushed the strawberry pink dressing gown over my head. I struggled and screamed, but he was stronger...and there was no one to hear. He forced my legs apart.

"Stop! Don't! Stop it!" I screamed as loudly as I could, not caring if I was being rude, or mean, or ugly. It was happening again. Only this time I couldn't run. With the weight of his body, Brother Charles pinned me down. Unable to move, my screams smothered beneath folds of silk and lace, I could not see, but I could feel and I could hear...rough fingers groping...nasty slurping sounds...slimy wetness drowning my fire.

"Stay as sweet as you are," he mumbled. I was powerless, numb, falling, a small round stone, no arms, no legs, dropping into a swampy pool, drifting, slipping into the unfathomable, bottomless deep.

When Mother called to see if I was having fun, Brother Charles asked her if I could stay another week. My head felt like it would explode and the cat had my tongue. I felt ashamed and embarrassed, shivering cold, without words strong enough to say "No!" He wouldn't have told the truth, anyway. I could see that. Beyond reach, one imprisoned week lengthened into two.

Morning sunshine streamed through open jalousie windows on Mamo's sun porch, cranked wide in the muggy heat of early summer. Overhead, the ceiling fan squeakily stirred stifling air to little effect. Tiny beads of sweat moistened my upper lip.

Spain had chauffeured Bodie, Brother Charles and me home to Longview three days ago. Then he had gone to stay with "his people," Bodie said. Only Bodie and Brother Charles stayed at Mamo's. *But what if Spain doesn't come back?* I worried and worried that he might forget.

Wild to get away, as much as I could I escaped to my wisteria arbor playhouse, hidden in dense bushes beside the garage. Digging in the warm earth, I could feel my arms and legs again. At first they felt numb and tingly like I had been sleepwalking and finally awakened from a nightmare. My eyes saw more clearly and my head started making sense again. *Brother Charles will not touch me! Never! Ever, again!* I vowed to myself.

Actually, he had not touched me. Even though he had tried, pulling me to him behind partially closed doors several times these miserably long three days. He seemed surprised when he grabbed me from behind and I furiously stomped on his foot and elbowed his stomach like Wonder Woman fighting evil. This seemed to discourage him.

Finally, just now, Spain had arrived to collect Bodie and Brother Charles for their return journey to Beaumont. Mamo, Mother and I walked outside with them to say goodbye before they got in the back seat of their black Cadillac. I had to raise a cheek to be kissed. This is what we always did. It was polite and would have seemed strange if I refused. But I felt sick to my stomach and struggled to breathe.

I ran back inside as soon as Spain closed the doors for Bodie and Brother Charles, and then climbed behind the steering wheel and started the engine. I froze in the vestibule, not knowing what to do. As the glass-shuttered slats on the jalousie back door rattled shut behind Mother and Mamo and they headed for the sun porch, I felt my heart jolt, twist and turn cold as ice. I knew what I had to do. I couldn't stay in this house one more minute. As much as I needed air, water and food, I had to have this whole day without anybody disturbing my retreat from the unhappiness of this past month.

My hand halfway turned the knob of the back door. "I'm going outside to play for a while!" I shouted toward Mother and Mamo as they settled onto the sun porch for their second cup of Maxwell House. They raised their heads and looked confused, as if they assumed I would follow.

"What's your hurry, Sandy?" Mamo asked with a puzzled tone in her voice.

"Tell us about your trip, Sandy," Mother said, looking at me suspiciously, her forehead creasing into twin wrinkles between her eyebrows. "Come here," Mother demanded in her most forceful, you-had-better-do-what-I-say voice.

I squirmed, wishing a hole in the floor would open up and I could drop through. I dragged myself to the sun porch wondering what I should do. *Do I tell them? How do I tell them? What do I tell them? Mother says she can read my mind. Maybe she can figure it out. I don't even know how to talk about what happened to me in Beaumont.* I looked down at my dusty bare feet and flipped a frayed edge in the braid rug with a big toe before I answered. "It was okay...I guess."

Mother lurched forward on the sofa with an alarmed look on her face. "You guess? You don't look okay. What's the matter, Sandy? Something is the matter."

My stomach churned. "You're blushing! Sandy! What is it? You know you can't hide anything from me. Out with it!" Mother shouted.

I felt like I might throw up. My palms were sweaty and my ears hummed as loud as a swarm of bumblebees. "It's...Brother Charles...he did things to me...."

They jumped to their feet. "Mama!" Mother shouted. "He did it again!"

Mamo clenched her hands into fists like John Wayne did right before he socked somebody. "That sonofabitch! I'll kill him with my bare hands!"

Feeling like I could explode, I screamed, "Again? Again!

You knew? And didn't warn me?" Mother and Mamo kept shouting at each other like I wasn't even there. Standing between them I was invisible, my words unheard, lost beneath their chins. The fury in their words flew around me like yellowjackets and red wasps. I grimaced and clenched my jaw, catching their words in my teeth like bugs flattened against the front grille of Mamo's Buick.

I took a step back and stood in the doorway with my arms braced on the door frame. I tried to run but couldn't make my feet move. Mamo paced back and forth, wearing a path in the braid rug. She held her head in both hands like it might fall off. Over and over she moaned, "What are we going to do? Poor Bodie. Poor Bodie. Poor, poor Bodie."

Mother collapsed on the sofa, pale and floppy as cooked spaghetti, but starchy enough to mumble agreement. "I know, Mama. You're right, Mama. It'll be all right, Mama."

They had never agreed on anything until now! My ears felt like they were on fire. I shrieked. "What about me? Me! Me! Me! I hate you! You don't love anybody but your Fine Old Family!"

Mamo wheeled on me, howling like a banshee, rattling a bony finger in my face. "Bodie can't know. She must never know. It would kill her to know." I couldn't find my words but managed only to glare at Mamo while I wished all of them...the whole family...would die right here and now. Mamo could probably tell how I felt. She grabbed my shoulders, shook me and hissed. "Do you understand me, Sandy? She can never know!"

White-hot anger smoldered in my belly and spewed out in a blistering stream. "I hate you! Hate you! Hate you! Go away! Leave me alone!" Turning heel I blazed through the house and dived beneath the four-poster bed that I supplied for emergencies with my secret stuff, hidden inside the torn box-spring lining: a stash of books, Big Chief tablet and pencils, flashlight and cookies.

I dare them to try and find me! They'll be sorry! Sobbing, I screamed in my head, wanting to rip into them, bite, scratch and pound them with my fists until they shut up. I hoped they would find me. Was afraid they might. But they never came. *They know better,* I supposed. *No telling what might happen if they were stupid enough to corner me.*

The sun was going down before I crept from my dusty hideout. My time alone had not been wasted. I needed to figure things out…and I did. *No matter why or how they got this way, my family means only one thing to me: danger.*

To make certain I never forgot what I knew, I bore down with my No. 2 pencil and wrote as hard and dark as I could, making a list in my Big Chief tablet:

DANGEROUS THINGS ABOUT MY FAMILY
1. **They act nice sometimes and they are not**
2. **They pretend to be grown-up and they are not**
3. **Gifts cannot make up for bad things**
4. **I am way smarter than they are**
5. **The only person I can trust is me**

When I finished my list, I hid it in the torn lining of my mattress as a forever reminder.

It was almost dark, my legs and back felt ache-y and I was starving by the time I crawled from beneath the four-poster. I felt nervous. How would Mother and Mamo act?

When I crept through Mamo's bedroom and silently stood in the doorway, I found them sitting on the sun porch — Mamo in her green chair, and Jo beside Mother on the couch. Beyond glass-shuttered windows, sinking sunlight filtered through branches of the giant cedar tree and transformed the perfect lawn into ponds of mossy gray shadow. After a few seconds, Mamo, Mother and Jo noticed me standing there. Mid-sentence, they halted their conversation about azalea blossoms, which had been more beautiful this year than any other. They stared at me, but said nothing. Absolutely nothing...not "Hello" or "How are you?" Not "We're sorry," or "Are you sorry?" Just nothing, like I was invisible.

And maybe I was. What happened to me in Beaumont was never mentioned again. We had to protect Bodie. No one would ever know.

Before the soiled summer was over, I threw away Brother Charles's books. One book at a time, so nobody could make me take them back. Mother took me shopping for a training bra. I quit biting my nails and convinced her I was ready for Tangee pink lipstick and pale pink nail polish. After all, in September I would go to ninth grade. My baby sister grew up, too. All of a sudden she was a real girl about to enter fifth grade. I didn't think of her as my little sister anymore, but my best friend. And finally, just before Labor Day, when cicadas sang their dying song and leaves crinkled and curled, blazing into fiery orange, red and yellow, I gave up my childhood.

III

THE HILL COUNTRY

Sandy and Amie on farmhouse front porch

THE MOON HUNG HIGH, scattering beams through twisting oak branches, patterning shifting pools of light along the dusty road that led to my farmhouse, caressing me with shimmering fingers as I stretched my legs on a hand-hewn cedar column and pumped the Tennessee rocker back and forth, back and forth. I couldn't sleep; wasn't even inclined to try. Over-tired but riled up, I was exhausted emotionally. The eight-hour return from Longview back to the Hill Country was grueling enough in itself, but a shaky sense of reality messed with my head. Memories of Christmases past had come to roost, and I felt alert as the barn owl, *whoo…whoo…whoo*-ing in the darkness.

The *whos* crowded my mind, with Mother topping the list. From her invisible world, she insistently pecked at me like an irritated mother goose. Past and present, no question, Mother dominated my thoughts. But she was only a part of my unrest. Fresh recall; raw flashbacks jarred my senses with distressing images, smells and sensations like they happened yesterday. Horrible Brother Charles, my mother and grandmother's lack of love and understanding on that sun porch at 815 Charlotte Drive and my own primal disgust for our *Fine Old Family* filled me with visceral fury.

Sliding down the rabbit hole that emptied into the Texas of my childhood chafed thoroughly enough, but future skinned knees were guaranteed. In the present, my brooding, angry father lived and breathed out there somewhere. Aunt Margaret toted far more than photographs in that Piggly Wiggly grocery sack I had just dumped onto the fall-front lid of the old secretary in the farmhouse front room at my back, grateful to lay it down. That unpretentious plastic receptacle of memory revealed a cast of characters unfamiliar to my eyes: a whole other family, a whole other life, missing for forty-seven years. How do you resurrect an identity — so long-lost it feels like fiction — after a lifetime of separation? In a mere week, the simplicity that was mine for the past two years had become incredibly complicated.

There was nothing for it but reckoning the past, a reckoning that began with Mother's death a week ago. I wasn't ready. I felt reluctant to reckon anything, except maybe shift the flat stone walkway into better alignment with the dusty earth. Caretaking this parcel of magical real estate had awakened a joyful appreciation for simple pleasures. At first glance, love for this patch of wild swooped down and swept me away without a question, thought or backward glance. I never wanted the magic to end.

In October — unbelievably, just two years ago — when I first bumped down the dusty roadway that led to this white clapboard farmhouse, making a radical move was the last thing on my mind. I wasn't picky. Mainly I wanted to reduce my overhead and cut down on the drama. In June, I had purchased pastel linen dresses for Sarah and Lacie to wear to their dad's out-of-state wedding. In July, I helped Mother move back to *Texas* — which meant Houston. In late August, we loaded Sarah off to college at the University of Texas in Austin. Lacie's boyfriend became her husband the first week of October.

Globally, 1994 had been a stellar year. Aside from Lorena Bobbitt messing with her husband's manhood and the gruesome Nicole Brown Simpson murders, things at home and abroad were peaceful. The Atlantic hurricane season petered out, leaving U.S. soil untouched. President Bill Clinton's positive political influence spread to Europe, where he and Russian President Yeltsin signed a stand-down nuclear-arms agreement.

As for me *sans* child support, financing Sarah at college stretched my finances, and through necessity I poured energy into my private practice twenty-four/seven. Downsizing in familiar Alamo Heights was the sensible plan. Probably I'd lease a small duplex or condo, possibly travel. And down the line, when I felt secure, maybe...maybe...open up to the possibility of a relationship.

Little did I know, the wild-woman side of me buried since childhood in service to life as a wife and mother — and a good life, until it wasn't anymore — was on the loose and would have her way with me. By chance — or perhaps fate — just as I began the search for a conservative crib where I could lay my head, a friend offhandedly mentioned that a friend of hers was done with chiggers and grasshoppers. This unlikely hovel, located in primitive mesquite and juniper backcountry, would be available for lease soon. Impulse grabbed hold, and I was jonesing to have a look.

Here it stood, positioned on a gentle rise in the land, surrounded by oak groves with fairy dust glimmering off the landscape and the theme from *Out of Africa* playing in my head. Even though he wasn't Robert Redford, from the beginning I felt tender towards the grandfatherly German landowner who puffed out his chest and reared back, military-straight, outfitted in khaki slacks and starched and pressed white cotton shirt. That first October morning still blistering hot beneath a blast of Texas sunshine, I shook his hand and cemented the deal before I even thought about it. Reason had nothing to do with this choice. It was pure romance.

Although I couldn't own this place and would be only a "tenant," as the prehistoric German gentleman made sure I understood, this gleaming parcel of land belonged to me at first sight. In my eyes, the whole ten acres — which I claimed as mine, to have and hold from this day forward — sparkled against the tangled mass of undergrowth, mesquite trees long neglected and bracken of young cedar, home to deer and rabbits. Each month, the pull of the full moon summoned a herd of feral hogs, which snorted and snuffed across the meadow, rooting the earth with their snouts. On the other side of the barbed-wire fence that separated the farmhouse from grazing land, white egrets and blue heron vied for water rights with a lowing herd of Herefords. And on cool nights with wooden window sashes thrown high, I drifted into peaceful sleep serenaded by a pack of coyotes, singing to the moon out back beyond the abandoned barn and ancient wrought iron-enclosed cemetery with gravestones etched in German.

The stately owner to these primeval acres was the stuff of Texas folklore. For ninety-five years he had lived on this land and his family before him, the original settlers. My imagination went wild picturing the untamed Texas Plains of 1800's which his parents civilized, and passed down as his heritage. The American Indians, rustlers, Texas Rangers, cowboys, sheepherders and settlers; the endless battles, scuffles and range wars these eight-hundred acres had witnessed. The old gentleman lived beyond hilly fields and rusted barbed wire, in the "big house." From my front porch on moonless nights, if a gusty wind parted the tangle of tree limbs I caught flickers of lamplight twinkling through his windows. His widowed son and his son's two teenage children lived in the third house, farther up the hill, impossible to locate in the dark no matter how brightly their lights shone. Our three structures were the only houses on this abundant acreage.

The curving rocky roadway that led from the highway to my shotgun-style farmhouse was all but impassable; deep gouges dredged by fierce Hill Country thunderstorms swallowed the tires of my Jeep. The ramshackle cottage was hardly in better condition. In truth, it looked like an old abandoned shack. A rusted television antenna hung precariously from a chimney. Even though it was substantially cracked, the cement-floored front porch was solid enough. The ceiling in the front room sagged and shed blobs of plaster, and one wall was papered with a silver foil, bamboo print, a little crinkly in spots. Water from the well leaked through pipes up-ground and trickled through my kitchen and bathroom faucets in a meager drizzle. Upkeep on the septic tank had been so neglected that rank waste water pooled in the side yard beneath the kitchen windows if I didn't control how much water dumped into the system all at once.

Who cared, anyway? These slight problems appeared entirely fixable. In New Braunfels, the closest town, surely the HEB grocery displayed green sheets that advertised services offered for the Hill Country area. Local handymen would be eager to hire on, right? How much could it cost to repair a doorjamb here, a window sash there, wrap a bit of lattice skirting around the exposed cinder block foundation and add a little paint and spackle?

With worried expressions, my friends and family questioned this radical departure from a manicured St. Augustine lifestyle. But when they asked, "Aren't you afraid living out there all alone?" I answered with what might sound like a riddle to them, but exactly expressed the fullness I felt. "I don't live alone. I live with myself."

Predictably, Mother would be underwhelmed about my choice of living arrangements. Her new Houston apartment — citified and civilized, patrolled and protected, lacquered and lovely — was emblematic of her refined taste, drilled into me from time immemorial. I dreaded calling and owning what could only be from her perspective, an egregious error in judgment. It took me two weeks to get up enough courage to tell the truth.

Mother had become increasingly frail over the past year,

and my country-girl fantasy set her off like Roman candles on the Fourth of July. "You what? Damn you, Sandy! You're going to be the death of me! I didn't raise you to be stupid! No woman in her right mind would move out to the country all alone like that! What is the matter with you, anyway? You can't do this to me! My blood pressure! I can't deal with this, now. I'll talk to you later."

A week later Mother — a woman of her word — and I continued our one-sided conversation. "Sandy! Now listen to me and don't say a word. I've been investigating. That godforsaken Mexican town of yours at least offers a reasonable burglar-alarm company. I've already made arrangements. They'll be contacting you about installing a system in your wretched farmhouse. Consider it done and leave me out of it. I don't want to hear a word out of you!" We lost the connection. I knew it wasn't a dropped call. I didn't call back.

Had Mother known the farmhouse's only door locks were simple hook and screw-eyes, she would have felt compelled to hire a locksmith. Panicked, I realized this place required civilizing renovation if I expected my mother to lay her head beneath towering oaks with low-hanging branches eerily scratching against the tin roof in the slightest breeze.

Deciding where to begin the restoration process was hardly an issue. Opportunities abounded. Fortunately, the ten many-paned windows with wavy glass — two in the front room, one in the teensy bedroom, two in the bathroom, two in the kitchen and two in the front study — were gloriously tall and wide, and I didn't want to cover a one. Nothing would block the meadow view of rangy mesquite, juniper, huisache, the cluster of oaks and tall burgundy grasses whispering in the breeze.

After I overcame the overwhelm of peeling paint and sagging plaster, the claw-foot tub taking forever to fill — forget about a shower — and a black pot-bellied iron stove in the kitchen serving as the solitary source of heat, I pulled on an old pair of jeans and chambray shirt and got to work. Climbing the ancient wood ladder I found in the tin shed out back, balancing joint compound, putty knife and paint rollers, filling cracks, resurfacing, rolling eggshell white and sunrise colors to the ceiling, the lyrics of Mama Cass Elliot's "New World Coming" hummed through my head:

There's a New World Coming. And it's just around the bend...
There's a new voice calling. You can hear it if you try...
Coming in peace, coming in joy, coming in love.

On Turkey Day that first year, my little dollhouse had her coming-out party. At sunrise a Blue Norther — the first of the season — swooshed down, clashing with the tepid air of Indian Summer, creating billowing clouds of foggy mists that settled on grasses and leaves like glistening diamonds.

By mid-morning when Lacie and John drove up from San Antonio, Sarah — who had driven down from Austin the day before — and I had already stuffed the pot-bellied stove with cedar logs for a trial run. With a nudge from a cheater self-burning log, the cedar immediately caught fire, and before long the humble black iron contraption blazed red hot. The old walls breathed in the warmth, soaked it up and within an hour the whole place radiated an even temperature that magnified the yummy aroma of the big bird browning in the minuscule oven. This was mother nirvana, milling bod to bod beside my brood, slicing, dicing and dishing traditional cornbread dressing, yellow squash and green-bean trailer-trash casseroles, mashed potatoes, Pillsbury midget croissants, Waldorf salad and pumpkin pie.

Physical warmth and an overfull belly, although extraordinarily superb, were the least I felt grateful for this first Thanksgiving. After the divorce — not so long ago, really — after the initial ache of separation and worrying that my house would never feel like home again, now to have my family living close by and sharing the holidays stoked my emotional fires, and banked them high with what felt like forever-burning embers. At no other time in my life had I ever felt so irrationally, completely at home. In my mind this was nothing short of a miracle.

Through the next months, family and friends came to witness this odd life that Sandy had created. Jo was the first to arrive. In jeans and boots, we tromped around the land. "Wow. Doesn't this remind you of the Farm in Kountze," she asked. "It was so special."

"Yes, it was," I answered, knowing my *yes* veiled a dark truth. To this day, the secret of Brother Charles had never been told. I wasn't ready to have that conversation, and might never. Sinking into a pit of confession was the last thing I wanted when occasions where Jo and I could walk on common ground were rare.

To protect relationships that are keepers and never going away even though they are difficult and dangerous, I've developed cautionary guidelines. With a soul-sister or soul mate who mirrors my deepest self, I share one-hundred percent of who I am — even the bitchy, confused, lonely parts — trusting they won't try to fix me, judge me, gossip about me, or blackmail me down the line. With others, like treasured career mates, I share maybe fifty percent. And with others I only share one-fourth of my true self. But that one-fourth is still a wholehearted fraction that both gives and receives, just at a playful, *olly-olly-in-free* level of being which is often satisfying enough. I wasn't planning on messing that up.

We laughed, joked and explored the day away in conflict-free sister time until night fell around us like an old quilt. Lazily slouched in rocking chairs on the front porch, we huddled together against the brisk, chilly night, caught up on

mutual Houston friends and reminisced about childhood,
without shame, blame or harsh words. It was beautiful. And
when we couldn't hold our eyes open any longer, we giggled
ourselves to sleep in my king-size bed that barely fit into the
slant-roof bedroom that had once been a back porch. At first
light, the *coo-coo* of doves announced morning. It was my
birthday, and miraculously, we would soon discover that
during the night the land had delivered a present.

With coffee mugs in hand, Jo and I pushed the grating
screen door aside and walked out into morning mist, dewy
fields of wild grasses winking in the breeze. From behind the
Tennessee rocking chairs, a gray, fuzzy creature rose from
sleep and fixed penetrating brown eyes on my face.

"It's a wolf!" I teased and grabbed for Jo, playing on our
shared memory of Aunt Bodie scaring us with that hairy wolf
foot after bedtime stories on the sleeping porch of Wil-Lou
Lakes Farm. But this animal didn't lunge or bare fangs. After
a heart-thumping second or two, Jo and I agreed this was a
girly, doggy-creature, smaller than any self-respecting wolf
and hardly menacing with that fluffy gray tail curving over
her back.

Hoping to communicate that I wasn't a threat, I crouched
in front of the puppy until our eyes met at the same level. She
stood motionless, surveying me with all-encompassing,
chocolate-brown eyes. Encouraged that she didn't bolt, I
tentatively moved even closer until we touched noses and
remained nose-to-nose for a few heart-opening seconds. In
that moment, we belonged to each other. And I swear, when I
asked, "What is your name?" she told me, thought to thought,
that she was *Amie.* "My friend," I translated. And so she was.

From the beginning, our intuitive connection was
stunning. When I needed Amie or just wondered what she was
up to, all I had to do was walk out on the porch and *think* of
her. There she'd come, loping through a field and under

barbed wire, running lickety split up the road or scooching on her belly from beneath the old water tower out back, which she claimed as her kennel. She rarely barked, but when she needed me, Amie took a position on the stone walkway, standing alert without moving, for however long it took for me to sense her presence. I am convinced that humans and animals can be soul mates. We were from day one.

Even though Amie looked like a mutt to me, when I took her to be spayed so she wouldn't have little coyote babies, the country vet had another opinion. "Got a Keeshond here. Not yet full-grown. They are an Arctic breed like the Husky, real popular with the Dutch. These dogs are accustomed to bitter cold. Trained to work on sailing ships. Warned the sailors of impending danger. They spook in a rainstorm. To them it is a life-threatening situation. You have got yourself a pure-bred dog here. No telling where she ran off from. Probably that last storm spooked her good. We have no shortage of strays around here. If you will have her, I think she is yours."

When I tried to put a collar and leash on Amie or attempted to coax her inside, she sprawled on her back in the dirt road and whimpered like she was being whipped. She just flat refused to be tamed. With the run of the land, it didn't take long for her idea of fun to turn into a bad reputation with the local ranchers. The irate landowners showed up on my front porch, banged on the screen door, shook their fist and hollered, "That damn dog of yours is chasing up my stock. If you don't keep her penned up, I'm gonna shoot her!"

I knew exactly what they meant, had seen it with my own eyes. On our walks down country lanes, my shouts did nothing to stop Amie from tearing out under a fence and across a field whenever she sniffed sheep. She didn't nip at the flock but only ran herd, not satisfied until she corralled them into a quaking huddle. I felt bad for the bleating sheep, but insensitive towards the ranchers' plight. My dog wasn't mean.

She was just doing what came naturally. But from their perspective this amounted to terrorizing their livelihood. They meant business.

And still, I couldn't bear to tie Amie up like any sensible doggie-parent should. Instead I refused to comply with the rancher's demands and took chances with her life. Even though I figured out why I couldn't talk myself into restraining my beautiful Amie, knowing the reason made no difference. In truth, she seemed a lot like me. Wise or unwise, I would rather have her die from a bullet than die of a broken heart mourning her freedom. Amie and I shared this grand adventure, and I dealt destiny the upper hand.

When the weather warmed up that first spring I became obsessed with yardwork, heavy on weeding. Once I hacked flower beds out of the dried-out, clumpy, root-bound sod and bordered them with round white river rocks I wheelbarrowed from wherever they lay, I loaded the back of the Jeep with Wolfe nursery mulch and topsoil, trays of hardy yellow, purple and pink lantana and red salvia, broad-frond purple liriope, blue plumbago and yellow yarrow. Once the meandering beds that cozied up to the house on all sides were planted with resilient nursery favorites, my eye roamed in search of more plants, more flowers, more beauty. Out in the grassy fields, purple iris grew wild so I transplanted those along with Black-eyed Susan and any other flowering plant I could wrestle from the parched soil. On weekends, between my first cup of coffee and a cold dinner on the front porch, I dug and planted until my body ached and my heart overflowed with happiness.

My boots were consistently clumped with dirt, so naturally I resorted to my time-tested practice of shamelessly — yet practically — peeing in the yard behind the house, out of sight of anyone except grasshoppers and hummingbirds.

And of course, Amie, who just squatted and peed in unison.

By the time the dormant fields exploded with shades of green, my lovely little shack had been transformed inside and out. Rusty screens on the ten wavy-glass windows were restrung. Fresh white paint wrapped the front porch and aging shiplap boards. The landowner had sympathetically re-angled the pipes from the well, and a consistent flow poured through my faucets. I hired a local plumber to install a doable shower rig, and a rancher willing to grade roadways for a small price — by city standards. I tossed an old Heriz rug on top of the beige carpet in the front room, and my gently aged upholstered pieces nestled into place like they had lived here since Texas was a child.

While I gentrified my homestead, I kept a San Antonio office and limited my practice to an intense three days a week. My forty-five-minute commute, rolling along grassy country highways, cutting through forested hillsides and settling into an easy clip down Highway 35 put me in a Zen state of mind. If this journey to and from San Antonio nourished my parched body, mind and spirit, then why wouldn't this be true for my clients as well?

At first I invited only high-profile professionals — doctors, lawyers, therapists — to the farm. Privacy was a priority, and the only warm-blooded creatures who would observe their comings and goings were sweet-faced Herefords, grazing in the pasture that ran alongside my property. But since clients referred their friends, networking webs of people connected all the time and word soon got around. Before long the phone was ringing and I answered, "Yes." "Yes." "Yes!" By late spring of the first year steady clouds of dust trailed up and down the lovely smooth roadbed.

Quickly my San Antonio office no longer made sense, so I negotiated my way out of the lease. When I shared my plan with my long-time soul-sister office manager, Emily — with a bubbly yet efficient personality and a mouth on her that could scorch concrete — she shouted, "Of course I'm coming. That's a vacation!" Quick as a lightning strike, Emily commandeered the land line and set up shop in the small front room with a separate entry door off the front porch. The whole setup was perfect — as if it was meant to be from the get-go.

Before I realized what was happening, my practice flourished in a retreat-center setting. Sometimes a client and I settled into the front-porch pair of Tennessee rockers that a former client gifted after locating his craftsman family in Appalachia. Sometimes we ambled around the land sharing and eventually propping our backs against an ancient oak within the grove of four towering branches, often burning a poison-pen letter — never intended to be read — in the fire pit surrounded by thirteen white stones. When icy storms rattled the window panes, I stoked embers in the pot-bellied stove, and clients cozied into an overstuffed chair in the front room. The third time someone sipped a warm mug of chamomile and purred, "This feels like home," I knew I had stumbled into something better than good.

One of my esteemed way-showers, mythologist Joseph Campbell, taught that the way to create a fulfilled life is to *follow your bliss*, lean toward what makes you happy. And so I had. Without getting in my head and figuring things out — the way I usually make decisions — I simply followed my heart and fell into my version of paradise. Since the first night I slept beneath the vast canopy of stars, I had never feared for my safety. But now I felt terrified of loss. I loved this place. I wanted it. I needed it. This land felt like holy ground, the pulsating center of my universe.

Feeling panicked, I asked my attorney to draft a lease/purchase agreement and in a large manila envelope delivered the legal document to the aging owner, praying he would consult with his son and they would jump at the chance to sell a meager ten acres. I had reason to trust that the deal would be accepted. The gentlemanly owner's widowed — and as yet not remarried — son had commented when he ambled up my road to check out what all the traffic was about, "This place has never looked so good." Shuffling his feet and stirring up dust with the tip of his boot, he declared, "I hope you stay here forever."

He was appealing in a Texas good-old-boy, khaki-butt sort of way. I'm pretty much a Texas good-old-girl myself, so we might have made beautiful music, although I'm not into the *oompah-pah* German variety that his band offered at local beer joints. In truth, even if this woman-less — clearly ready to mate — heir to eight hundred acres of pristine raw land pregnant with limitless potential *was* interested in me, I couldn't come to it. I was already occupied.

These two magical years, Amie, clients, family and friends were not the only gifts the land attracted. No matter her age, a woman is magnetic when she lives from the center of who she is. My heart opened wide and men tumbled into my life. One was a broker, one an attorney, and one a spiritual guru. The broker hung his fishing pole in the rafters on my back porch. The attorney asked if he could dig a fire pit for roasting a whole pig. The guru stayed for a while, then flew away to California and purposeful work in a legendary retreat center. The relationships were sweet and ended well. Not because there was anything wrong, but because we just weren't right.

My guru was the hardest to let go. Not because I loved him more, but because we shared spiritual beliefs and a passion for facilitating healing. On the front porch with Amie looking sad at my side as if she sensed my tears, my lover and I kissed our final goodbye. As he turned and walked away, I slumped into a Tennessee rocking chair and bit my lip, promising myself I wouldn't cry and ruin our last moments.

He hesitated as he opened the door of his sedan and looked back, bathing me in a broad smile. "You look pretty sitting there on the porch."

I answered, returning the compliment. "I feel pretty. Being with you makes me feel this way."

"You should." He tucked his chin and showered me with a slow, sexy grin. "I can't be celibate, you know. Will you come see me?"

I returned his warmth with my eyes, but was shocked by my reply. "No, over is over. My life is here." Realizing this was harsh, I cleaned it up. "But I'll always remember you with beautiful thoughts." As he drove away in a cloud of dust, I realized with a thud: *I've taken this land as my lover. How can any man compete? Unless, that is, he shares my passions, my dreams.*

In quiet front-porch moments as I sat with this distressing awareness, I saw how I had come to this point. For twenty-six married years — twenty-nine, really, if I counted the three years my husband and I were together in college — my freedom had been restricted, caged and cut back a meaningful lifetime too long. A question hung there, and I feared knowing the answer: *Honestly, am I capable of completely opening my heart to a man again? Even a loving relationship feels like tender entrapment.* Not alone, but with myself, seemed the only way I could now live my life. I felt deeply sad. I felt deliriously free.

More than partnership, I wanted this place for myself, my family and all the clients who had come to love it. With the never-ending flow of blessings coming my way, I felt convinced that fate had a hand in my settling on this land. Deep in my soul I just knew this place was mine. And while I patiently waited for sure ownership, I sketched plans for renovating the ancient barn out back, all the while feeling happy, joyous and free as iridescent hummingbirds flitting from flower to flower across my front porch...and the waning moon floating high and white until it drifted out of sight.

REARRANGING MY LIFE INTO manageable order had taken the greater part of the month following Mother's funeral. Tying up loose ends, I located a memorial company in Longview and ordered Mother's gravestone, strangely deciding to have *Wilma Flewellen Miller Foster* inscribed, instead of *Wilma Miller Foster* — her legal name. Plain and simple, the inscription was a lie, but sometimes heart-truth is greater than mere factual details. My mother was Flewellen all the way to the marrow of her bones.

Clearly, her ghost approved of creative license, giggling in my ear as I finalized the memorial-company order after also deciding to inscribe, *Nearer God's Heart in the Garden*, a paraphrase from a favorite old Flewellen hymn. Most likely, Mother implanted the *Flewellen* idea in the first place. Her ghost had mastered the art of subliminal suggestion. Pretty scary. In the same way I had grown accustomed to the purring presence of my fuzzy children — Pookie, a black-and-white short-hair with a Hitler mustache, and Maximilian the Great, a fourteen-pound, orange-and-white beast with long hair and a lion's mane — ever so stealthily draped across clients' folders when I transcribed sessions, Mother's commonplace suggestions affected me at the level of familiarity. There, but not there. So constant, so usual, I had begun not to notice…at least consciously. Nor did I pay attention to the critical fact that being ignored is abhorrent to a queen.

I was too busy trying to stay sane to give much consideration to Mother's state of being. For as long as I could remember, meaningful work — like my private practice —

translated into salvation. Sweating my way to beauty on this land these past two years, my heart lurched when I recalled Annie wisdom: "Best yo' can do is jes be yo'self. God don' 'spect no mo' from any of us," coupled with the Flewellen brother's pride about Papaw's Puritan Work Ethic. When I played barefoot beneath the Wisteria Arbor, the Green-Eyed Monster grabbed hold of me because I wasn't J. J. Flewellen's child. I didn't think Mamo, Bodie, Nana, Junie and Gene were good enough children for Papaw…like I would definitely be if I had the chance. Annie was my secret weapon, but Papaw was my secret devotion. And now that I was full-grown and able, it was time to walk my talk. Staying focused — in spite of Mother's self-centered demands — challenged my everyday quality of life even more than divorce, or any other heavy-duty losses past.

This mere month since Mother's death and burial felt like eons. A reality check confirmed it amounted to only four weeks, twenty-eight days and — more or less — six hundred and seventy two hours. What was one piddling calendar month within a lifetime bent toward meaningful work? Everyone loses parents. We grieve. That's normal, as evidenced by many sympathy cards, phone messages and emails from clients. What they couldn't know is that Mother still hung out, or that I molted emotionally…unless I told them…which I wouldn't. Only an idiot would stir up suspicions that the therapist herself had gone around the bend. Without the stabilizing support of work, I would be a total wreck.

Fortunately, my practice didn't even hiccup. One-on-one client sessions stayed steady. This month I had mailed flyers for a couples' workshop, and organized an ongoing group with six strong and gutsy women who I suspected would become best friends. One weekend I had retreated to Austin's Lake Travis and reconnected with my therapist soul-sister friend, Connie — older than me by eleven years, but equally eclectic as I about spirituality. I trusted Connie and gratefully laid down the truth about Mother. With every word I felt relief from the heavy burden that hunched my shoulders. Connie didn't seem to think I was nuts, because we went ahead with plans for co-facilitating monthly workshops to be staged on her Austin turf. There was *kumbaya* everywhere, except between me and Mother's ghost — or when I considered establishing a relationship with my found Foster family.

Fear of opening Pandora's Box felt almost paralyzing. *I'll call soon*, I told myself every time the image of Margaret in that blue print dress crossed my mind. But I simply hadn't gathered courage. Was there anything left of the innocent little girl Margaret remembered? I feared disappointing her, but more, I feared disappointing myself. It had to be done, but did I have to hurry?

Like a homeopathic cure, every morning — whether I wanted to or not — I digested *one* of the tattered childhood photographs Margaret had shared at Mother's graveside. And with each image, I brooded over the groundswell of renegade childhood memories: tried, convicted, forgiven and put to rest years before, now on the loose again, disturbing the peace.

The worst of it, sifting through family memorabilia stored all these years in the dusty attic of memory, led me to admit that in fact, like it or not, I am Mother's lineage bearer — present tense. *Look at me. I'm doing it — turning up the dirt, digging the roots. So then — horror of horrors — could it also be true that I am destined to do something — like, right now? What, for instance?*

I was just lying to myself. I knew that Mother meant for me to tell the *Fine Old Family* story. But I wasn't a fan of this idea; it gnawed at me like those voracious little mice that noisily scurried around inside the tin shed in the side yard. How would I go about sharing her precious lineage, anyway?

I lacked enthusiasm for Tara. And what about the secrets? She would never want those told.

Besides, I wasn't a writer, other than penning research papers and a column about emotional and spiritual healing that I wrote for *Whole Health*, a free Hill Country magazine stacked bimonthly in bins at the entrance to Whole Foods. Those little eight-hundred-word articles kept clients flowing toward me like the Guadalupe after soaking rains. Granted, as a freshman at the University of Texas, I had intended to major in journalism. Things got off-course, though, when I was assigned to *The Daily Texan*, UT's student newspaper and proving ground for future journalists. Wearing Jesus sandals and dreadlocks smelling of weed, the eager staff had crowded around their new recruit and assured me I should "make love, not war," while one of the great unwashed idly flipped my long pageboy and breathed behind my right ear — therefore radically inverting my original intent.

They scared me. I couldn't handle their raw energy and passion. I beat feet. I did not pass go. I did not collect $200. As fast as my Bass Weejun loafers could carry me, I hauled across campus and signed up for a safe elementary-education degree. I couldn't afford to be wild. The instability I grew up with was enough for a lifetime, thank you very much.

But in spite of swerving from a journalistic path, I could string a few nouns and verbs together and throw in an adjective, adverb and a prepositional phrase or two. *All right Mother*, I thought one night as I sat at my desk after writing client notes. *I'll give it a go.* I opened the laptop and started a new folder, "Mother's Story." This was not, actually, *her* story. How could it be when she was not alive to write it? This was *my* version of her story...and...it was fairly vicious.

With every word, the stifling smoke of Mother's displeasure pressed around me. She said not a word. Many times I had seen her like this: brooding, fuming and belching volcanic ash until she generated energy for eruption. I sat in the shadow of Vesuvius. Several pages down the word.doc road, the computer crashed.

Faulty connection, I assumed. At a stopping point in the story, I automatically glanced at my watch and realized it was late, already midnight. I tried several times to reboot the laptop before I gave up, deciding that in the morning I would email Lacie's husband, John, for help. As I completed the busywork of sorting papers and checking my calendar for tomorrow's therapy sessions, I glanced at the clock that hung on the wall above the desk — the battery-operated clock. It still read 12:00 AM. I checked my watch again. The hands registered thirty minutes later, 12:30 AM. I froze, momentarily stunned motionless. My head felt like it would explode. "Oh my God!" I screamed, and Pookie and Maxy dove for cover. The computer and clock *both* crashed exactly at midnight. And they ran on completely different power sources.

Gooseflesh crept up my arms and stood my scalp on end. Feeling livid, I shouted out loud to the — judging from visual evidence — empty house, "Mother! Quit it! Pretty impressive, aren't you? You have dominion over hard drives and super-cells. Simultaneously! Stop messing with my life! What is it? You don't like what I'm writing? Can't say I blame you, but it's all I've got. Well, alrighty then. Who needs it? I quit!" I stormed out of the office and foraged for chocolate, determined to forevermore dump the insane idea of chronicling Mother's life.

But her ghost possessed the tenacity of a prehistoric mole, a crawling cretin burrowing through the underground psyches of her descendants, depositing mounds of discomfort in her wake. The enormity of Mother's devilish determination and the futility of defensive measures filled me with desperation. Somehow, someway, I had to get the upper hand.

Pity I wasn't a primitive woman. If I belonged to a tribe, the local shaman would probably smoke up a healing ritual. Maybe he — or the Medicine Woman — would encourage me to cry, rant, paint my face and shred my clothes. Perhaps give me a new name, necklace, feather, tattoo, or possibly a new bone for my nose. Everybody would know what I was going through. They might even throw a campfire in my honor. I'd smoke a peace pipe, summon my demons and the demons of my family, dance until we dropped and feel better in the morning.

However, it was highly unlikely that a stray shaman would cross my path. Instead, I could shred the copy of *Mother's Story*, sob until I was spent and torch the paper in the oak-grove fire pit. White puffs of spiraling smoke would represent my willingness to release resentment and anger, and claim both forgiveness and excessively longed-for acceptance. On rainy days, flushing torn fragments of rage down the toilet could substitute as my pagan ritual of exorcism.

And then there was my altar, a humble contrivance created from my grandmother's mahogany secretary wedged into a corner of the minuscule front room. When I lowered the slant front and pulled out the first drawer to support the weight, I called the exposed shelf *sacred*. Every morning after rolling out of bed, I encouraged my eyes to focus by staring at my holy place, shaped by the remembered thud of the heavy slant top all those years at Mamo's house, and pedestrian objects that to me symbolized worlds of meaning. I lit the white candle and reminded myself that there had been times when my thoughts were clean and unpolluted by negativity. A heart-shaped black seed pod washed ashore on Galveston Bay from far-flung West Indies isles spoke of the universality of love. An *Ichthys* paperweight suggested I was never alone when I connected to *Christ Consciousness.* In my mind, the meaning of this ancient Christian fish symbol was not limited to the historical Jesus, but represented the universal source of *Higher Love* common to all people, of all races and religions, since the beginning of time. A tiny, ivory-colored Buddha challenged me to seek contentment and laughter. A smooth white river stone plucked from the Frio River on a silent retreat years ago encouraged me to be still. When my life was rich with opportunity for angst (like now), my altar sagged under a plethora of meaningful objects. And in times of deep peace (like the last two years), only the single white candle burned (or maybe two when I believed true love had come again).

Pouring a cup of joe prepped me for the next phase of my morning ritual. Lifting my journal from the table beside my wing-back, I pushed the screen door aside, plopped into a rocking chair, propped my feet on a post and poured my heart into the pages of a spiral notebook which I called my *God Book.* Since the *Holy* was the most likely friend to forgive my rants, pages of discontent tumbled out first. These white-hot feelings were prime contenders for burning or flushing later in the day. Eventually I got down to the business of measuring my options, and asking questions of God. Such as: *Would you please take my mother? Like, immediately?* Or, when I felt more loving: *God, since I'm not doing a very good job of being a decent human being, would you take over here?*

Dreams, when I could remember them, went into my journal, too. Years ago, Carl Jung's work awakened me to the curative role dreams play in healing a bruised psyche: "The dream is a small hidden door in the deepest and most intimate sanctum of soul, which opens to that primeval cosmic night that was soul long before there was a conscious ego and will be soul far beyond what a conscious ego can ever reach."

With Mother's spirit unpredictably visiting around, I recorded Lacie and Sarah's dreams and haunting experiences as well as my own. Praying that one fortunate day I might read back through my journal and feel grateful that *Morgaine le Fey* had faded into the mists of *Avalon,* on November 14 — two weeks after Mother's supposed burial — I wrote: This is big. Sarah just called. As she drifted off to sleep last night she had a dream. Not really a dream, more like a waking visitation. She heard a voice say, "Tell her I'm sorry I hurt her and held her back. I did it all for love." Sarah bolted upright and burst into tears when she heard Mother's voice. "Bebe was there, Mom! Not like human there, but ghost there — wavy and cloudy. I knew it was her. Nobody else talks like that."

Sarah was a basket case, fighting tears, her voice gravelly and hoarse. "There was no emotional buildup, Mom! You know it's not like me to be so emotional! I'm not even sure what I sobbed about...but I couldn't stop. I only know Bebe was talking about you. Apologizing to *you*, Mom. And then after she spoke, there were five flashes of light. What does five mean?"

I told her I had no idea.

"Well, anyway, Bebe's ghost disappeared into the light. Here's the scariest part: the light was so beautiful I wanted to follow it. Mom! I think I might have died if I had. I was so pulled! It was horrible. I don't think I've ever felt so scared. But I grabbed hold of the sheets and stopped myself from running into the light."

This has got to stop. I'm thinking to myself while I'm trying to decide what I should say to Sarah. *Screwing with my computer is one thing. Screwing up Sarah's life is completely unacceptable. Why isn't Mother sharing her come-to-Jesus, "I did it all for love" awareness with ME? Apologizing to ME?*

Because she knows I'll call her on her stuff...always have. She knows she can't shame, blame or charm me into doing what she wants. So does she think she can scare me into complying with her wishes, whatever they may be? NOT.

Can you hear my thoughts, Mother? Are you listening? We've got to work things out − together − just you and me learning to love. Not buying into fear or rage. Here's what I think: Our anger toward each other is only a secondhand emotion. We're fighting because we're scared of being murdered with words, meanness and wicked judgments. Love and fear…the one you feed is the one that grows.

I've got to love you, Mother. No choice. Mainly because I believe we become what we fear. I can't allow myself to hate you, fear you and be forever angry, because that's how I could become like you. Cold hard resentment buried like a stone, growing huge in the nests of my obsession. A boulder rolling out of my mouth, sounding like you, acting like you.

Listen up. I've changed how I act toward you. Have you noticed? I realize I'm pissed right now. Because I'm scared of what your antics will do to Sarah. This is only a temporary condition. I'm no longer invested in our "Anger Will Get Me Through" game. Like it or not, I'm gonna love you until you love yourself enough to quit being a scared little girl acting big and bossy.

I hoped I handled this right with Sarah. Hearing her sheer terror broke my heart. She's my child − not my client. I was hardly objective. I talked her through near-hysteria best I could, when I wanted to scream and tear my hair, furious with Mother for her kamikaze terror tactics. I advised Sarah to call on her angels, pray to Mother-Father God for protection and ask that she be surrounded with protective God-light. To hold the image of the Light, covering and shielding her every waking…every sleeping moment. I said that she has free will and ultimate control. Neither Mother, nor anyone else on the Other Side, can make her do anything she didn't want to do, not even God. I reminded her that she instinctively knew how to protect herself. She didn't rush into the light. She could trust her judgment. She didn't need to be afraid.

Keeping my head on straight and processing the Bebe Happenings was becoming a full-time job. A few days after

Sarah's white-light experience, Lacie phoned. "Okay, Mom. Here's the latest."

"Shoot," I said, beginning to feel the mice gnaw at my gut.

"I had a dream last night. I'm standing in front of a beautiful medieval door, all carved and intricate. Round at the top. It's shut. White light is pouring through the cracks all around the edges. Bebe walks up to the door, opens it and walks into the light."

"Oh my, Lace. That's wonderful. So, you think she's gone to the light and won't be back?"

Lacie quickly shot back, "Bebe? Gone for good? I doubt it. I feel her. She wants something pretty bad. Don't know what, but she's too stubborn to give up without a fight."

This is not what I wanted to hear, but I could hang with it. I was practicing loving acceptance, letting go of control, what will be, will be, *que sera, sera*. My attitude seemed mature and the results felt profoundly peaceful, almost normal, even hopeful and positive. But my Zen state of mind left me completely unprepared for Mother's next move.

Although it was already December, the rusted thermometer on the front porch registered eighty degrees. The Christmas tree sparkled with twinkling white lights and random ornaments collected through the years, but Mother Nature wasn't cooperating with the Christmas spirit. As often happens in the Hill Country, a humid gush of Gulf Coast air delivered toasty days of Indian Summer. Notoriously slow in coming, winter would soon descend. This was hardly evident today.

First thing this steamy morning, Lacie called, mysteriously saying she wanted to *talk*. I doubted my still-acting-like-a-newlywed daughter would make this solo effort just to deliver her Christmas wish list. Since their marriage two years ago, Lacie and John had glommed together, making Lacie's mitosis today all the more suggestive. I had a hunch what this *talk* was about and why protoplasmic metaphors fertilized my mind.

In the blazing sunlight on this thirsty Saturday afternoon my skin felt itchy and dry, all my senses on alert. My grown-up baby girl and I cooled off on the front porch and surveyed the parched fields where grasshoppers nosily foraged in scorched brown stubble. Lacie rattled ice in her tall glass, took a sip of Crystal Light, cocked her blond head to one side and amplified our chitchat to a whole new level. "Mom?"

"What, sweetie?" I took a deep breath and leaned back, anticipating news worth rejoicing about.

Lacie's forehead creased with apprehension. "I don't really want to tell you this." She threw her feet over the broad arm of the rocking chair and faced me head-on. Inside of me, a warning siren started to wail. "Okay. Here it is." She hesitated and sighed, impaling me with her eyes. "You know the dream I told you about? The one with the round door and light seeping around the corners?"

"Yeah, I remember. It was awesome. Sarah had a similar dream. We thought Mother walked into the light? Right?" This wasn't going exactly as I expected.

"Um, yeah. That's the problem."

"Problem?" I felt like a bag of rocks suddenly dropped into my lap.

"I haven't told you this part. The next night after the door dream, as I was going to sleep I had a premonition that I was pregnant. We've been trying, you know."

"I do know. I sort of imagined you drove out to tell me you're pregnant." I smiled hopefully, imagining my confession would steer her toward the real message, the good news, and quick.

Lacie swiveled her head back and forth. "Hold up, Mom." She breathed deep and let the air out with a loud *whoosh*. "So...I put my hands on my stomach and opened my heart, asking God to tell me if I was. That's when I heard her. You know how she talks. '*Tee hee*,' Bebe giggled in her little-girl voice. It couldn't have been anyone else but her. 'You *are* pregnant, Lacie,' she said. 'It's me. I'm coming back!'"

"Jesus!" My body slammed against the chair, flattened by a surge of emotion. In a nanosecond, a shiver of fear freeze-dried me to pulp. Weakly, I managed to speak. "What are you talking about, Lacie? This can't be true. She wouldn't."

"*Oy*! Of course she would!" I nodded in miserable agreement, unconvinced by my feeble protest. Now that I thought of it, I hadn't really felt Mother around for a month. Lacie continued in a rush, clearly relieved to share this unthinkable possibility. "The next day, I bought a pregnancy test. It was positive." Anger seeped into her voice. "I believe her, Mom! Bebe is strong enough to make it happen. But it's wrong! She ought to be learning her spiritual lessons. It's not time for her to come back yet!"

"Oh, darlin'...sweet, sweet, darlin' girl. I couldn't agree more! I feel sick...sick...sick. I'm so, so sorry." In mind-drooling shock, I reached for Lacie and folded my fingers around her forearm. "Sorry you have to even consider this bizarre possibility. I don't want to believe she's doing this!" Another troubling twist occurred to me. "Have you told John? How does he feel about Mother coming back as his child?"

Lacie stiffened and looked at me with disbelief. "Mom! Are you kidding me? No way am I telling him this spooky stuff with Bebe. He already thinks we're all nuts."

I nodded my head up and down, once again agreeing, but wishing I could throw up and stop the front porch from spinning."Can you blame him? This is completely insane."

Lacie wriggled in her chair. "Well...no, I don't blame him.

But he isn't the major problem here, is he? It's just not right, Mom. Bebe needed to hang out with God a while. It's too soon for her to come back."

Mentally, I shook myself. This wasn't my drama. At least not yet. I couldn't go there. Couldn't think about Mother returning as my grandchild, or having a grandchild, period, when Sarah wasn't even out of college. This was Lacie's body, Lacie's baby. She deserved my support. "Honey, tell you what. Let's not get our panties in a knot over this. We don't know for sure. But we do know you're having a baby. This is beautiful. How about I treat y'all to a celebration dinner at the Grist Mill? And, hey...prayer is probably a good idea. I'll do that with you. Then let's leave the rest in God's hands. Does this sound like a plan?"

Lacie squeezed her eyes into slits of don't-screw-with-my-reality displeasure. "It's a plan. And I *do* know for sure."

LACIE KNEW WHAT SHE KNEW. My insightful daughter had proven her intuitive abilities many mind-bending times. I had a choice here — we all did. Either these bizarre intuitive experiences could transform us or take us down. A relationship with Mother for real was challenging. A relationship with Mother un-real pushed every emotional button. But Lacie's intuitive download announcing that Mother would soon reappear in this family as a live human being made me crazy as a road lizard.

Searching for a sane standpoint, one fact could not be denied: My girls and I have inherited Mother's *sight,* as ancient Celts referred to clairvoyance. How? By actively accepting intuition as garden-variety equipment that comes with tending a human garden, no more curious than the garden hose I taught the kids to circle in order to prevent tripping. No owner's manual comes with intuition; I learned to believe through observation. When Mother said she could read my mind, I took it for granted and assumed I should, too. And so I did. My girls picked up the slack without questioning, especially Lacie, who found intuitive abilities useful. Sarah, not so much.

Doesn't everybody sometimes experience knowing who's calling when the cell sings? I'm not talking about iPhone rings programmed to specific people, but about a sixth sense — a.k.a., intuition. We mindlessly duck into Starbucks for a latte and just *happen* to bump into someone who's on our mind. We turn a corner and everything changes because it felt right to make some random choice. Most everybody has clairvoyant hunches, that magnetic pull toward people, places and things that can't be explained using common logic. We connect to someone through what appears to be meaningless coincidence…and the bond is so powerful we become lovers, go into business together or become best friends forever. Perhaps as ancient Gnostic Christians supposed, every human being possesses the spiritual capacity to dig deep and connect with inner wisdom – *gnosis* – inner knowledge. Intuition is an automatic human download.

But we have the option of choosing to pursue inner knowing…or not. If it's too scary, we usually don't. Lacie has been finding my keys and warning of police just around the bend since she could talk. Sarah wasn't a fan of *the sight* because of circumstances that occurred before Mother showed up in a blaze of seductively dazzling light. But she wasn't always allergic to intuition. When Sarah was five and we lived in Houston, I realized her window to the other world was wide open. At this point, sharing intuitive experiences was as ordinary as asking for mac and cheese for dinner.

With Bunny under one arm, my freewheeling daughter was up with the sun, padding into the den and plopping in my lap where I slouched in a comfy chair, drinking coffee and reading, hoping to find peace before the day of carpools and meetings began. "Fill me up, Mommy," was always Sarah's first line. One particular sunrise she was especially talkative. "Mommy, I 'member somethin'. Do you wanna know how God made you my mommy and Daddy my daddy?"

I wrapped my arms around her and squeezed. "Filling up…filling up. There. You're all full. Of course, honey. Tell me."

Not needing much encouragement, she launched into a lengthy story with vivid descriptions. It seems that once upon a time before Sarah was Sarah, she was an angel floating around with God. One day He asked if she wanted to become a real girl. "And I said, 'Yes!' So God took me to that green church and showed me you and Daddy sitting up close to that man standing up high and talking. God asked me if I wanted you to be my mommy and daddy." Sarah gestured with her arms and pointed to show our exact location in the church.

I got it, right not left. I remembered precisely what she meant. St. Martin's Episcopal Church, our church home before Sarah's birth, was carpeted in green. We changed to St. John the Divine, carpeted in red, not long after her one-month baptism. Our family never revisited the green church where her dad and I always sat in the second pew on the right, in front of the lectern. In the red church we claimed pews on the left, in front of the lectern where the minister preached. Sarah wriggled and grinned with excitement as she delivered her denouement. "I said yes I wanted you and Daddy! And that's how I became your little girl!"

Through the years Sarah shared garden-variety intuition — like reading my mind and charming a "yes" out of me when I was firmly into "no," or picturing where a kitty was hiding. But in college her clairvoyant abilities became unmanageable. On her way to class one day with friends, as they crossed the Main Mall and rounded the Tower, Sarah impulsively dove for the graveled pavement and flattened out with arms folded over her head. Shocked, she lay there "feeling crazy, Mom!" Then she became aware of the *whap…whap…whap…* sound of a helicopter dipping low overhead. At that moment she experienced memory of herself — or someone — as an American soldier dying in Vietnam. Horrified, she shared the incident with me only once — clairvoyance was just too weird to wrap her arms around. And so she shut it off…until Mother made her white-light appearance.

From the beginning I've experienced a helpful relationship with my intuition, so I've stayed with it. Reading Mamo and Mother's minds gave me the advantage of a running lead — most of the time anyway. But in high school surrounded by hordes of friends, I had to trick myself out of mind-reading to stop the annoying habit of finishing my friends' sentences. Pretending I was Sandra Dee cured me from intuiting anything, as long as I stayed in character. Her charmingly uncomplicated Gidget was innocent, funny and quite useful. Gidget definitely didn't converse with animals, birds and a fairy godmother like Cinderella and I did.

Today, I've developed my own code of ethics about tuning into clairvoyant knowing. It's a deliberate choice. Voyeuristically invading people's privacy isn't cool, whether on the level of brain waves or otherwise. Unless I'm in need of self-defense, I don't go there…except with clients. They pay me to be aware, so I am. But I don't nurture or develop clairvoyant abilities, or aspire to be a working psychic, although I respect and admire profound practitioners like healer and oracle Edgar Cayce, psychiatrist Judith Orloff and medium James Van Praagh.

Intuition happens. It is fact. In spite of gallows humor about Mother's being "a witch, you know," this family has exhibited intuitive clairvoyance in varying degrees — in many guises — for as long as I can remember. What are we talking about here anyway? *Clairvoyance* is a French word originating in the seventeenth century. *Clair* means clear and *voyance* means vision — or the observation of events separated from us by some distance. But this specific *seeing* term — clairvoyance — is commonly used in a blanket sense to cover all forms of intuition. *Déjà vu,* the experience of feeling like we've been somewhere or done something before, is a related form of clairvoyance — seeing at a distance.

Clairaudience — hearing what is beyond the senses — describes what Lacie and I experience when Mother's disembodied spirit speaks. We don't see her. We only hear her. That's probably a good thing. Sarah not only heard Mother speak, but she saw her — "wavy and cloudy" — and felt impelled to follow as she watched her ethereal apparition escape into the light.

Then there's telepathy, in which thoughts are transferred from one mind to another. Mother's mind-reading, although irritating to the max when I tried to get away with something — like stashing booze in the back of my high-school boyfriend's car as we headed out on a date — became quite handy when I perfected the tool for my own use.

In the experience of retrocognition, an event or a series of events are drawn into present memory out of a distant past remembered in an unlikely way. The whole clairvoyant shopping list is improbable. Past-life recall is among the showiest revelations and might be what Carl Jung refers to as cellular DNA memories. Psychic mediums also exercise retrocognition like I experienced at Mother's dying bedside when her life flashed before my eyes. But then again...maybe I was reading her mind.

Precognition is awareness of future events. Mother was powerfully precognitive and frightened of her ability to foresee. She believed she caused bad things to happen because she intuited the occurrence. When it came to pass she felt intensely responsible and guilty, believing that her dream or vision was the cause, rather than a gift of perception meant to warn and perhaps invite intervention. If seers — like Nostradamus and the Biblical prophet John — do truly foresee world disasters, what if we took them seriously and intervened diplomatically to facilitate peace instead of making war? Would it make a difference?

In psychokinesis — or *PK* as it is known in ESP circles — the human psyche, in the body or out, directly influences matter. People with this gift make things move just by wishing it so, for instance, ramming an old guy's blue sedan into an intersection, jamming clocks and computers and making things bump in the night. Psychic healing is a beautiful example of this ability and one this family could use about now.

Acknowledging potential believability in the plethora of psychic experiences does help normalize unscheduled flights of fantasy. Countless people, for years and years, have gracefully accepted their exceptional experiences and steered them toward good…even orthodox versions of the Bible tell of bushes that talk and seas parting, not to mention manna dropping from the clouds. Getting with the program would surely do me a world of good.

Regardless of potential higher purpose, my mental machinations continued to march in protest. *Mistake! Wrong move! If Mother was determined to reincarnate, what could be done?* Surely there was something. *Clearly, she feels incomplete. Not finished with this family. But how could coming back as a helpless baby – probably with no memory of the previous Wilma Flewellen Miller Foster incarnation – be anything but totally dumb? I mean, this family is great, but surely there are greater familial situations from which to choose. What about royalty? Wonder if she thought of that? Proud as Mother was – is – of her Fine Old Family, why doesn't she kick this reincarnational thing up a notch? Why us when she could probably swing Queendom, maybe even King if she was into switching? Could she? Even now? I hope. I hope.*

Finding no way out, over the Christmas holidays I faced the possibility of Mother's soul jumping back into this family as Lacie and John's child. Wilma Foster's second coming labored toward us – like, next August. Before her reincarnation I had heavy-lifting to do. If I didn't resolve my conflicted feelings, I would freak out when I held Lacie's baby. Maybe this precious infant would be Mother incarnate, but thinking about an innocent creature this way seems seriously unhealthy. The role Mother played in my life would never come again.

We have only one mother. I loved her. I hated her. I didn't even know how I felt about her. Same blood, same worldview about many things. Even when I determined to create a much different life, I came through her, from her. No matter how I wished to sever the relationship when we dueled over a contentious issue — like her precious lineage — for better or worse, in sickness and in health, for richer or poorer, this woman created me, my very own, no-matter-what mother.

Defeated by fates dangerously in cahoots with my dead but not departed mother, my mind churned with corrective self-talk. *Get a grip, Sandy. You might consider a few grounding principles: All you've got is today. The only thing you can control is your attitude. Maybe if you burn enough, flush enough, cathart and wail enough, you'll offload this anger and resentment...and just possibly might remember when you loved your mother. Not because she was perfect. Not because she was necessarily loving, but because she was a human being.*

It was 1994. A year rich in more family drama than any human would sensibly prefer. Mother had moved to Houston and I had moved out in the middle of nowhere, about which Mother continued to rant. And yet, rather than ignoring me entirely, which was her usual operating procedure, with every phone call she claimed neglect and insisted she deserved a visit. This was most unusual. Mother was seldom whiny: plus, the pleasure of my company normally rated second behind trepidation that I might crash and burn on the interstate and cause unnecessary aggravation. This decided shift in attitude meant something was up. In the spirit of peace, as soon as I could catch a break from renovation projects and clients and when Sarah had her first free weekend, I slipped Alabama into the tape deck and we headed on down the road.

Mother's new Houston digs were west of downtown

along the Memorial Drive ribbon of green forests. When I helped her move, I left Mother ensconced in a hotel while she waited for the movers to arrive. I hadn't seen her new place. Doglegs and cut-backs made the going tricky — if lovely — as I craned my neck in search of the street address. Around a bend in the road, the lush garden apartment complex screamed refinement…just as I would have expected.

Regardless of her fluctuating income from oil royalties, Mother possessed seismic skill for locating affordable beauty. The term *meaningful work* might just as well be Serbo-Croatian. This was my vernacular, not Mother's. To her way of thinking any job was a *tacky job*, definitely beneath her status as a woman *to the manor born*. Not that she lacked resourcefulness or ingenuity. Mother gardened with ferocity and maintained standards of impeccability within her domain. Yet — in her mind — even the thought of receiving remuneration for her efforts tainted her reputation.

Mother's financial health depended solely on unpredictable supply and demand — oil and gas prices set by global commodity markets continents away. Much as I begrudged her elitist attitude, I felt slightly charmed by Mother's Wilma-isms — to the manor born, tacky job and on and on — which unapologetically expressed the personality of a woman willing to pay the price for living life on her own terms. *Sweating bullets*, she waited for the postman to deliver royalty checks each month, and chewed the end off erasers as she slumped at her Italianate desk *pushing a pencil* to figure out how to make ends meet.

The *all bidness* was different today than in the 1940s when the Big Inch pipeline funneled Texas Black Gold to Northeast refineries. In that era, U.S. petroleum products were more than sufficient to propel America's war effort. It was commonly acknowledged that "America rode to victory on East Texas Oil." Texas oil production so far exceeded our needs that the

U.S. actually exported.

But in the 1950s, Middle East oil was seductively less expensive than domestic production, and the balance shifted. By 1970, eighty-five percent of America's oil came from the Middle East. Once fiercely independent and proud of it, American Spirit lost its muscle, grew fat and flabby, and got drunk on cheap oil...bought at a great price. With governmental regulation and disincentives toward America's homegrown oil production, in the global economy of the 1980s domestic drilling was down, and imports were up. Dependence on bargain-priced Middle East oil eroded America's economic singularity and leached national sovereignty. By 1993 the spigot was wide open for foreign oil, whose price fell to $17.49 a barrel, gutting Mother's income.

As Sarah and I wound our way along stone pathways that led to Mother's front door, I suspected Mother still sweated out her dependency on an American industry that was drifting into irrelevance. Perhaps she needed a house call for a little *all* therapy. Black gold had always been her unfaithful and destructive lover, giving love when it wanted and then abandoning her for years.

Stooped and diminished, Mother swung the leaded-glass entry door wide and beamed with a hearty voice, "Come in this house right this very minute!" She reached to envelop Sarah. "I am so happy to see my favorite granddaughter!" I smiled, appreciating the effortless connection between these two.

Sarah purred, "I've missed you, Bebe!"

Mother turned to me, "Well, Madame Psychologist, how are your crazy people?"

I took the bait. "Oh, Mama! Stop! They're not crazy! They're ordinary people caught in painful circumstances. I should think you would know about this." We were off, predictably assuming our contentious roles.

The aroma of Claire Burke potpourri wafted over me as I crossed the threshold, the flowery fragrance almost camouflaging the odor of stale cigarette smoke. A nasty habit absolutely discordant with elegance, yet worn like a World War II Medal of Honor.

"Sandy, sit there." Mother motioned toward the far end of the sofa, down-cushioned and upholstered in silk, arranged beside the French doors with the patio beyond. "And Sarah" — Mother *pat-patted* the down cushion closest to her. "And Sarah, you sit right here by me." A broad smile spread across Mother's face as she wriggled into a crewel-embroidered wing-back, and sighed with satisfaction. All actors onstage, raise the curtain, the performance can now begin. On the butler's table in front of the sofa, a porcelain bowl of Golden Delicious apples, "…just the right shade of green," masked the scar left from a burning cigarette which once slipped unnoticed from the ashtray. A sherry-filled Waterford decanter for *afternoon tea* and a thin novel which spoke volumes — *A Woman of Independent Means* — completed the arrangement. Nothing about Mother's personal space felt homey, but she was my home and I relaxed into our history — good, bad and in-between.

While Sarah and Mother chatted in animated hieroglyphs, I drank from Mother's outside terrace. Artistically arranged, every lush clay pot and wisp of vine visually created a still-life begging to be painted. The tender love Mother lavished on gardening spoke louder than her laser-beam eye for interior design. However Mother envisioned God, I knew where they met — in the garden.

As the weekend progressed my intuition sent out distress flares. What was this visit about? I would soon find out.

In the steamy afternoon of the second day, Sarah decided to catch a few rays by the pool. The apartment fell into stillness. I lounged on the sofa flipping the pages of *House Beautiful*. Mother lit a cigarette and purposely arranged herself in a straight-backed chair pulled from beneath the dark cherry dining table just off the seating area. She loudly cleared her throat, "Ahem! Sandy! Madame Psychologist, come here." She inclined her head and nudged a green silk upholstered dining chair with her foot. "I need a little therapy. I have to tell you something about my daddy."

Feeling nervous and not understanding why, I carefully repositioned *House Beautiful* in the array of shelter magazines that fanned out on the coffee table like a winning hand. As I took my seat, I acknowledged Mother's summon. "Okay. You've got my attention." I couldn't let it go. "But you know I'm not a psychologist, Mother. I'm a psychotherapist."

"Oh, I know that! Just listen to me. You know how nervous I get. I've got to tell you the truth about something that we've always kept secret in the Flewellen Family — a big secret. It killed my mother." My heart skipped a beat and took off running.

Mother looked pinched and grave. "Always you've been told that my daddy was unfairly murdered." Mother hesitated with pain rising in her eyes like the Mississippi before the levees break. "Well, that's a boldfaced lie. It is the truth he was shot and killed on October 31, 1925, right there in the middle of Tatum. But it wasn't an unfair killing."

I had never seen Mother struggle this hard to rein in her feelings. She bowed her head, placed her hand across her eyes, took a breath and then, with a rush of words, she continued. "I always told you — we told everyone, all of Longview — that Daddy was shot by that horrible man, one of the cotton pickers in Daddy's fields who he loaned a lot of money, feeling sorry for his wife and children because they were so poor. Then one day that man told Daddy he would pay him his due and they set up a meeting for that purpose. They arranged to meet in that cotton-picking shantytown, Tatum. There was never a more godforsaken place on earth! But Daddy never saw the money. Instead the man lay in wait with a loaded hunting rifle. Ambushed my daddy and killed him. Shot Daddy through the heart. He died right there in the dirt of that one-horse road with practically the whole town looking on."

My heart hurt and I reached to grasp Mother's hand. "I know, Mama. You've told me. It must have been horrible for you."

Mother slipped her hand from beneath my fingers, shifted her weight and wriggled upright. "But I didn't tell you the whole truth and nothing but the truth, Sandy. I don't want to admit this...swore I would never tell...but...it's time now. So...that's the story everyone knew." Chain-smoking, Mother snubbed the cigarette to light another as thick smoke clogged the air. A shadow of pain creased her face, visibly aging her as she spoke, her voice so weak and hesitant it rattled when she spoke. "Well, that's not the way it really happened at all. Mama's best friend, Julia Acker — the Society Editor for the *Longview News* — fed that bogus story to the paper and they printed it. I guess everyone believed the lie. At least they never let on if they didn't and the story stuck. There was no evidence of the truth ever published in Longview. The paper just carried a fuzzy account about how Tatum rallied in protection of its own against the landowner, Angus Miller. The story implied that my daddy was money-hungry and greedy. and that is why the law forgave the murderer. What they didn't print is that those Tatum-ites murdered my daddy like he was a rabid dog on the loose." Mother appraised me with oceans of grief in her eyes. "Do you want me to tell you what really happened?"

"Are you kidding? Of course I wanna hear. You can't stop now! Go on. Please!"

"All right." Mother took a breath and sighed from the top of her head to the tip of her toes. "Here it is: My daddy was carrying on with that man's wife. That's it. Plain and simple. The husband killed my daddy, and the law didn't do a thing with the cold-blooded murderer." Mother drew in a gulp of air and exhaled with deflated resignation, staring through glinting French doors before continuing in a small, faraway voice. "A crime of passion, they called it. Justified by what my daddy did."

"Mama…I'm so sorry." Instinctively, I reached for Mother and again covered her frail hand with mine, forgetting to abide by family rules that forbade demonstrations of tenderness. But this time she didn't pull away. In stunned silence Mother and I unflinchingly stared into each other's eyes, both of us in shock and needing a few moments to absorb the enormity of what she shared. Propelled by an emotional charge, my mind rocketed back into childhood. *The drives in the country…never once visiting a cemetery. How can this be?* "Mother! Where is he buried?"

Mother stared me down, cagey eyes promising that even in this moment of truth there were still secrets she hid. "Why do you ask?"

"I want to know! He's my grandfather."

"That's for me to know and you to find out. We never visited Daddy's grave." Mother spoke unblinkingly as if she were on the witness stand and I was the prosecuting attorney. Clearly, she was not going to answer. *Why all the mystery? Still!* I felt sick at my stomach and speechless.

Avoiding my gaze, Mother lit a cigarette and stared through the French doors, seeing something I could not. Crumpled under what seemed an interminable length of time, in a faint voice Mother pressed on with her story. "I will never understand how Daddy did that to Mama. How could he be so stupid! Of course the husband found out! And why did Daddy need another woman anyway when he had my beautiful Mama?"

"I dunno, Mama. This is more than I can take in." Strands of limp brown hair grazed her cheek as Mother dropped into the memory. Cataracts faded her hazel eyes to gray, creating the eerie impression that her view had turned inward and away from the outer world. "Daddy was such a good-looking man. Mama said he used to stand in front of the mirror, throw out his chest and say to himself, 'You good-looking devil, you!' To which Mama snorted, 'Oh, Angus! Stop it!'"

"He was, you know." With vulnerable childlike innocence Mother took my hand and led us to the place she turned when hope wanted to die: the Dead People's Wall and ornate gold-leaf framed portraits of husband and wife, Angus and Elizabeth Miller. "Look at him, so handsome in his World War I uniform. Do you think I look like him?" Without waiting for an answer, Mother rushed on, the tone of her voice stronger with every word. "Everyone said I do. He was handsome and he knew it. But look at Mother...such a beauty. Who could have been prettier? They're so handsome together! It killed Mother. Just killed her to know what Daddy did. She never quit loving him...even when she married Lacey Eddins and he made her feel safe again. No wonder...look at my beautiful daddy."

After countless neutral glances over the years, seeing the image of my grandfather for the first time as a fleshed-out man made my mind run rampant with unanswered questions. *What was the affair about? What was her name? Did Angus love Mamo or was theirs a marriage of convenience arranged between landholding families? Painful as it must have been, how could Mamo refuse her daughters a visit to their daddy's grave, even if she needed to wait until they were older? How can I ever know the answers to any of this?*

Returning to the straight-backed chair and bending to light another cigarette with a sterling-silver lighter, Mother haltingly pushed on with her confessional. "I was so little all I could see were knees. Daddy lay in state for a week at the Millers', his parents' house in Henderson. What an awful way to do things! Mama, Louise and I stayed there the whole time. The living room was so crammed with people, I could barely move. One day, Mrs. Jameson, the Henderson Postmistress, looked at me sadly and said an awful thing: 'You poor little orphan. Do you want to see your daddy?' Orphan! What a horrible thing to say to a little girl. I said 'Yes,' because I didn't know what she was talking about. I wish I'd never seen him. *Ooooo...*" Mother moaned, buried her face in her hands and spoke through her fingers. "It was awful, awful...so cold, gray, stiff...that wasn't my daddy."

Stopping to regain her composure and stem tears rising in her eyes, Mother pressed on with the story. "I don't know where Mama was. Visiting with all those people in the Miller house, I guess. The coffin sat right there in the living room with people coming and going for days. Daddy was buried a week later, but Louise and I were sent off to Bodie in Beaumont...for the funeral and everything. Then when it was all over Mother came to Bodie's for a long visit. Finally we all rode back to Longview on the train, a puffing, jostling old thing. Bodie returned with us so she could take care of us."

Mother snorted contemptuously and rearranged herself in the straight backed chair. "That was a joke. Mama sat in her seat, not crying, not talking, not moving. *Boogedy-boogedy*. It was scary. Bodie couldn't take care of anybody. She cried and then swooned, took a whiff of smelling salts and went right back to crying even harder. We were just little girls — Louise was five, and I was only two! We sat across from Mama and Bodie not knowing what to think or do. Bodie made such a fuss and Mama looked so strange just sitting there staring that the black conductor kept eyeing us. Finally he approached our seats and whispered to Louise and me, 'If you gals need help you just holler.' Of course we didn't need to call on him for help after that because Bodie straightened up."

Finally, Mother's story appeared to be winding down and her voice softened, sounding far away as if she spoke in a dream. "But it got better when we moved into the Old Home Place with all the family coming and going. That's what they did, you know. Everyone moved back home when trouble came. Papaw and Mamuvah kept adding rooms onto the Old Home Place so they could fit everybody in. I know Mama felt better living with her own mother and father again."

"And Sandy, you know the really strange thing? After a while I almost forgot I ever had a daddy. I couldn't remember what he looked like, so I'd stand in front of the picture I showed you. It hung on the wall of the front room of the Old Home Place. I'd look at that proud face...but he seemed like someone I never knew. No matter how long I stared I couldn't remember a time when my daddy looked back at me. You know how Mama was. She could just block anything out by saying, 'You can't cry over spilt milk.' How did she do that? She never talked about Daddy again for as long as I can remember."

Struggling not to cry, I couldn't think of anything to say that matched the overwhelming sadness I felt. "I don't know how she did it, Mama, but I'm glad you're sharing what happened. I don't know how you've kept this awful secret all these years."

As if anticipating a question, Mother raised her hand and pushed the flat palm toward my face. "Maybe I'm more like my mother than I want to admit. Don't expect me to say how I found out the real story of Daddy's death. And I'm not telling you where he is buried, either. I promised Mama I would not, and you know I don't break my promises. Do you know

Louise never believed the real story about Daddy's death? I tried to tell her, but she was so furious she wouldn't speak. Sometimes we would go months at a time without talking."

"It's the secrets, Mama. They tear people apart." A wave of shame washed over me. "The sisters in this family have a history of shutting each other out. It's really painful, Mama. I've always felt sad that you and Louise fight and don't love each other. Maybe you can now."

Mother didn't pursue my comment about Louise and, by implication, Jo and me. I knew she knew where I was leading, but this was one of those gray areas about which family wisdom suggested "Let sleeping dogs lie." In a flat voice depleted of emotion, Mother followed her solitary train of thought. "Well, it really is over now. I just needed to tell someone." We sat in silence as she lit another cigarette, took a deep drag and gazed again toward her garden, drawing strength. After several minutes that felt like hours, Mother shifted in her chair and stubbed out the cigarette. Our eyes met for a searching moment as age-old female understanding passed between us. In that look lay all the loves and losses of all women for all time.

In my imagination I heard ancestral gears grind into sync with a metallic thud. The drawbridge lowered: the gate swung open on its creaking hinges. *So this secret lay at the root of exaggerated Flewellen pride, a cover-up to hide the depth of shame surrounding my Grandfather Angus's murder. Toxic waste buried in the depths of a dark well, polluting my grandmother's psyche, year after deadening year.* Horrendous damage had been done. I struggled to bring myself present past the ringing in my ears.

Insight after insight ticked off in my brain. *Mother held her mother's secret, pitied her and at the same time taunted her. Their endless fights seemed always to be about men — the unwise choices each had made. Instead of supporting each other with the truth, they hated each other with their secrets.*

As if I were seeing my mother for the first time, tenderness seeped into my heart. I shivered. A chill ran down my spine. *And it has been the same for me...probably for all of us. I suspect every woman alive shares a gut-wrenching loss we would have given anything to change.*

While I sat transfixed by Mother's vulnerability and brokenness, she resurrected. From some deep place, a fire of resolve took possession of her eyes. With determination she rose from the chair, smoothed wispy strands of brown hair, pushed the folds of her denim dress into submission and giggled. A smile crinkled the corners of her mouth. She lifted her head and threw her shoulders back. "But I won't think about that now. I'll think about that tomorrow."

In this weekend of terrible beauty Mother let me into her heart. But my Grandmother Mamo had been gone two decades before I learned the truth and without thought forgave every cruel thing she had ever said or done. Now I solved the riddle of the obscure Victorian verse that Mamo quoted in odd moments, motionlessly gazing onto the back yard as if a dark shadow had obliterated her light. "It is great, it is good of the Wise One above, to throw destiny's veil o'er the face of our years."

ON MY FRONT PORCH — the beginning and ending of all things good — the chrysalis of night and misty mornings enveloped me in boundless compassion for my grandmother, my mother…and myself. We are women who gaze. Mamo had her back yard; Mother, the garden beyond the French doors; me, the meadows and open fields. Mamo shared once that when she thought of her mother — Mamuvah who lost three of her seven children — she pictured her on the back porch of the Old Home Place, hour after hour, stringing green beans, shelling peas and shucking corn. When Mamo missed Mamuvah and began searching, she would find her crying, with tears dripping into the colander. I know what drew Mamuvah to that back porch — gazing. Truths unforgettable make a woman weep.

With a flood of understanding, Mamo's stories washed over me; loving stories, rock upon rock, childhood founded on secure stepping stones. I could see, smell and hear…as if I were there: sunlight dipping low, air crisp and clean, smelling of lofty pines. Little Beth — as the family called their last baby girl — clung to the wrought-iron gate of the Old Home Place. Eaglet's eye fixed on the sidewalk, she climbed the bottom rung and rode the squeaking gate back and forth, watching and waiting for homecoming footsteps of her Papaw, in anticipation of their ritual of afternoon delights. Before he climbed the front steps of the Old Home Place or kissed his wife and older children hello, Papaw took my grandmother's small hand in his callused palm and led her along tree-lined Green Street, tipping his hat and nodding to neighbors who rocked on porches decorated with gingerbread trim created at the Castleberry and Flewellen Mill, "How do you do? Good afternoon to you." Hundreds of times they strolled just like this — hand in hand.

"Upsy-daisy!" Papaw lifted Little Beth to the commissary countertop rimmed with glass jars of rainbow-colored sweets, humoring clanging tin lids until his littlest angel chose the special candy she couldn't resist popping into her mouth. My grandmother grew accustomed to special time, special tolerance, special choices. Her Papaw would forever be the most faithful man my grandmother would ever know.

What does every little girl want? Big hairy bear daddy who holds your arms and swings you in circles until you're dizzy, wrestles and tickles until you giggle so hard you can't breathe, scream stop but don't mean it, and then he wraps his bear arms around you and your heart warms like the sun. Tucks you in at night smelling of soap, growls and nuzzles your cheek with his scratchy face, kisses your forehead. "You're my girl. Sleep tight. Don't let the bedbugs bite."

You listen to conversation, muffled through their closed bedroom door, Mommy laughs, then silence. The house is quiet and you dream, "Someday my daddy will marry me."

Like baby ducks quacking after the first living creature they see, you will marry daddy someday, big hairy bear of a man. And you'll wear pink ribbons in your long curls and know all the way down to your painted pink toenails that you deserve love.

Of course my grandmother idolized her Papaw, Junius Jefferson Flewellen. Mother worshiped her father, too — the romanticized memory of Angus Pitser Miller, not the actuality. After all, Little Wilma's father faded from her life when she was two and a half years old. These women I trusted to teach me to become a grown-up girl, searched and searched for that good father who would rule the land with fairness, honor, concern for all; love and loyalty for one woman. He was there…somewhere…they just needed to keep looking.

My father didn't feed into a good-daddy fantasy. I longed for a tough-guy brother who would beat up the bad guy, and I found my Don Quixote. In truth, King Arthur and Lancelot live within the pages of *Le Mort d'Arthur*. Real life and myth aren't truly related.

The Velveteen Rabbit says that becoming real takes a long time. By then most of our hair has been loved off, our eyes drop out, and we get loose in the joints and shabby. Some enchanted evening once we're real, maybe we'll see a mature stranger across a crowded room…and run to their side…and make them our own…grown-up to grown-up. How lovely it would be if the stranger turns out to be the transformed grown-up who has shared our bed all these years. For my mother and grandmother…and me…this storyline didn't play out too well.

She put it off as long as she could, but at forty-four Mother crashed into her long-overdue nervous collapse. The unfortunate combination of *Valley of the Dolls* drugs — Miltown, Dexedrine and Dexamyl — brought her down. At least that's how Timberlawn psychiatrist Dr. Johansen's report read. Jo and I knew better. Mother's true demon was love found then lost…all over again.

Marriage was Mother's ruin. In 1964, a few months before I married the love of my life, she married her good King Arthur, whose arm I held to walk down the aisle. Mother's single-woman-on-her-own years had been unkind, and resulted in an emotional climate beyond ready for a husband. He showed up when she was parched and aching to be filled.

Following my enlightening summer vacation at the Farm in Kountze — and extra vacation in Beaumont with Brother

Charles — Mother had pulled up her big-girl panties and signed a mortgage for her own home located in an up-and-coming Longview neighborhood. We walked down Mamo's red concrete sidewalk one last time. Feeling tearful, even though crying wasn't allowed, my other mother and father, Annie and Anderson, and I said goodbye — but only through loving eyes and without the warmth of a hug. In a black-and-white world, our relationships had no value. This goodbye was absolute.

Mother began her first-time-ever independent life in the space-efficient ranch-style bungalow at 704 Sylvan Drive: one-half white limestone and one-half natural cedar shakes, with a willowy pink mimosa shielding the expanse of picture windows across the front. Missing Annie terribly, I worked toward liking our new home. Holidays were indubitably the best, because Brother Charles wasn't around to *accidentally* stroll through the bathroom.

Mother's passion for fit-to-kill outfits now served our dollhouse. I forgot she knew how to cook, but here she was, appearing very Flewellen work-ethic-ish: rolling scratch pastry for lemon pies with mile-high meringue, laboring over homemade spaghetti sauce and homefries, grilling sirloin outside on the red brick patio; sweating from sunrise to sunset dressed in "work clothes" — khakis and a white cotton skirt. We had the bloomingest azaleas and gardenias on Sylvan Drive. For ten standing-on-her-own years Mother autonomously ruled her kingdom without the help of a man. And she grew weary.

Good King Arthur was a friend of a friend: a high-ranking military officer granted early retirement because of heart problems, negatively affecting his genius not in the least. Gathering around Mother's round pine kitchen table on a weekend visit, my husband and I tested Cooksey for sleight of hand, some magician's trick. One, two, three…slight pause...turn page...one, two, three...slight pause...with complete concentration he flipped the pages of *Newsweek* or *Time*. Under interrogation, he accurately answered questions about specific information, from any page, cover to cover, without breaking a sweat. Jo, my husband and I debated whether Mother fell in love with this guy because of his uniform, photographic memory or the Cessna private aircraft they flew from city to city.

With Mother's bungalow as home base, the ink had barely dried on their marriage license before he returned to doing trade deals: exporting Santa Gertrudis cattle to Russia and Cessna aircraft to South America, importing Canon cameras to the U.S. from Japan. A few months after the wedding, the sheriff knocked on the door and hand-delivered a warrant for his arrest. Conveniently, he was out of the country. It was all a mistake, you see. Cooksey simply forgot to deposit checks in time to cover withdrawals on their joint bank account. At about this time, Mother became acquainted with a psychiatrist who treated only the wealthiest, fashionably sad women in Longview.

It was 1967, and Mother and her army guy had been married for three brain-bending years. My mother couldn't even realize I was pregnant, and here I was about to deliver a baby. Husbands weren't allowed in Labor and Delivery so I was alone, waiting for "productive contractions to begin," so the labor nurse said as she switched off the light. I checked the hands on the large wall clock across the room — 10:00 PM — as she swooshed from the room. "We'll look in on you. I phoned the doctor telling him not to expect anything until morning." Labor and Delivery at Baptist Memorial Hospital nudged me toward a sleep cycle. I could not go.

This whole night stood before me, precious time to reflect

on the miracle scheduled to arrive with the morning sun. *July 8, 1967. If the baby waits past midnight, he* — I felt sure this was a he — *will be born on Mamo's birthday. How sad is that? I haven't even seen her since my wedding three years ago! Really, since Mother, Jo and I moved from Mamo's, she has been more and more out of it…a hermit, setting small fires with her cigarettes, forgetting stuff. Maybe our moving didn't affect Mamo at all, but I feel responsible and guilty. Even if Mother was protecting me…and Jo…from Brother Charles, we left right when Mamo started liking us. She won't even know she has a great-grandson…born on her birthday! What kind of family cuts people off like we do? It's just wrong.*

And Mother? My heart hurt as I thought about her. *She's so far gone I can't even let her know I'm in labor. Basically, I don't have a mother. No point calling. She's in a Houston hospital — out of her mind — incapable of understanding anything. Jo has her hands full. She's barely twenty. Managing Mother is a lot to deal with. Jo will just be upset if she knows this baby is coming and she can't be here. Wait 'til this is done…then call.*

It's been a bad scene for Jo for two years. Mother pulled her out of the University of Texas this sophomore year fall semester…sent her back to UT this spring. But now it's summer and Jo's college future is in jeopardy. Funny how embezzlement can wreck your finances.

Things definitely aren't good. Of course Mother's marriage is on the rocks. Jo and I knew it would be. That husband is a goldbricker…an absolute con. That's ironic! Mother is a bankrupt heiress pretending to be rich so she could snag a wealthy sugar daddy.

Emotionally I shook myself…. *STOP. Quit thinking about it. Rest. You've got work to do. You'll be a woman soon.* I breathed deep and traced the roll of my son's body, rushing to shore like waves on the sand. *I know. I know, little one. You're impatient. You'll be here soon, Trey.*

I laughed remembering a funky dream. Even before my husband and I married, we agreed that if we had a son he would be named after his dad, a Junior, and grandfather, a Senior. In the dream the boys kept coming year after year: a number IV, V and VI. *But tonight there is only you, Trey...our precious III...beautiful first-born boy.*

Overcome with a rush of love, I pledged to this creature who would soon require grown-up parents: *I will love and protect you like a mama bear. Even while I wrap my arms around you, I release you to find your own way. How will I do that? I have no idea. But I want to. Your dad and I will make it up as we go along. And you will help by showing us who you are.*

A wall of midmorning humidity blasted us as the ObGyn nurse wheelchaired me and our teensy infant down the Baptist Hospital ramp. Grinning like a Cheshire cat, my husband stood at the curb beside our sea-green Volkswagen and settled us into the front seat. He actually did the dad thing and passed out cigars, even to female nurses. I was required to wear a robe — turquoise-floral-cute but embarrassing. Not only did I feel naked in public, but I felt overwhelmed with responsibility for mothering this warm little body I held in my arms. I had zero experience caring for an infant. I never even babysat. But I did feel reassured knowing that Mrs. Edwards — a baby nurse who rotated from newborn house to newborn house among our friends — was scheduled to arrive after supper.

Those same friends from our UT college days promised to keep the casseroles coming, at least for a week. Besides, my husband could run out for groceries. We could do this. As if he sensed my growing excitement — and probably felt it too — my husband reached across our swaddled bundle and wrapped his arm around my shoulders. I felt a rush of happiness and joy...in short supply for weeks to come.

Through a Shakespearean trick of fate, Mother occupied a bed at Kelsey-Seybold Clinic — right here, right now — for another round of tests to diagnose the reason her health had hit the skids. Her break with reality was absolute. Jo and I talked on the phone as often as we could, but I didn't fully realize how bad things were. Mother's state of mind wouldn't be a mystery much longer. Without deliberate coordination of discharge plans, she was released from Kelsey-Seybold the same hour that Trey and I were discharged from Baptist. Two cars drove toward the same apartment.

I had barely tucked Trey into his hastily assembled crib set up in the living room of our tiny one-bedroom apartment when I opened the door to mayhem. I hardly recognized my own mother. Rail-thin, crumpled and bent with straggly brown hair falling into her face, she looked like the old witch who fed Snow White the poison apple. She wore a loose-fitting beige dress which — had she been in her right mind — would never have entered her house, much less found its way onto her body.

With a grimace, Jo steered Mother around the baby bed. Mother was incapable of noticing her newborn grandson snuggled into a corner beneath a puffy animal mobile, slowly circling with "Lullaby and Goodnight" grinding on the music box. Feeling ashamed of my family, I looked at my husband and mouthed, "I'm sorry."

He shrugged his shoulders and mouthed back, "It's okay." Swinging into action, he stirred around offering food, drinks; a seat on the deacon's bench, solitary upholstered chair, or one of four straight-back dining chairs. Cooksey apologized for the intrusion. I felt nauseated even looking in his direction. Buying time, I offered the excuse of needing to change out of the robe and retreated to the bedroom where I stared at contents of the unpromising closet, wondering if anything would button around my smooshy stomach. It would have to be a maternity dress. The one I liked best — the orange tent with white collar and cuffs, UT colors.

Whispering to keep from upsetting Mother, Jo and I ushered her into our bedroom, tucked her into bed and prayed she would sleep. Peacefully…like my baby boy.

I felt shocked and scared — not only about Mother's physical and mental meltdown — but because of Jo's appearance. Her young face looked drawn and pale, years older than twenty. She shuffled along, energetically limp as Mother's hair. *How long has it been since I've seen her? I don't remember.* I taught third grade almost to the end of my pregnancy and had been completely absorbed in my own life. *It was probably Christmas. This is July. My God, things have gone downhill fast.*

After her spring semester — marked by hysterical phone calls and mounting mayhem — Jo played nursemaid twenty-four/seven. Before this Houston hospitalization, Jo shepherded Mother through two other diagnostic events, both in Dallas, both with the same results as those Jo now reported.

"There is nothing physically wrong with her," Jo whispered as we retreated to the corridor kitchen, leaving the living room to that husband-person and my husband, practically doing handstands to keep him away from us. "The doctors can't find anything. But what they *have* discovered is the horrible combination of tranquilizers, muscle relaxants and sleeping pills…" She grimaced. "…which her Longview doctor prescribed for *nerves,* have driven her over the edge. They say it's a nervous breakdown. You see her, Sandy. Unbelievable. She's totally out of her mind. Makes no sense at all. I lead her around, and she acts like I'm her mother. It's horrible!"

"Oh my God, Jo," I whispered. "I had no idea. I'm so sorry you're going through this. It can't go on. We've got to do something!"

"I know." Jo nodded, her forehead pleated into anxious horizontal creases and a deep vertical line that knitted her eyebrows together. "The doctors at Kelsey-Seybold recommend hospitalization at a funny farm in Dallas — Timberlawn. How in the world can we get her there? *He* keeps creeping around." She rolled her eyes toward the living room.

I peeped around the corner. Mother's husband of three years sat military-straight with his back pressed against the one comfortable armchair, head down, buried in the pages of *Newsweek,* which he had tucked under his arm when he walked through the door. My husband doggedly interrupted Cooksey's reading and attempted to steer the conversation toward man things like birds, guns and hunting gear. It wasn't going so well.

"God, Jo. We're under siege!"

"See? I know. It's awful!"

"I'm starved. We've gotta eat." I opened cabinets and peered into the refrigerator. "Here, this will have to do." We slathered mayonnaise on crackers with slabs of rat cheese on top.

With resignation written on her face, Jo continued dissecting the facts. "I don't know what to do...guess we'll have to go home to Longview." Normally determined and strong, she sputtered like an almost extinguished candle. Clearly, she couldn't take much more. And still, responsibility for action fell squarely on her drooping shoulders.

Attempting to envision a workable plan hammered the twisted drama home. My brain threw up irreconcilable images, scrolling across television screens splayed in my head like a bank of newsroom monitors.

On one screen a prosaic story plays out. A twenty-something couple bring their newborn home from the hospital. They began their professional married life in Houston — not even a year ago. He has a promising job in an insurance firm. She teaches third grade. They live in a brand new apartment in an ideal part of town, close to his mother and father. They have University of Texas friends without number, a new Volkswagen, a dachshund and a life filled with promise.

On the other monitor an addled bag lady has lost her mind over love gone wrong. She clings to her twenty-year-old daughter — her lifeline. The young girl has no place to turn. She is financially dependent. Forbidden from getting a driver's license, she is prisoner to her mother's insanity. The plotting husband stalks the family, palpating the purse strings, looking for the next windfall.

After too much for too long, my capacity for response was rusty as lead pipes in a broken-down shack. In my relationship with Mother, a fierce drought had taken hold and the well was dry. The sink had a worn spot where water once flowed. Turning the handle was pointless. There was nothing left to give.

The Queen of Outrageous, one minute Mother was a wounded sparrow, the next a scratching bobcat and in-between, obsessive beyond belief. At least drug-induced insanity put her out of commission so she couldn't stand at my refrigerator opening Rubbermaid lids, smelling the contents and quizzing me on the questionable shelf life of the leftovers she located. Or climb on a chair, Reynolds Wrap, scissors and scotch tape in hand, bent on shrouding the air conditioning vent so it wouldn't *blow* on her. The bobcat I could handle; I struck out in return and slammed away. Somewhere along the way I quit reacting, period. *Not going there. Zip. Nada. Done that. I'm through. Bone dry.*

I married. I escaped. Jo was up to her eyeballs in misery with no relief in sight. I felt awful about it. "My God, Jo," I whispered. "I can't bear your going through this alone. Remember what Mamo used to say: There is more than one way to skin a cat. Going straight home to Longview guarantees the same results — insanity. Doctors advise Timberlawn. So okay. We'll find a way to get her there."

"Sounds good, but she won't," Jo rasped. "Their suggestion registered with Mother. Even in her confused state she refuses to go. She says when *we* get *home* she'll *think* about it."

"Very clever. And you know it will never happen. She wants *you* to go back with her. She can't manage if you don't. She needs you. You're her nurse. But if you keep doing this…you'll crack up yourself. That can't happen. Without you to run interference, the creep will milk her of every last dime. Come on. We've got to think of something. And quick. How can we get her to Timberlawn?"

Jo hung her head and her face fell. She looked like she might cry. "It's hopeless. She won't go. You know how she is." Of course Jo felt hopeless. This experience had worn her down, sucked the life out of her month after wretched month.

"Right…but she's still dependent on you. She can't do anything without you. You're her sun, moon and shining star. What if you refused to go back to Longview and said you would only go with her to Timberlawn? Then the loser can't get his hands on her. Do you think you can pull it off?" I was warming to the possibilities. "Mother opened her bank account. She can freeze it. Lock him out. Maybe that would convince her she would be safer at Timberlawn where he can't touch her."

With a rush, color returned to Jo's face. "Hum. I like this. It might work. I *really* don't want to be stuck with *him*. But you know she never let me learn to drive a car. I've got to depend on him to even get her to Dallas at all."

"Um. That's right. Okay, then. We'll have to figure out how to convince *him* that Timberlawn would benefit his interests. Can you lie? Pretend you think they should stay together. Say Mother is just crazy right now. When Timberlawn psychiatrists help her come to her senses she will be *so very happy* to have him in her life."

"Gag." Jo's hands flew to her throat. "I don't know if I can bear dealing with that slimy worm! But I've got no choice…do I?" We held silence for a few seconds, neither of us daring to trust how this was going. "If Mother was at Timberlawn…I do like the idea…I could get him off me. Maybe I can pull it off." Jo smiled weakly, lifted her chin and threw her head back. "It will be interesting to see what happens."

I smiled and nodded as I repeated the line. "It will be interesting to see what happens." The beginning of the quote goes, "It doesn't really matter. Here goes nothing." Stolen from cool Gregory Peck in *The Man in the Gray Flannel Suit*. Jo and I co-opted the fatalistically ballsy dialogue as our mantra for charging onward, ever onward, through Mother's emotional storms. I grinned, "So we've got a plan." We reached for each other and hugged. "I know you can do this, Jo. You've got to…that's all. And Jo…"

"Yeah."

"You can come live with us. That's not such a great deal with a new baby. But you can't live in that house all by yourself, can you? Mamo is on her last leg, right? Unless you think she might pay for UT and you could move back to Austin."

"No." Jo frowned and shook her head left…and then right. "To keep him out of jail Mother has covered the crook's financial disasters. Mamo has rescued her over and over. She's done. Anyway…I can't think about school now. I'll get to it when I can. But thanks. I may not have anywhere else to go. "

Mother revived and stumbled into the living room when our baby nurse rang the doorbell. Feeling mortified that a stranger would witness the insanity in my family, I scooped

Trey out of bed, plopped him in Mrs. Edwards's arms, steered her toward our bedroom and closed the door.

With Trey and Mrs. Edwards out of the picture, Jo and I huddled around Mother, hemming her in. The time was now. Jo took a deep breath, squared her shoulders and announced in a firm voice with fire in her eyes, "Mother, the only place I'm going with you is Timberlawn." Mother crumbled and almost dropped to the floor. But Jo caught her and eased her into the one armchair, quickly vacated by Mother's husband. With tears spilling from her eyes, Mother accepted the inevitable like a small bird with a broken wing, incapable of flight.

Our first purchase after we moved into a two-bedroom apartment was a twin bed. Even though she would have to share the room with a newborn baby, Jo loaded up Mother's copper-toned Buick Electra and moved to Houston. But not before she marched into the Gregg Country Courthouse and walked out with a Power of Attorney. The small legality of owning a Texas driver's license before you get behind the wheel was no bigger than a button off her shirt when the first day of the rest of her life was a happening thing.

Jo bought her second tank of gas to go on job interviews. Before she needed a third, she nailed a receptionist job in the Personal Trust Department of Texas Commerce Bank — awash with young attorneys.

Mother could have second-guessed hospitalization and checked herself out, but she submitted to therapy and made Timberlawn her home for two months. Communication wasn't allowed — a major relief — except for Dr. Johansen's faithfully mailed progress reports that sounded more positive every week.

When she was released, Mother returned to Longview, filed for divorce, put the house on the market and moved to the Towne Oaks garden apartment complex with a pool and lush landscaping. A lovely, Fine Old Family, sherry-sharing friend, Kathryne — the mother of Ann, one of my Longview BFFs — lived right next door. Twice each week Mother drove to Dallas for one-on-one sessions with Dr. Dixon, her therapist. This man gave her life. She gained twenty pounds of muscle and her face radiated happiness — actual happiness! The spoiled-food and blowing-air obsessions vanished, and her optimistic view of the future made a therapy true-believer out of me.

After a few months of 2 AM feedings, Jo moved into an apartment with friends. Within a year our son was climbing trees — or at least trying — and Jo was married. Yep, to one of those hot attorneys.

Mamo always said, "It is darkest before the dawn." On a good day she was genius.

FIRST LIGHT FILTERS THROUGH leafy branches of Live Oak trees that rim the ten-acre plot and hide my farmhouse from the farm-to-market road. A Blue Norther blows in: stark line of gunmetal gray cutting across the pale dawn, cold air against warm, smoky mist softening the dried, brown grasses into pewter. I rush around, slam the windows shut, stuff the black pot-bellied stove with cedar firewood. It catches. The smell is intoxicating. First fire of deep winter and I embrace the womb-feeling, a gift from bone-chilling storms, driving me inside, making me sit still. I've been working too hard again, running to avoid emotional sorting.

I pour a cup of coffee, claim a pastel quilt musty from storage and settle into the wingback. My vantage point faces the twisting road that leads to the tiny farmhouse, dark green oak branches whipped first one way and then the other; lifeless meadow grass lying flat before the fierce February wind. The cold front bears down, kicks up a racket, batters the aged window panes...*bam...bam, bam, bam.*

I take my fill of watching all hell break loose, then like every morning, drag my journal from the chairside table and plop it in my lap, scribble a beginning sentence from last night's dream: *A dark stranger is chasing me, threatening to do me harm. Sigh*...I don't want to do this. Not today. Not any day. The pen slips from my fingers onto the journal page. No energy. None at all. My thoughts wander, heading in the only direction they can sensibly take me.

That dark stranger thing again...yada, yada, yada. I know what the dream means. I'm not paying attention and my psyche is scaring me so I'll notice, listen, deal with it. It is a him. My father. One long-lost aunt in a blue print dress shows up at my mother's funeral, hands me faded photographs from a life I've repressed, all but forgotten, don't identify with at all anymore, and I'm coming unraveled. I don't like it. Invaded by the mind-snatcher. Okay...it's dark...it's cold...it's winter...time to resurrect my own unresolved past.

My gaze fastens on yellowed photographs from childhood, propped on the fall-front secretary since the day Aunt Margaret delivered them to Jo and me at Mother's graveside. I promised my sister I'd have copies made, but I haven't been able to relinquish these startling images, even for a few days. I'm morbidly fascinated. No need to rise from my chair and scrutinize each photograph. I've memorized every face, every pose. Forty-seven blissful years of denial go by with little evidence that this family, this marriage existed except for my father's surname — Foster. Now here we all are, smiling, captured by the lens, caught for eternity in happy family poses. I'm trying to piece it all together, mirrored glass shards, hidden in corners and crevices of childhood.

The phone line between San Antonio and Hughes Springs pulsates with emotional current. Hearing echoes from long ago in Aunt Margaret's East Texas drawl, knowing that Margaret is the only living link to that generation, and like Alice eating too much of the cookie, I'm suddenly small. "I don't remember much, Margaret. Mother hardly ever talked about that life, except to get all starry-eyed about George and say how in love they were during The War."

"That they were." I was getting used to Margaret's terse, no-nonsense way of speaking. She told it like it was. I liked that. I was beginning to trust her. "I remember bits and pieces of some pretty scary stuff. What was wrong with him, Margaret? Was he crazy?"

"Your father wasn't right, Sandy."

Wasn't right...wasn't right. A gust of wind slams against the windowpanes. Margaret's words echo down rabbit holes in my mind. *My stomach hurts. Oh God. Here we go.* A dark memory lurks behind my eyes....I see....I'm there again....

It's September in Los Angeles. In our cute new yellow convertible, my mother and father, my two-year-old baby sister and I just drove all the way to California from Texas. Mother said, "To have a better life." War is over and everybody is happy. But my father starts drinking on the road. Mother starts crying, and I haven't felt right since.

We live in the San Fernando Valley, and I'm in second grade. My new red Buster Browns have rubbed blisters on my heels. I opened my yellow Snow White lunch pail at school today, but my thermos is broken. Little pieces of glass float in my milk. I'll get in trouble when I get home. I'm always in trouble at home. I hate school.

It's like this every afternoon — homework time. My father doesn't have a regular job. He's an "engineer," Mother says when I ask why. She looks at me like I'm stupid. "George is like lots of soldiers home from The War. There are many more men than jobs. Don't be critical of your father!"

To him she says, "It'll be better soon, George." Mother hugs him and pats his big back, talking into his shirt. They look funny together. He's so tall. She's so short, but for sure she's the only one I can count on. Size isn't the only thing that makes you strong. I hope she's right and things are gonna get better. Since my father is home all the time, he's decided to teach me stuff. With him I have to get it right...and quick. Today I'm supposed to learn to tell time.

He calls me to his and Mother's bedroom. He smells like whiskey and sweat. The smell makes my stomach tumbly. The Big Ben wind-up alarm clock sits on the bedside table. The fat white face and long black hands remind me of the late-for-an-important-date white rabbit.

My father, all red-faced and sweaty in his army-like pants and shirt, twists his wrist hard and makes the alarm clock mind him. He

*sets the time, slams the clock on the table so it rattles, then he frowns
at me and demands, "Now, Sandra...tell me what time it is."*

A full-blown flashback unfolds in my head, with images
so strong I smell the odors, hear the sounds. The air is charged
with that peculiar sort of stillness that settles over the San
Fernando Valley in the fall, excluding even a whisper of a
breeze. With metal screens slightly ajar, the windows are
raised for relief from the stifling heat. Slipping in through the
cracks, noisy flies drone around the room.

*My mind goes blank. I don't know a thing except he is smelly
and the flies are loud. "What time is it?" he shouts again, angry,
with veins popping out. I shake my head and say, "Don't know."*

*He does it again. Twists the hands on the clock. Slams it on the
bedside table, "What's the matter with you? When both hands are on
top what time is it?"*

*I can't think. All I can see is the mad scratch on the bedside
table. I put it there. Got punished for being destructive. I don't care.
It felt good to do it. I'm wishing I could take Mother's bobby pin and
drag it through the wood again — hard. My father is still frowning
at me...waiting for an answer. Sweat drips down the side of his face.
"I don't remember," I say.*

*"Stupid! Good-for-nothing..." His face is fire-engine red. "Pay
attention to what I say!" He pulls the brown belt from his pants,
snaps it together...pop. The sound is so loud I jump. Then he does it
again, smiling meanly. My heart beats* thump...thump...thump
*really loud, but I don't think he can hear it. "Lie across that bed.
Maybe this will teach you a thing or two."*

*My hands and arms feel cold and numb like they felt in Illinois
last summer with my cousins, when I dragged them through an icy
cold creek. My head feels as tight as the too-small headband on my blue
straw Easter hat, making it hard to think about anything except it hurt.
I'm falling down the hole in Alice's Wonderland. I can't be reached.*

*I pray as hard as I can for an earthquake to come and swallow
him up. Then maybe the noise will stop. "George, please open the*

door!" Bang...bang...bang. Rattle...rattle...rattle. *I can't handle this racket much longer. Mother pleads, "Don't do this, George! You don't mean it. Open this door!"* Wham...wham...wham. *"George! Stop! Boo-hoo, boo-hoo...." Something has to be really horrible for Mother to cry.*

No earthquake came, at least not literally, but something cracked loose that day. Nothing was the same after that. It took the whole wretched year, but Mother was done with California — and with George.

It's night and my father is "out for the evening," Mother says. "Hurry up! Stop dawdling! He'll be home soon." She packs her bags and supervises my packing. Looking worried and scared, Jo toddles from room to room, first to Mother, then to me. She may only be two years old, but Jo knows something horrible is happening. I try to make her feel better by saying, "It will be okay, Jo-Jo." But I don't feel at all sure of this. I feel just as scared as Jo looks.

Mother makes me think of the Wicked Witch of the West. She swooshes and swoops from her bedroom to our bedroom, dragging clothes out of drawers, snatching the lavatory cabinet door open, dumping bottles into her square brown suitcase.

We are only allowed one small suitcase each, and this means I have to leave almost all my things. So my father won't figure out what we're doing: running away. I drag the small blue suitcase off my bed, open it before Mother and ask, "Is this okay?" She hisses, "No! Only one animal. Get that tiger out of the bag. Too big! Take the lamb." With each word her face gets redder, her voice hoarser. I'm afraid she'll fall down, melt into a puddle and disappear. "Keep quiet!" Mother warns. "Don't you breathe a word of this to your father when he comes home! You hear me?"

"Yes ma'am." I fuss with Jo and she fusses right back. I don't blame her for being aggravated with my bossiness, but I have to do something to keep from worrying my father will come home early and figure out the truth. I can hardly stand to wait until the plane takes off in the morning. I'm beside myself with relief that Mother has

decided to take us away, and so proud of the way she lied to him.

She told him, "We need to go to Texas to visit Mama, George."
Sickly-sweet smile. "You two don't get along, so why go?" She dips
her chin, bats her curled eyelashes and sticks her lips out like Betty
Grable. "You need to keep trying to find a job, don't you?" Kiss,
kiss...pat, pat...hug, hug. "It'll work out all right. You'll see."

The next morning my stomach is so jumpy I can't even eat my
corn flakes. I hope he can't tell I'm nervous. I can't, can't let on to
what we're doing!

At the big and noisy Los Angeles airport, I'm so jittery I
squeeze Jo's hand until she screams and jerks away. "`Top it! You're
hurtin' me!"

My father frowns at me, grabs my hand and hauls me into a bar
where I sit on a high stool with my feet dangling in the air. I don't
say a word. But I'm thinking: They're gonna leave without me! He
slams his hand on the shiny wooden bar and shouts to the bartender
in a white apron, "Wild Turkey, and keep em coming."

The bartender smiles at me. "Do you want a Shirley Temple, little
lady?" I shake my head. "No, thank you." I feel sick at my stomach.

After what seems like forever, Mother rushes in, kisses my
father for the last time, snatches my hand and drags me away as the
loudspeaker squawks, "First call. Boarding flight for Dallas, Texas."
I can't understand what the announcer said...couldn't make out the
flight number...don't know what to do or where to go. Just so Mother
knows, we'll be all right.

We never see my father again — or any of our worldly
possessions — until once when I'm full grown and wonder if
maybe he misses me, finally loves me. It didn't go well. Forty-
seven years. No father. Most everyone who knows me thinks
my father is dead. I never said so. I never said — period.

"He's alive, living in Marshall in your grandmother's
house," Aunt Margaret says. "He's lived there since she died
sixteen years ago and not seen that the place is cleaned since."
*Humph...*she snorts with obvious disgust. "Might as well take

a look. Come see me, Sandy. It's a close enough drive to Marshall from Hughes Springs, where I live."

"How about Easter?" I say, wondering if I've truly lost my mind.

"Fine," Margaret says. "Do you wanna try and see your father? He's a hermit, you know. Let me see if he can be civil...just this once."

I say, "Yes." I'd rather eat a roach.

With scheduling in my own hands, I didn't see my first client until noon. And then I was scheduled straight through until the last client drove away in the dusky glow of headlights. Mornings belonged to God and me.

My God wasn't the white-bearded old Jewish patriarch of classical canvases, frescoes and friezes. Really, I couldn't imagine God as solitarily *HE*. My God was a *WE* − a Mother-Father God. Male *and* female combined into one. Like Jung's teaching that both men and women embody the opposite sex within our-selves: *anima* − or female − within men; *animus* − or male − within women. In my mind, God and Goddess are a couple − a married couple. I know this sounds simplistic, maybe even silly; for sure not terribly theological. But for those very reasons, it works for me. Sometimes I change it up and call God, *Spirit*. I don't think it matters to the Holy what we call it, just so we do.

The sun was up, midway between daybreak and high noon. I shivered in a brittle gust of wind, zipped the Gap fleece and pulled the hood over my head. The world felt still, dried grass crunching beneath my feet. Herefords on the owner's side of the barbed wire chomped on scattered hay, but apparently noticed my movement. As one, the cattle nearest the fence line lifted their heads and raised their snouts, sniffing at the wind, taking me in. I smiled, feeling full, part of everything and everything a part of me. I identified with the Herefords' animal instincts, sensing the wind of Spirit, unseen yet stirring my senses. Morning stillness drew me in, called me to remember that God was close. All I had to do was believe. I definitely did. I needed faith in something bigger than me. I needed support. I ached for love.

And here it was: God and I wandered around the land, poked in desolate flower beds, commiserated over naked plant stalks and withered iris fronds. I itched to dig an iris bulb and see how much it had multiplied. But as I bolted for the tin shed to find a spade, God nudged my thoughts with a felt-voice: "You must wait, Precious One. Your impatience does not serve you well. The time of ripening has not yet come. As it is with the earth, so it is with you. Do not hasten tomorrow. Love yourself each day as I love you, nothing more."

I stuffed my hands in my pockets and sighed with appreciation for God's loving reprimand. Our mornings together were more important to me than food...or even sex, which was unlikely anyway. Right now, I had room in my life for only one man — my father, out there, somewhere. How our connection would play out was yet to be revealed. I had no control over that relationship — or lack of one, as I expected. Nor could I control Mother's return to earth. Until God's gentle reminder, I had forgotten my mantras for invoking peaceful thoughts: It will be interesting to see what happens. What will be, will be. Everything is unfolding exactly as it should.

At least for this moment, I breathed deep and my body relaxed. But my Amie was having a harder go at winter. Wailing winds and roiling storms drove her crazy with fear. When lightning cracked and thunder rolled, she took off running. Nobody and nothing could stop her. After she ran herself to ground, a rancher's chicken coop several miles down the road was her favorite hiding place. He would call — foaming at the mouth — and I would penitently rescue

Amie, aching to give her comfort.

She still refused a collar and a leash, wouldn't darken the door of the farmhouse and insisted on kenneling on frigid earth beneath the abandoned cistern, exposed to the vicissitudes of nature. There was no help for Amie, except to do the next right thing — as much as I was able.

With every sunrise, belief in the organic rightness and simplicity of life grew. God and I would get through Mother's return as Lacie's child, and the Easter confrontation with my father. Hard-headed as I am, it took a while, but finally I stopped struggling. Not only did I believe, but accepted with gut intelligence: change is the only constant. And everything is unfolding exactly as it should.

Little did I know. This interlude of tranquil acceptance — although hard-gained — would soon evaporate like a desert mirage.

The last week in February, I answered the phone and immediately assumed that the uncontrollable sobbing on the other end belonged to a client. This was no client. Wailing until her tears became a whimper, Lacie could finally speak. "Mom...my baby is dead. I'm coming to see you."

Miscarriage is a silent death seldom shared. Even though that fragile life had been conceived in the crack between the worlds, like most every woman who loses the hope of new life, Lacie was shattered. But determination is the bedrock of her personality and she heard her OB's encouragement as a promise: "A woman is especially fertile following a D&C, Lacie. If you and your husband want to conceive, now is a good time."

Who can know whether Mother's soul had a change of heart, or whether her physical return to this family flew in the face of fate? I have learned — and am certain — that a woman never forgets the death of a child. Over time, the pain doesn't come as often and it doesn't last as long. But when grief is stirred, the ache feels just as excruciating as it did that first day.

MARCH 4, 1973. American soldiers slogged their way through the jungles of Vietnam. Within months America would be racked and torn by Watergate, war protests and gas shortages; endless lines encircling Houston's city blocks — odd days for odd-numbered plates, even days for even-numbered plates — with the price of gasoline skyrocketing to a pricey seventy-five cents a gallon. I felt the tremors of unrest — who didn't if they tuned in to Huntley/Brinkley — but my emotional fiber was stretched as thin as a rubber band about to snap. I didn't have enough patience to ponder the state of the world. Or feel guilty that my husband avoided the draft by marrying me and fathering our two children. He was a warrior and would love to get into the fight. But he was my warrior, and I had never needed his strength more.

It was Sunday, and we piled out of our boxy Chevrolet wagon after returning from early church. I dumped my purse on the kitchen counter and made it no further than our lemony yellow den/dining room combo beside the kitchen. A chill settled over me in spite of the unseasonably warm spring day. Absent-mindedly I gathered my blazer around me, but remained rooted to the oak floor.

Falling within my unfocused vision, a rascally brown squirrel flattened himself spread-eagle against the gray bark of the ash tree just beyond the tall windows and French door. Craning his neck to stare, the squirrel's alert brown eyes observed me intently, transfixed and still, as if this creature sensed my mental strain.

On a whim I made direct eye contact and in my mind

spoke to this blatant voyeur. *Hey, little guy. What's up? Don't worry. I'll be all right. I just have to sort it all out.* As if satisfied, the squirrel popped his tail, scrambled up the tree and was immediately hidden in dense new leaves.

As background music for my dark mood, the family created a dissonant racket: tossing church clothes, rifling through drawers, swinging closet doors wide with a bang. *They sound so happy, so purposeful. Good, maybe it will rub off on me. The Episcopal service failed to inspire, but then maybe nothing could today. Something is bothering me. So here I stand like a lump, talking to a squirrel, staring into the sunshine and hungering for warmth…any old warmth will do.* What *is the matter with me? Of course…it's Lacie.*

I turned and soaked up the almost life-sized print of a little girl — probably five years old — that spanned the length of the love seat. She stood in a field of wildflowers on the other side of a split-rail fence. In her hands she held a wildflower bouquet; wind tossed her wispy blond hair and parted tall field grasses. On a visit to Mother's in Longview last year, I spied this print and snagged it from her garbage. "It's so tacky!" Mother protested. "I'm getting rid of it. Why would you want to hang such a tacky print in your pretty little house?"

"Oh, Mother!" I moaned, as I hauled the print to the station wagon and decisively locked the door. "Why should you even care? I like it, that's why. It's how Lacie will be in a few years. She'll stand in a field of wildflowers and her hip surgeries will be history. Your *tacky* print is, to me, a symbol of hope. I'll feel encouraged every time I look at it."

A dislocated hip — discovered not long after Lacie's birth — was hardly a fatal condition even if it did mean she couldn't walk until it was fixed. If I had the choice, I would vote for sand castles and sea shells on Bolivar Peninsula over hospitalizing our two-and-a-half-year-old Botticelli angel for a *second* hip surgery. From last year's experience, when she was eighteen months old, I knew what was ahead of us. This second *rotational osteotomy* to prevent *aseptic necrosis* would amount to five hours — give or take a suture or two — and then ten weeks encased in a full body cast. I hated medical lingo, a likely target for my impotent anger. Really, I was eaten up with sad. Lacie's surgery was scheduled in two weeks…and I wasn't ready.

Last year's experience had forever altered my reality. Not Lacie's surgery, which went well considering another was required. It's what happened afterward that blew me away. I mean, I'm the kid who fainted when I was eleven or so and joined the First Presbyterian Church. After Tommy Talbot — the round-faced preacher who reminded me of a storybook gnome — completed the ceremony of confirmation, we confirmees reverently clasped our hands over our stomach, and silently returned to our pews. I do recall shuffling into the long wooden pew with white-frocked and white-shirted confirmation classmates on either side. But that's the last I remembered until I opened my eyes to find myself wedged in between the seat of one pew and the back of the next. I came to with Mother and Jo fanning my face and the anxious minister close by. When I opened my eyes he smiled and then, with a booming voice, announced to the hushed congregation, "Well. I guess it took!"

I wasn't so sure. But I was fairly certain I didn't faint because of reverent awe for the Divine. I fainted from relief that the scary old man in the sky who smote people regularly — so I was taught — hadn't decided to smite me as well. I wasn't exactly anti-Christian, but I couldn't quite get with the program, either. Between my childhood confirmation and Lacie's hip surgery the previous March, my attitude toward religion had changed little. God and I remained polite strangers. I had little context for dealing with what happened only an hour after returning home from Lacie's first hip surgery.

Granted, Texas Children's Hospital was designed for patients, not parents. The turquoise plastic window seat — cum-bed — while adequate, was not conducive to rest. Sleep deprivation can cause hallucinations, so maybe that's how it happened. I just know I have never felt so completely loved in all my life — before or since.

By the time Lacie and I vacated Texas Children's, the whole family was worn out: my husband, because he had shuttled between work, home and hospital for all ten days of Lacie's hospitalization, and Mother, because she had become a quintessential grandmother, solitarily taking care of our wild and woolly five-year-old son. Lacie and I were on our last nerve because hospitals are an unwholesome environment — if essential — for maintaining and/or regaining health.

Trey's deposit for his first grade year at Second Baptist School was due, and I couldn't wait to get behind the wheel of a car, and do something for Trey at the same time. In just five months he would be in school all day, and I missed him already. He was growing up way too fast. But he was crazy excited about school, and I needed to begin the process of giving my son wings.

We had all crowded into the infinitesimal den, and by some miracle, Mother and my husband declared a truce. They sat side by side on the loveseat, chatting amiably about Lacie's surgery and recovery. Lacie giggled from her forty-five degree angle position in the stroller — an ingenious rigging that accommodated her full body cast — while *Bubba* Trey created a barnyard of Playskool animals just beyond the tips of her bare toes. *"Moo…moo. Neigh...neigh.* How does the piggy go, *Wacee*?" With a satisfied smile, I quietly slipped from the house.

I let the car windows down all the way and breathed deeply for the first time in weeks. Second Baptist was just a quick hop over and back. For these few brief minutes I felt like a butterfly fluttering on the breeze. The scent of gardenia and ligustrum blooms filled my senses, and wind buffeted me as I drove. I switched on the radio and sang an off-key duet with Neil Diamond, "Song sung blue, everybody knows one. Funny thing, but when you sing it with a cry in your voice. Before you know it you start to feeling good. You've simply got no choice...."

Rounding the corner from Westheimer and turning onto Voss Road, I suddenly regretted leaving my sunglasses at home. The sunlight was so glaring I could hardly see the road. *I must be extra sensitive because I've been inside so long,* I thought. *But no...that's weird...what's up with the light?* I steered into the boulevard's slower right lane, and craned my neck to inspect the sky. A strange greenish-yellow permeated everything. *Like before a tornado,* I thought, but then quickly reasoned: *That can't be. We don't have tornadoes in Houston. Besides, there isn't a cloud anywhere. What is this?*

The more I concentrated on the light the more it glistened and glowed. I began to tremble uncontrollably. Not in fear, but with anticipation, then suddenly, I gasped with surprise. Firmly yet softly, the unmistakable pressure of a hand rested on my left shoulder. I whipped my head around to scan the back seat. No one was there. I shook my head to clear my thoughts. *No, I'm not making this up. I feel the pressure of an actual hand on my shoulder.* Long fingers extended well toward my chest, while I felt the heel of the hand on my back below my shoulder blade. *It's such a big hand. It's got to be a man's hand.* With startled recognition, I assumed this hand could only belong to God.

I don't know why I made that assumption. I showed up at church only to satisfy my cherub husband, who cut his religious teeth as a falsetto choirboy in the Washington Cathedral. I had little religious reference point. No reason whatsoever to imagine God knew I existed, much less would make the effort to reach out and touch me. But everything happened so fast, I couldn't argue with the experience, or stop clear thoughts from forming. Stronger and more certain than my own thoughts, separate yet emanating from within my own mind:

"There will be difficulties. I will be with you. Never forget. I am always with you."

That was it. A matter of minutes, and then it was gone. As if by magic, the meaning of Neil Diamond's lyrics amplified the experience like a soundtrack: "Song sung blue, every garden grows one…." Just when I realized the meaning of Diamond's lyrics synched with God's words, the pressure of God's hand disappeared as the last note faded away.

In a daze I maneuvered through Houston traffic, parked in front of Second Baptist and turned over Trey's first grade registration, even managing chatty conversation with the office staff. Moonstruck like a woman in love, I took the long way home.

When I arrived, my husband's car was no longer in the driveway. *Oh yeah*, I remembered, *he returned to the office*. I burst through the front door shouting, "Mother! Mother!" I found her in the kitchen facing the sink, frozen in position as she twisted around speechless, a dish towel hovering motionless in mid-air, her eyes big as saucers. I must have looked crazed. I certainly felt energized. "Oh, I'm sorry," I giggled. "I scared you. There's nothing wrong. It's all good. Real good. Come, come sit down." Lacie and Trey had moved into the living room and played on the yellow shag carpet. I took Mother's hand and led her to the love seat, where she remained speechless, and I remained Chatty Kathy with no string to pull to stop my talking. "This is incredible. Unreal! When I drove past Cornelius Nursery on Voss Road I felt God's hand on my shoulder. He touched me. I'm like crazy-in-love feeling. Can you believe it?"

Mother answered, "No," followed by, "Are you losing your mind? You're scaring me, Sandy. You're tired...that's it...you need rest."

I showed up at a Christian bookstore the next day, bought a Bible, and had paid close attention in church this whole year. I wanted answers. What was this thing? What did it mean, and what was I supposed to do with it?

Quickly, I learned to limit fervent sharing. Any information about the experience was too much information. Friends — even the minister — looked at me like I was a weird mutant and gave me space rather quickly. My husband, accustomed to incense and high church drama, took it all in and regarded the experience as something special. I never wanted to lose the feeling of complete and absolute love that still warmed me in the deepest, darkest parts of my soul — but special?

Now that I'd had time to process it, the experience felt a little daunting. The message God spoke in my mind wasn't exactly exalted. The Episcopal minister even suggested that God's touch — like in *Job* — was a "heavy hand," divine warning of difficulties to come. This interpretation did not provide comfort. Unfortunately, his reasoning made sense. Didn't I pat someone in hope of offering comfort when they were going through a rough time? A pat isn't exactly a high-five, is it? Regarding the God-thing from this doomsday perspective, I started feeling paranoid. Unable to settle on an explanation — even though second-guessing God leased significant space in my head — I persisted in watching my back while feeling slightly unhinged.

Interrupting my thoughts, Trey bounded around the corner. "Mom! Look at me! I dressed myself." He grinned and rubbed his chest up and down with both hands.

I crouched to eye level. "I can see that." I couldn't keep from smiling as I appraised his surfer-dude look—an orange-

and-green plaid shirt and blue-and-white striped shorts. "Good job, little guy."

"Mom!" Trey scowled, squared his shoulders and tucked his chin. "I'm not *wittle!* I'm big! And I'm hungry. What's for lunch, Mom?"

I laughed, "My mistake! Of course you're *big.* So hey, *big* guy, go ask your dad what he wants." Trey roared away and thumped down the hall." *Whew. Such a thundering little guy!*

Buying time to get myself together, I cracked the French door and stepped onto the brick patio. Sighing with pleasure, I closed my eyes and turned my face to the sun. *Farmer's Almanac* proof of early spring, a flock of robins pecked in the thick St. Augustine lawn. Not caring that I wore a suit and heels, I crouched in the flower bed beside the patio and continued soul-searching as I haphazardly freed Ajuga ground cover from withered ash leaves, twisted in among the tourmaline green, new growth.

So...I'm resigned to Lacie's surgery and okay about it. But I still feel heavy. What? Layers of anxiety and fear wafted into awareness like water vapor drawn toward the sun. *Oh. No wonder. Mother's unsettling phone call this morning. What was that about?*

"Sandy?"

"Yes, Mother. Good God, it's early. What's up?"

"I need to know if you're okay?"

"*Yes.*" I tried to stop, but impatience crept into my voice. "You sound stressed. What's wrong? I only have a second. We're leaving for church."

"Okay. Just a minute! I need to tell you this scary, scary dream I had last night. In the dream I'm coming to Houston. But I'm not driving. I'm riding in the back seat of Kathryne's car with her friend Mary driving. Very strange. Kathryne and I are friends, but we don't have plans to travel together. I'm sick or something...stretched out across the back seat. I can't even sit up. What could be wrong? Boogedy-boogedy. I would never come to Houston like that. What do you think it means?"

I felt somewhat concerned. Why *would* Mother come to Houston with Kathryne, my Longview friend, Ann's mom? They did live next door and share "tea time" — the 5 o'clock sherry hour — but Kathryne was several years older than Mother and they ran in different circles. Unsettled or not, I didn't have time to get into it. "I haven't a clue. We've got to go — now. I'm sorry. I really can't talk. I'll call you later." Before she could protest, I hung up.

As I reflected on this early-morning phone call, I was still not ready to deal with it. *It'll have to wait. I feel strange today myself. Two creeped-out women can't make anything right. Ever since Timberlawn five years ago Mother has been another person. But when she freaks out about something I flash back to all those unhappy times. I get mean. I feel ashamed to admit it, but I do. I feel anger rising and it's hard to stop. I need time. I'm not ready to listen. It sounds like one of her precognitive dreams. And somehow we're involved. I don't like it.*

Another troubling circumstance bubbled to the surface. *That thing with Trey last night....*

I tucked my almost six-year-old, Mr. Bubble-scented little man between jungle-print sheets, folded a fleece cheetah-print spread over his camo pj chest and nestled a lumpy Snoopy into the crook of his arm. I kneeled beside his bed and listened as he thanked God: "...for Mommy and Daddy and Wacee and all the animals in the jungle and everybody in the *whole wide world.*" I brushed damp blond corkscrews from his face, kissed his forehead, turned out the light and murmured, "Sleep tight, pumpkin," as I crept hopefully toward the door.

"Mom?" Trey called, with the urgent tone that usually preceded "I'm thirsty." Or "I need to go potty."

I stood in the doorway with light from the hallway dimly

outlining his face. "What, honey?"

"What happens to you when you die?" he asked, with a catch in his voice.

My throat tightened. "What makes you ask that, sweetheart?"

"'Cause I wanna know."

"What for, honey?" I felt alarmed. What was going on in that innocent head? "That's such a serious thing to wonder about. How come?"

"'Cause...you know, like in Sunday school they talk about 'dose many mansions you go to when you die. But the teacher wouldn't tell me what happens to your *body*, Mom. I wanna know."

It was awful. Trey asked one question after another...pressing me for details. Did I say too much? But he wouldn't let me go until we covered the body with dirt and a slab of marble marked the grave. Before we were done I was crying. Hiding my tears...feeling sick at my stomach. What are they teaching him in Sunday school? This is distressing.

As I stood and stretched, I realized I had crouched over the Ajuga bed an obscenely long time when there was lunch to prepare, and a family that humored my need for solitude. My body felt stiff and creaky, but I now had something to give.

As if on cue, the French door slammed against the den wall, and Trey vaulted onto the patio waving a piece of paper. "Mom! Mom! 'Member Bryan's letter? Dad's talkin' to Art and Ann. We're goin', Mom. Pretty, pretty please. Can we? Can we go to Art and Ann's?"

"Let me see, honey." Printed in careful script, the letter from Trey's big-guy idol read: "Dear Trey, I miss you. I want you to come see me. I have a minibike and a horse. Her name is Granny. She is real *gental*. Come soon. Your friend, Bryan."

I laughed and threw my arms around Trey. "Kinda exciting, huh?"

Trey bounced up and down like Tigger. "Yes! Yes! Yes!"

"Okay, honey. Okay! Give me a second to find out what's going on! I'm sure we can go if they are inviting us. Dad and I miss them, too."

Of all our Larchmont subdivision neighbors, Art and Ann and their children — Jana, who was ten and Bryan, eight — were our closest friends. They lived next door and our families joined at the hip until they moved away six months ago. Larchmont was a starter neighborhood for newly married, twenty-something husbands making their mark in the business world, and their wives, stay-at-home moms. As soon as the guys conquered Wall Street, we all planned to move on — to Richistan River Oaks estates for the more ambitious, maybe an upgrade to modestly larger *casas* for the rest of us. Art and Ann migrated to ten acres an hour north of Houston in the Conroe countryside, reasoning that a retro country town would inoculate their kids from the viral drug culture that infected Houston schools.

My husband and I weren't this far along. Trey and Lacie were still young. We would cross the relocation bridge when we came to it. Really, it hurt to think about moving. I loved this place, especially in the spring. No one had to send an engraved invitation for the front-yard party beginning now, right through summer and into fall. With a *whomp* the garage doors went up. Out came the barbecue pits, aluminum and blue, yellow, red and green plastic webbing lawn chairs. The *clack clack...clack-clack-clack* of Big Wheels roared up and down sidewalks, mowing down both man and beast who dared cross their path. Prissy little princesses pushed baby-doll carriages. The *thump* of basketballs filled the air; shouts of victory at the hoop, shouts of defeat.

The deafening roar of lawnmowers almost drowned out boomboxes perched on window sills, wailing Willie Nelson, Johnny Cash, Jerry Jeff Walker. The most irreverent and downright nasty song of the bunch, "Up against the wall, redneck mother..." was practically our theme song, eliciting an off-key chorus from anyone within earshot. Now *this* whole scene was *tacky*...and highly predictable behavior for twenty-somethings on steroids, sucking the last drop out of barely legal, college crazies.

Regardless of our raunchy taste in music and low-rent driveway socializing, Larchmont was exactly the right environment for raising kids. Hordes of little people squirmed underfoot, living in and out of one another's houses. The neighborhood wasn't exactly a commune, but close — with the exception that we didn't mingle our finances. It seemed naturally expedient for our 5500 block of Judalon to operate by an unspoken code of ethics: I will treat all children as if they are my own. The children of Judalon trembled. Nothing could they hide from the parent police.

I completely understood why Art and Ann moved. The glamour of drugs seduced even the best kids like Jana and Bryan. But how would our families ever replace the 5500 block of Judalon on the Fourth of July? By city ordinance, all Larchmont streets were barricaded. With every house streaming red, white and blue crepe paper, beginning at steamy mid-morning the games kicked off: sack races, relays, volleyball, beer-chugging contests. And then at noon, after the mommies and daddies tapped the second keg of Lone Star, the full-out parade of bikes, Big Wheels, and floats — with a makeshift fife and drum corps attempting "Yankee Doodle Dandy" — made a grand tour of every street, every block.

The event attracted an impressive crowd. Jo and her husband, and their Jennifer, age-wise wedged between Trey and Lacie, pulled on red, white and blue and contributed to the standard mayhem. Mother wouldn't miss it. She considered patriotism of this magnitude a priority, almost a religious pilgrimage...and redemption for Larchmont. "You've finally got it right. This is America. Just like after *Dubya Dubya Two*."

By 5 PM on this arguably hottest day of the year, guaranteed the mercury would rise to one hundred degrees in the shade. Curling gray clouds of smoke from the guys' cookers permeated the heavy, humid air. Barbecue brisket, ribs, chicken, sausage and burgers smoked in pits up and down the street. Red checked picnic tables sagged under the weight of potato salad, beans, coleslaw, deviled eggs, pickles, chips and garlic bread, cookies, brownies and pies.

One year, our patriotic fervor drew so much attention the *Houston Chronicle* ran a feature article that spread across two pages under the banner head: *Go Fourth Judalon!* The collage of photos made us famous for a day. But the elder Larchmont lifers, Pat and Tom — with their matching Cadillacs, white for Pat, black for Tom — achieved the greatest notoriety, thanks to Boy Dog, their white poodle who Pat dyed blue for the occasion. Fame, however, did not alter the fact that Boy Dog slunk around looking pretty mangy until the next Fourth of July when he got a fresh dye job.

Every quirky Judalon experience bound us tightly to our best-ever friends. Now, after six months of lonely separation, as if there were some way to legalize our closeness, Art and Ann had asked for legal custody of Trey should anything ever happen to my husband and me. After much discussion, we were ready to say "Yes," hire an attorney, draw up documents and make it official: We feel as close — or closer — to you than we do to any of our real family members. If we should die, Trey is yours. Probably, we would grant the Halls' wish before the sun set on what promised to be another glorious country Sunday.

AS THE TIRES SCRAPED noisily against freshly laid gravel, our friends spilled out onto the deck surrounding their country escape. Everyone talked at once. "You guys look great! Country air does you a world of good!" I shouted as we piled out of the car. "Damn good," my husband hollered.

With a wispy shag haircut, and wearing tight jeans and a white shirt, Ann bounced towards us with open arms. "What took you so long?"

"Little Lacie!" Jana scooped Lacie from my arms. So like her mom, gentle and good-natured, Jana was the mirror image of Ann both in looks and temperament. Slung on Jana's hip, Lacie wriggled with pleasure.

"Hey, buddy!" With ritual male bonding, Art clapped Trey on the back and threw an arm around his shoulder as we picked our way toward their new home, completed only this week. "Y'all watch out for those cedar stumps," Art cautioned. "Gotta rout those out. One thing at a time!"

Until today, with his scruffy cowboy haircut — or lack thereof — I never realized how much Art resembled Clint Eastwood. Or how much their natural cedar, ranch-style home would pay homage to early Texas. On other weekend excursions when construction was in process, our friends bunked in a drafty old line shack on the property, and we only saw the skeleton of their home taking shape. Now, the myth had come alive. "Built this place out of those cedar trees. Milled in town. How's that for living off the land?" Art grinned, a sense of accomplishment oozing out of every pore. "Come on! Let me show you around."

To the left of the house, the five-acre pasture had recently been fenced. So new, the barbed wire hadn't rusted yet. This wasn't a working pasture with stock, but a playground where Bryan rode his minibike, and grazing land for Bryan's *gental* horse, Granny. Like ranch *podnahs*, the weekend cowboys moseyed toward the vintage red barn to inspect Art's new toy, an ancient John Deere tractor, recently refurbished.

With the kids giggling and laughing at our side, Ann and I headed for the kitchen. The boys wrestled their way down the hall, leaving nicks in the wall. While Jana and Lacie giggled their way into Jana's room, Ann and I straddled bar stools arranged beside the cook island and squished hamburger meat into patties.

"So how are you? What's goin' on?" Ann asked, as we slid into effortless sister-talk. But as all moms and dads know to expect, peace on the ranch is as rare as caviar. Trey and Bryan soon tired of Pac-Man and stormed the kitchen. A rangy replica of his dad with sandy hair and sparkling new braces, Bryan slouched coolly up to the cook island and straddled a bar stool.

Not quite so cool, Trey tugged at my denim shirt and whispered in my ear, trying to camouflage the fact that he interrupted. "Mom? Mom! Can Bryan and I have a walking-around sandwich instead of waiting for supper?"

"A what?"

"A walking-around sandwich! You know, we can walk around with it."

Visions of my childhood and endless picnics under Mamo's wisteria arbor swam before my eyes. "Who's got time to eat? Right?"

Ann shot me a conspiratorial grin. "Yes! Of course! I'll fix those walking-around sandwiches right now. Wash your grubby hands, both of you!" No encouragement needed, Bryan upended the stool and bolted for the powder room.

"Thank you, Aunt Ann!" Trey wrapped his arms around her legs and crushed her with a hug. Ann swatted him on the back. "Go...go...wash your hands."

My heart turned in circles and danced a two-step. *Of course you can rush and tumble through that door, sandwich clutched in your dirty little hands. Of course you can dash headlong into the adventures you are creating for yourself. Of course you can roll around and cover yourself with life. It's yours. Live it. Vicariously through your joy, I'm in ecstasy.* With an unruly slam, walking-around sandwiches in hand, Bryan and Trey bolted through the back door and were gone.

The big boys thundered across the cedar deck and tore into the kitchen. Balancing Lacie on her hip, Jana rushed into the room to see what all the activity was about. Brawny and brash as his Scottish Highland ancestors, my husband grabbed me from behind, wrapped his arms around my waist, swung me in circles and nuzzled my neck with his weekend scruff. I squealed and grinned at Lacie, "Daddy has a scratchy face!" mimicking her line when her daddy nuzzled her with his five o'clock bristles.

"You'd better watch who you're messin' with," my husband teased.

Art chimed in, "You girls wouldn't mind if we took the kids out to the field to watch Bri perform on his minibike, would you?"

"We'll be crying in our beer missing you, won't we, Sandy?" Ann laughed.

Art slapped Ann's bottom. "Just see to it that you women have dinner a-waitin' when we're done. Isn't that right?" He winked at my husband, thumped him on the back and drawled, "Let's head 'em up and roll 'em out, *hombre*," as the wannabe cowpokes slammed through the ranch house door.

Ann jiggled a blue-and-white mixing bowl overflowing with potato salad still naked without mayonnaise. "Come on,

Sandy! Free at last. Let's get this done!" In a Julia Child minute, our cooking projects slid into the refrigerator. Ann hollered over her shoulder as she headed for the deck, "Let the screen door slam! It's one of the rules around here. You have to!"

On the deck out back, we pulled director chairs side by side, and twisted the tops off Lone Star longnecks. Through tall pines, fading sunbeams cast lacy afternoon shadows along the wide cedar planks. Ann and I settled into needlework projects and conversation. In the distance I heard the drone of Bryan's minibike and smiled with satisfaction. "Trey loves being here, Ann. Bryan is like a god to him. I'm so grateful for Bryan's older-good-guy modeling."

Ann's eyes blared in agreement. "Oh, my God! You know how much Bryan wishes Trey was his little brother. This family thing we've got going is perfect for all of us!"

Time drifted as we stitched and settled into comfortable, silent, all's-right-with-the-world camaraderie. There was no warning when Bryan's shrill scream pierced the air. *"Treeeey!"* Muffled in the distance, yet clear, the distress in his voice was unmistakable.

Ann and I shot to our feet. Her wide-eyed terror mirrored my own. Tossing the needlework canvas, I ran. The scrunch of my boots on the earth seemed far away, disembodied as if these feet were not my own. The length of the house took an eternity to traverse. As I stumbled forward my mind's eye brought me a picture: *The day is clear. I have rounded the corner from Westheimer onto Voss Road. The light is entrancing, numinous, glistening. I feel God touch me and speak in my mind.* "There will be difficulties. I will be with you. Never forget. I am always with you."

I screamed as I ran, "Oh God! Oh God! Oh God! No! It *was* a heavy hand!"

Sobbing and shrieking, Jana ran past me as I rounded the corner of the house. "Mom! Mom! Mom!"

At a distance, crumpled forms huddled in the center of the pasture beyond the barbed-wire fence. My husband. Cradling Trey in his lap. I could hear nothing but my heartbeat slamming against my chest. Frantically separating barbed links with my boot and hand, I stooped and lurched forward, snagging my denim shirt on a barbed wire prong. I ripped free and stumbled to the feet of my son's blood-stained, writhing form. Lacie stood and screamed hysterically a few feet from Trey. "Bubba! Bubba! Bubba!" Crouching, I lifted her into me, shielded her eyes; held her against my heart.

An eerie calm wrapped around me and held me upright. Unbearable images imprinted on my mind in black and white, colorless frames, jerky, flickering like an old silent movie; blank spaces in between. Kneeling, I reached to touch Trey, horrified by the red pool rapidly saturating his dad's white western shirt. *Skull crushed…left side…completely…a plate of spaghetti…a plate of spaghetti…* My thoughts hammered against the inevitable like the thundering force of water plunging over Niagara Falls.

Fiercely hanging on to Lacie, I stumbled backward, almost losing my balance on rocky ground. Righting myself with effort, I scanned the deep meadow, drawn by the dissonant metal groan of the abandoned minibike that spun in erratic circles and gouged the earth. With arms and legs pumping Bryan charged towards us, his face contorted by screams. "Trey! *Treeeeeey!*" Across the field, Art yanked Granny towards the barn. Images and sounds summoned the inconceivable. *No. Not Granny. Gentle Bryan's gentle mare…spooked by the minibike. Fear in her eyes. Feet planted. Ears set back. Trey hurtling across the field. Eyes fixed on Brian and the cool minibike. Not seeing Granny. Deaf to his dad's warning screams. Granny turning heel as Trey flew past…. No. No.* My heart knew what my head could not accept and without thought formed a final prayer: *God take him. He's yours. Always was. Always will be.*

The trauma unit of a big-city hospital is all about saving lives, little else. Houston's Ben Taub lacked the cushion of soft lights and comforting sofas. Impersonally strewn along hospital corridors, stretchers supported human beings badly hurt, but not in danger of dying from their wounds. *Triage*, my mind translated. *We won't find Trey in these hallways.*

In a dingy back hallway outside the OR, no one gathered around the lost-looking man in a white, bloodstained Western shirt. I threw my arms around him, overwhelmed with relief. "Oh, honey! I'm here." He stiffened and backed away. His eyes glazed over with shock, as though he had gone far, far away, traveled alone down a road I couldn't know...or touch. He averted my gaze and spoke toward the worn and dirty linoleum floor. "As good as can be expected, I guess. The ambulance ride was awful. They're working on him now." His eyes were closed. He had drawn the blinds. *Dear God. Will I ever see him again?*

Feeling grinding despair, I stumbled backward and braced my hands against the peeling green walls for support. We didn't have long to wait. Ashen-faced, our beloved pediatrician, Dr. Bob, pushed through the dented and scarred metal surgery doors. With his face contorted, Bob shook his head. "It was too late. He's gone. There was nothing we could do."

Numb with grief, at almost midnight we pulled into our driveway. Having entrusted Lacie into Ann's care while Art drove me to Ben Taub, I knew she was safe. And would soon learn that Jo had intervened and Lacie was with her, here in Houston. Up and down the street, lights shone from windows. Bumper to bumper, parked cars strung out on both sides of Judalon like Christmas lights. "There was an announcement on the news," one of our college friends explained. "That's how we all knew."

Looking into our friends' faces, I felt paralyzed by a nauseating tide of finality. In the violent race riots and assassinations of the Sixties, and now in the Seventies with Vietnam, America felt like a strife-torn Third World country. Even in college, when I crouched beneath a desk as Charles Whitman took aim from the University of Texas Tower and in the space of ninety-six minutes gunned down forty-five innocents going about their daily life, I still felt some sense of separation from death. Tonight, our friends' gray, slack expressions mirrored the despair that stared from the pages of *Newsweek* and *Time*. *We aren't the only ones who face death tonight,* I thought. *This is happening to all of us. None of us are children anymore.*

Neither my husband nor I truly slept. Way too much…too much to process…too much to bear…too crushing to deal with in any sane way. We didn't talk, didn't kiss, mumbled goodnight and curled inward, turning our backs to one another, as if acknowledging each other forced us to confront Trey's death magnified times two — an unbearable burden neither of us could carry.

Our bed had gone cold like our son, the house chillingly still, every tick of the kitchen wall clock skipping across wood floors and bouncing off walls. In my mind I tracked the sound, where it originated, how it arced, where it landed and how it came to my ear. No other soul lay under the roof except the wretchedly isolated parents of a deceased son.

I could say, "Honey, are you awake? Hold me! I ache to feel your arms around me." But what if he hasn't got it to give? What stops us from holding each other? What's the matter with us?

He must feel guilty that he was responsible for Trey when this happened. It's not his fault. I should shake him and say so. Hold him until he cries…I cry. Should say I believe this was going to happen no matter what either of us did. God's hand on my shoulder. Trey

*asking what happens to your body when you die. Mother's
precognitive dream.*

*No. Too much. Not tonight. Let him be. Let myself be.
Tomorrow. Tomorrow we'll be close.*

Over and over again, my mind replayed the meadow
scene: Trey's writhing body cradled in my husband's lap, the
white shirt rapidly wicking our son's blood. When I couldn't
bear it any longer, I directed my thoughts toward an alternate
movie that my mind obediently spliced onto the frame of
truth: *Trey rising from his convulsing form…laughing, running
across the pasture into the sunlight…running…running…running.*

Telling your mother something makes it real. Finally
unable to escape sharing the story any longer, far past noon I
placed the call. "Sandy! Oh, Sandy honey. Don't explain. It's
okay. I know already. Early this morning Kathryne showed up
at my door and offered to drive me to Houston with the help
of her friend, Mary. Ann had called before dawn to tell her
about Trey. Kathryne had to tell me. I saw it in her eyes. Knew
something awful was wrong. I got it out of her."

As I explained anyway, Mother sounded disjointed and
fractured but still sharp. "I understand absolutely. Of course
you couldn't call. I'm packing to come. Just like in the dream.
I knew it showed me some horrible premonition. I don't
understand why I know things before they happen, but I
do…always have. Anyway I'm on the way. We are. As soon as
I can pull myself together. My precious baby, Trey." Her voice
broke. "I've got to go now. I'll be there soon…."

Mother moved in for months, sleeping on the living-room
sofa, serving, doing what was needed. Beyond casserole
dishes with names scotch-taped to the bottom, guest registers
and flower card enclosures carefully recorded, she
uncomplainingly accomplished the necessary. Lacie did have

her scheduled hip surgery as planned. She needed it. Life goes on. We would never have made it without Mother.

Until then I never dreamed that Mother was capable of selfless acts of kindness. Flabbergasted, one morning into Lacie's recovery after friends' visits were fewer and life assumed an almost normal cadence, I asked, "Mother, how can you keep being here day after day? I know you loved Trey, too. You've got your own grief and this isn't exactly a vacation."

We stood in the kitchen — sacred woman space — where we usually talked. Mother's face softened. "Of course, honey. Being here helps...I feel useful. I can't stay away. I need to be here. You're the Mother, and still stronger than I am. I get depressed. I fall apart."

I shrugged and began unloading the dishwasher while Mother coarsely sliced onions, carrots and potatoes for pot roast. "I dunno' about that. I'm not at all sure I won't lose it."

"I don't think you will. I can see that something holds you together. You've got faith. I don't know where it comes from." She paused, her forehead creased with concentration. "Maybe that weird hand-on-the-shoulder thing. You sure didn't get it from me. You know how Papaw scared us to death about the *blood of Jesus*. I hardly ever darkened the door of First Presbyterian. You remember." I nodded in agreement. "But I can see you've got something I don't, and it gets you through."

She paused as she slid the pot roast into the oven, wiped her hands on a red apron and, looking like a little girl with her chin tucked in embarrassment, took my hand, "Come here, Sandy. Come sit with me a minute." Leading us from the blindingly bright kitchen, Mother patted the love-seat in the little sitting room. We sat side by side beneath the "Dream for Lacie" print — clasping a bouquet of wildflowers, wispy-haired watercolor girl stands in windblown fields of grass.

Mother shifted her weight and turned so she could look

me in the eye. "Did I ever tell you about my baby boy?"

"What? No!" I flattened my hand against my heart and my ears buzzed from shock.

Eyes brimming with unshed tears, Mother began a conversation that headed in the direction of confession. "After I had you, a couple of years after, George and I had some pretty good times. He was stationed in the States, and I saw a lot of him. The drinking wasn't so bad. We were happy. And I got pregnant again before Jo. But I was sick, Sandy — the whole time. I lost weight instead of gaining like I had done with you. And when I was five months pregnant, I lost the baby."

"Oh, Mama, I'm so sorry." In this shared moment between mothers, I endeared her for the first time with an intimately loving name.

"Old Doc McCrea was with me. I had labor and everything, but the baby was dead. A boy. I had a boy. He was sick, Dr. McCrea said. And he made me sick. But Sandy, I never got over it. It took some of the life out of me, and I never got it back." Her head dropped and her chin quivered. "Why did God let that happen? Is it me? Being punished?"

"Oh, Mama. How sad for you." I leaned forward, guided her head to my shoulder and gently held her in my arms. "Mama. Mama. Mama." I murmured into her hair.

Mother straightened. "Just a minute. I need Kleenex."

After she returned to the love-seat — clearer-eyed — I continued with my train of thought. "It breaks my heart to imagine your thinking you're bad and that is why your baby died. Is that really what you think?"

"What else am I to think?" Mother shrugged.

"Well not that! I believe things happen just because we're human. Your baby wasn't supposed to be here. Wasn't strong enough somehow. I don't understand why." I flung my arm in a wide arc. "Besides, if whys were written all over this wall would it make any difference? Trying to figure out why is my definition of hell."

I felt agitated, jumped to my feet and paced. "I'm sorry…only not really…I absolutely refuse to believe God punishes us by killing our children! That's what I hate about the Old Testament. So much bloodshed, violence: *Vengeance is mine saith the Lord.* What is that? I can't conceive of a vengeful God like that. Look at Mamuvah and the Flewellens. Mamuvah lost three of her children. Three! That's what life was like back then, and this is just life now. Poor sweet Mama. I'm so sad for you."

I hung my head, flopped on the love-seat, stuck out my lower lip and shook my head back and forth. "A mother never gets over losing a child. Even a miscarriage. Things get back to normal, but you're a one-armed woman now. You learn to cope, but you're never quite the same. I'm not any different from you, Mama. But I won't believe God punished me or the Flewellens…or you. I just won't, that's all. " Mother's eyes were open, receptive; sorrowfully agreeing, she listened intently to every word. Feeling encouraged, I kept on with my soliloquy. It felt really, really good to talk and be heard.

"Some days I can't accept anything. Others I have the perspective of life's long trajectory. You're right about God's hand on my shoulder. I still feel the deepest, surest love I've ever known before, or since. That's why I can't accept a punishing God. He's just not like that. At least the God I know. Without believing in love I would probably feel bitter. But it's all that matters. And I'm grateful Trey was ours for almost six years." I leaned forward and touched Mother on the shoulder. "I'm so very sad you didn't have your baby boy, Mama. That's really harder than what I'm dealing with."

"Oh, honey." Her cheeks were wet with tears as she placed a firmly reassuring hand on my leg. "I hadn't thought of losing Trey the way you are. You did have Trey and I had

Trey. We all did. That makes me feel better. See. How do you know to do that?"

"Do what?" I frowned and shrugged. "I'm the mom of a son, that's all. No matter what happens no one can take that away from me. Today, that's enough. Tomorrow, who can tell? I may collapse into a puddle and ask you to scoop me up and put me in bed. Today I've got Trey covered. But a brother? I'm so glad you're telling me, Mama, even though knowing is painful. I remember wishing for a brother to take up for me. Did I know somehow that my brother was almost born? Do you think his spirit hung around us?"

Mother looked like she had touched hot coals. "Oh hush, Sandy! Do you mean was he a ghost? That's too weird. Boogedy-boogedy. You know how I feel about that creepy stuff." She stood and smoothed her apron. "Okay, honey. That's enough. Let's just think about all that tomorrow." She patted my knee and turned towards the kitchen. "I need to check on the roast." If Texas women didn't *pat* one another, a lot of conversations would have no beginning and no end.

A month after we lost our son, my husband began training for his first marathon. With his carbo-loading, stretching and icing buddies, he ran ten miles a day, seven days a week. In my way I ran, too. I poured myself into church, volunteer work, family and friends. Within a year I was pregnant with Sarah. Little Lacie, our sorrowful only child, couldn't possibly absorb the volume of parental love meant for two. That burden would be too great to carry. Most of all, she needed our strength. She had sorrows of her own.

My husband and I set out on different paths, separately cauterizing our wounds, growing away from each other. I knew the statistics: Ninety-nine percent of marriages that lose a child end up in divorce. It wouldn't happen to us. I wouldn't allow it. So for ten years we signed on for serious therapy. This is what I learned: Love alone is sometimes not enough. Our marriage endured for seventeen years after the death of our son…at least in form. In truth, it ended on a glorious country afternoon in March, only nine years after we married.

Mother's emotional health, which began at Timberlawn, blossomed like wildflowers sprouting through cracks of cooled molten rock after Trey flowed into his greater life. Two months after Sarah's birth, when Lacie was four, Mamo escaped this world. Within months Mother moved beyond her East Texas past and embraced new life in a hip Houston loft on the banks of Buffalo Bayou.

Death brought new life. Mother turned around and saw us: her daughters, her grandchildren. As for me, sharing our mutual loss of a son opened my eyes and allowed me to know Mother as just another human being. A person of strength, far from perfect, but with the exception of a few wrinkles, exactly like me — a woman, no longer a girl.

That achingly beautiful spring, our relationship changed. Ever after, when good intentions leaked into spite and malice, Mother and I patched the split as soon as we were able. After all, this family didn't have extras we could afford to throw away.

AS I STUFFED CLOTHES into my duffel, packing for Easter with Aunt Margaret, I felt lonely for Mother. Not the haunting relationship since her ghostly visitations began, but the Mother whose story I envisioned at her dying bedside. The fiery lifetime relationship neither of us could let go and mutual respect that eventually endured. Her spirit had been conspicuously absent since Lacie's miscarriage a month ago and for a couple of pregnant months before that. Without a "see you later, alligator," or "hang ten," Mother vanished in a burst of light. Surely this abrupt exit couldn't be the end. I felt unfinished and hanging in the dangle. After all the transformative struggles our relationship had survived, Mother and I deserved a happy ending.

Considering a reunion with my father summoned less fulfilling emotions. Even thinking about him felt uncomfortable. I tried to go easy on expectations, but I wanted a father. This was the truth, and I couldn't hide it from myself. Fortunately, Easter arrived early this year, March instead of April like normal. I felt lathered up like a wild filly galloping toward the barn, parched and in search of cooling waters to heal forty-seven arid years.

Getting to know Margaret face-to-face was the carrot that kept me going. Our many phone conversations these past months erased all awkwardness. Plank upon plank, she laid the foundation for understanding the Foster side of my family. Seen through her eyes, my father sounded like a broken man who had once been a lost boy, a far different picture from the Frankenstein monster I remembered. As she told it, whatever innocent vulnerability he may have possessed was beaten out of him by his two-fisted, man's-man father — Woody — the grandfather I barely remembered.

"How awful, Margaret. You mean Woody actually hit him?"

"I do. The drivers of Daddy's trucks for the butane business were like that. Physical. It was just joshing for them. But Daddy put George in the middle of a circle of his men and tried to teach him to box. When Daddy knocked him down his boys hauled George up and threw him back at Daddy. It got bloody. Daddy thought he would toughen him up. All it did was make George mean. So mean, one of his favorite tricks was shocking my cat with an electric charger stuck in the cigarette lighter of a truck. He worked at it. And I stayed out of his way as much as possible."

I felt sick at my stomach. "Where was his mother while all the chaos was going on?"

"Watching. Wringing her hands. Mother couldn't do anything with Daddy. She got back at him in quiet ways. She patched George up. Gave him sympathy. Raised him the way she wanted and didn't pay any attention to Daddy."

"That's no good, Margaret. Two parents raising their child with opposing values? That's crazy-making. So what happened to you in all that?"

"Nothing. With all that going on, I got by pretty easy. George was real smart, Sandy. Too smart for Daddy. He wanted George to be a man, not a mama's boy. Mother was a schoolteacher, you know." As she spoke, wisps of memory floated at the edges of my imagination: my gentle grandmother, sparkly necklaces and soft flowery dresses.

"Her daddy — my grandfather, your great-grandfather — was unusual for his day. He was a lawyer in Georgia with three daughters. Granddaddy Porter believed in girls bettering themselves. Mother went to college when most girls didn't.

When his three girls got to the marrying age, he didn't like the prospects in the town where they lived, and moved the whole family to another Georgia town where the prospects for suitors were more promising. That's where Mother met Daddy. He was a salesman — did well. After they married, they settled down in Marshall and then bought the butane business right before The War."

"Remarkable. My great-grandfather was a male suffragist. Too bad some of that didn't rub off on George." My head was spinning. "Mother never told me any of this, that I remember, anyway. All this family — all these stories — and it's *my* family."

"Yes indeed. That it is."

"It's so sad I didn't grow up knowing Cherry went to college." The line was silent for a few seconds. "Margaret? You there?"

Her voice was measured as she answered. "I am. Sandy… you used to call her Grandmother."

I felt shocked and embarrassed for casually using my grandmother's first name, as if she meant nothing to me. "Oh…I'm so sorry. I didn't mean to be disrespectful. I forgot. Of course she's *Grandmother*. The few times Mother talked about you all she always said 'Cherry,' never 'your grandmother.' Well…she would. To Mother she *was* Cherry. It's hard to get my mind around all this, Margaret. I did have another grandmother. It feels so odd, like we're talking about someone else's life, not mine."

"Understood. Mother would be so happy seeing us together again. All those years she was bedridden, pictures of you girls hung on her wall. I think Wilma sent them. Mother used to tell stories about you and Jo as children. She never quit loving you, Sandy."

"I believe you, Margaret, and maybe I'll feel it the more we talk. I think I remember *Grandmother* taking me with her to church. I was little — probably two. I hiked my short stubby legs on the back of the wooden pew. Banged white hightops in rhythm to the music. *Grandmother* had a soprano voice. Right? And her neck quivered when she sang."

"Yes, indeed. Mother played the organ most Sundays. When you stayed with us, she took you to church."

"So, I do remember."

"That you do. Do you remember playing *Sunny sool?* You couldn't pronounce words right yet." Margaret laughed a deep, resonant chuckle. "I will never forget coming to the house one day and you told me, "*Sunny sool* is about to *sop*.""

The phone line vibrated with insight. "So, of course. Grandmother took you and George to church, too."

"Yep. With me it was expected, but not with George. Daddy hated it. Said church was for sissies. The only thing George could do better than Daddy was slug a shot of Jim Beam. George had one colossal poor opinion of himself, Sandy. Mother took him to a psychiatrist when he was little. Never said why. And I didn't ask."

"That's awful, Margaret!" As the back-story came into focus, I felt sorry for George. I wasn't completely ready to forgive him for threatening Mother — and me. More than once when they screamed at each other, I pushed in between and demanded, "Don't hurt my mother!" He just knocked me away with the back of his hand like I was a bug. But if I detached, turned the wheel a few degrees beyond my own story and looked at my father as a desperate little boy aching for love and approval, I felt compassion. The Foster household worshipped at two holy altars: God and Grit. Caught between polar opposites, how could a young boy ever get it right?

With only two more hours to go before I reached Margaret's, the digital dashboard clock registered time in slow-mo. Slanting rays of late March sunshine warmed the earth. Patchwork fields, pastel wildflowers, curving furrows neatly plowed and standing tall, tiny mountains of dirt waiting for seed sped past as I careened around one hairpin curve after another.

Like a desert mirage, memories shimmered on the horizon in my mind and around every bend in the twisting road. Yet nothing looked familiar. Of course it didn't. I knew Marshall — the Foster home — and nearby Longview, but not the Hughes Springs home that Margaret shared with her husband. Only a few miles north of my Pineywoods childhood, yet continents apart, highway markers indicated towns I couldn't fit into the East Texas I knew. The town of Lone Star rang a bell because somewhere in the recesses of my mind I remembered Lone Star Steel. But Ore City and Pittsburg belonged in the Pacific Northwest or Northeast, not here.

Dwarfed by monumental structures, I skirted industrial graveyards marked by steely skeletal remains. Dull tin roofs, rusted heavy equipment and caterpillars, cranes, eighteen-wheelers abandoned on grimy gravel roadways overgrown with high weeds. Out the back door of childhood while my mud pies dried in sunshine on Mamo's pristine concrete bench set before her picturesque goldfish pond, teeming hordes of laborers sweated beneath hard hats and overalls, feet shod in steel-tipped boots.

As I snaked through the center of pocketbook towns sparsely populated, weathered signs hung at an angle and flapped as my red Jeep whizzed past. Dangling posters nailed to creosote-coated light poles advertised long-since-scheduled events. Crudely scrawled information, sprawling across the grimy plate-glass window of a deserted diner, announced: Blue Plate Special $3.25.

This world existed only an hour away from Longview…and I

never saw it? Where did all the people go? Mama, where are you? I wish you could explain.

As if she had been waiting for an opening, immediately Mother spoke. "It was different then, Sandy. It was The War, and East Texas did her part in preparing our boys for battle."

"Mama! I thought I'd lost you!"

She giggled. "Well. I should go away more often."

Oh, stop. I've been missing you.

"I know you have. And I'm here now. I had a few things to clear up."

Like what?

"Well, I got in a bit of a mess with Lacie. I made a grave mistake in exercising my will to come back to this family. I didn't consider the consequences. I didn't think of Lacie and what she would go through. I don't know if she heard me crying, but I was there with her in the operating room when she had the D&C because of me. I couldn't live inside of her, Sandy. I was selfish to think I could. God wouldn't let me have my way. It was wrong. I've had to learn a few things. I see it now. I'm sorry for the hurt and concern I've caused all of you."

Oh, my. That sounds hard. It's okay. I guess. I don't understand. What brought you back? Why didn't you just go on once you returned to the Other Side?

"You need me. That's why. And I need you. I feel unfinished, so I applied for a leave of absence and it was granted for good behavior. This family has a lot of healing to do. When it's done, I'll be gone. You see, this is how it works: Being of spirit is not a virtue in and of itself. Without human hands and feet we can do nothing. We are in this together, Sandy."

Well. Now it's my turn to apologize. I'm not exactly a rose myself. I'm sorry for being mean and impatient.

She giggled. "Well, you know...the apple doesn't fall far from the tree. So I'm here to share this adventure with you,

Sandy. We don't have much time. I need to prepare you."

I want you to. I'm listening. Talk to me.

"You need to listen to Margaret. She's right about George. Woody ruined him. Taught him to drink and fight. George could be scary when he drank, Sandy. He kidnapped you several times. You were gone for days. So strange. He would never say where you went. Do you remember?"

No. A shiver ran up my spine. *If it's all right with you, I'd rather not.*

"Okay. You don't need to remember everything to heal. You just have to forgive. I do. I loved him, Sandy. And he loved me. A woman is lucky if she has that once in a lifetime. And when she does, she never wants to lose it."

I understand. I had it too, once. I know you loved him. You married him twice. I still don't understand, but maybe I will.

"I know George frightened you. But he is no longer a threat. You will see. You will understand and you will forgive. You must in order to become whole. There is more to George's character than you know." She giggled. "And what Margaret shares about me will come as a surprise. You and I are different women. You can accomplish what I cannot. For all your strengths, you are still blinded by childhood prejudice. This must be transformed. I am here to help. I love you, Sandy. Really, I do.

I have to go now. Watch that lead foot. You drive like a bat out of hell. There's a county mounty waiting just up the road."

Exactly as Mother predicted, a black-and-white lurked around a bend in the road. Fuming and poking along at fifty when I had been going seventy, I watched him trail after me until his Ford did a loop-de-loop and headed back in the direction from whence it came. A grove of trees to hide in until another fat fly buzzed past.

I felt anxious and jittery and in need of soothing self-talk. *Slow is good. Stop running. George can't hurt you. He's only a seventy-something-year-old, burned-out, worn-down, crippled old man. It's gonna be okay.*

I wrenched on the radio and tuned into sing-along Sixties tunes. R-E-S-P-E-C-T. Find out what it means to me…. Aretha sang my song. *This is perfect. That's it. He'll have to respect me now. Maybe not love me. That may be too much of a stretch. But I'll take respect.*

Eight-hour drives are brutal and ought to be against the law. But finally…at last…there she stood: the small woman with a transcendent smile standing in the doorway of a white clapboard cottage, accompanied by a hallelujah chorus of fuchsia azaleas against spring green grass.

I couldn't climb out of the Jeep fast enough. "Margaret!" She opened her arms and I flew into them.

"My little blond Sandy," Margaret beamed and stepped back to get a better look. A quizzical frown creased her face.

I laughed. "I know. A lot of water has passed under the bridge. No more little blond Sandy. It's colored, Margaret. I'm getting gray around the edges. Can't let that happen. I'm trying on auburn. But if it makes you happy I can do blond again before long."

"Well *my Sandy*, your hair color doesn't matter to me. The high point of my life is the day I came to Wilma's funeral and saw you and Jo again." Her eyes softened like they do right before tears roll down our cheeks. Margaret wriggled and shook herself. "What are we standing here for? Come in!"

Blond or not, I felt like Goldilocks with much to explore. Before long, we settled into Margaret's not too hot, not too cold, but just right family room, knees together on the loveseat, with piles of photographs, scrapbooks and forty-seven years to resurrect.

"Do you remember? After dinner, we'd all sit back. Then

it would start. Mother swore you were vaccinated with a phonograph needle. You were such a little thing, sitting in your high chair, barely able to talk. Mother could ask just about anything: 'Sandy, now what do you think about the price of tea in China?' How you could go on!"

"Weeeeeeel I t'ink da' teee....' Margaret mimicked me. "Didn't matter what you were asked. You had us all in stitches — me, Mother, Daddy." I felt shamelessly in love with myself as a small child and wondered if Margaret had any idea what she was doing for me.

"That was before I married Alvis. He was a good man, Sandy. I wish you had known him."

"Me too. But I did, sort of. This is where we came in. I was a flower girl in your wedding."

Margaret beamed. "That you were!"

After we exhausted the first pile of photographs and family memorabilia, Margaret scoured a top closet shelf and dragged out a pastel floral hat box stuffed with more photographs. Side by side we meandered through our life together, much more extensive than I had imagined. "Do you remember your cousin Bill, our only child? Here he is with you and Jo. You're seven here. That's right before George took you to California. We spent a lot of time together in those days. See. That's you in the middle. The big girl."

"Bizarre. I don't remember this at all. Look at us. Jo and I are perfect."

Pointedly, Margaret looked me in the eye, as respected elders do with their errant young. "You girls were always tidy. Dressed alike. That was important to Wilma. I liked her, Sandy. She was a good mother. We were friends. We had great times shopping together."

I felt shocked. "Even after all that happened — that you weren't allowed to see us after the last divorce — you still like her? You and Grandmother and Woody came to see us that day at Mamo's. I won't forget it. Mamo and Mother were loud. Jo and I stood in the hallway and peeked through the cracked front door. They wouldn't let you in."

"That was bad, I'll admit. But I've forgiven Wilma now. She had a hard life, Sandy. It wasn't easy during The War, and your Grandmother Mamo — Beth, we called her — was a difficult woman. When Wilma and George were still married and she went to visit Beth, she'd come back to Marshall in tears. They got along like oil and water."

"You're right. Poor Mother. My relationship with her — and with Mamo for sure — wasn't much better. They were so wounded. Now I feel bad."

"Don't. It's just the way it was." Intimate truth telling had begun. "Now, now." Margaret patted my knee. "We're here now. Mother would be so happy." The sun was going down, casting shadows. Margaret clicked on a lamp, enveloping us in a buttery glow. "She knew about Trey, Sandy."

My heart thumped and my body went limp. "She did?" Unable to speak, my mind raced. A rush of tears filled my eyes, and Margaret let me be.

"Yes, she did. When it happened, Wilma phoned George. He came to see me, worried if he should tell Mother or not. She was so sick then, bedridden, living in that house with George. I told him that Mother could handle it."

"That's remarkable. George was concerned? That surprises me...and feels good. I'm glad. It means the world to me to know that you all knew."

Margaret placed a supportive hand on my shoulder and said with soft eyes, "Love you, Sandy." In a rush she hurried on. "And now we have this Easter lunch with George to think about. I've talked to him, and he's agreed to come. I didn't know if he would or not. When Mother died one of the last things she said to me was, 'Margaret, take care of George.'"

She groaned and shook her head. "I wish she's never told

me that. I do it for her. He doesn't even own that house; I do. Mother saw to that. She knew he was irresponsible. Poor man. He pays me rent. Drives over from Marshall to Hughes Springs. Sits in the chair over there." She pointed to a yellow armchair across the room. "We eat a chicken salad sandwich. He pays me. And then I don't see him again for another month. Don't know what he does with himself. And I warn you, he doesn't say much. Talking to him is like pulling teeth."

By Easter Sunday, when Margaret and I visited Grace Hill Cemetery, we had collapsed forty-seven years. She almost felt like a mother — certainly an aunt — the closest relationship with an older female family member I had ever experienced. I giggled as I read the inscription on the marble slab that marked Mother's grave. "Wilma Miller Flewellen Foster." I turned to Margaret and confessed, "Mother was never actually a Flewellen, you know. Something came over me when I instructed the tombstone company what to engrave. It's okay, right? Who but us will ever know or care?"

Margaret's face clouded over with sweet sadness. "She was proud of her heritage, Sandy."

"I know. It made her feel good when nothing else did. The Flewellen family was the one thing she could feel proud of." The force of Mother's deep ache to hide her shameful secrets — their shameful secrets — coursed through me. I knelt and gently placed a branchy white bouquet on her grave, cut in the early morning from Margaret's dogwood tree. "She loved these flowers, Margaret. Mamo had two dogwood trees in her yard. She transplanted them from the Big Woods, the Flewellen timber land where they found all those oil wells." I slid my hand back and forth, tracing the etching on the new marble slab. Set close — just as Mother had instructed — right by Mamo's weathered and pockmarked stone with moldy gray stains in the etched crevices. This inscription read: Elizabeth Flewellen Eddins. "It didn't feel right not to give Mother the

Flewellen name too, when it meant the world to her."

Before lunch we made a pilgrimage to the First Presbyterian Church in Longview. As we climbed the dogwood-lined front steps, in my imagination I heard Mamo's gravelly voice just as if I returned to childhood and sat on her sun porch, listening to her tales. "Papaw finally had enough. He pushed his chair back from the table where all the town leaders sat, reared to his full height and said, 'Hellfire, I've got the lumber. I'll build the damn church myself.'"

Inside the dimly lit vestibule the smell of musty red velvet lit my senses. Ushers — antique white-shirted gentlemen in business suits reminiscent of Uncle Gene, Mamo's brother — distributed printed programs for the service of worship. They smiled and said, "Good mawnin'," with a resonant Southern drawl that set my insides quivering from flashes of Easters past. Margaret and I chose a pew in the front — three rows back on the left — where I had fainted the day of my confirmation, terrified that God would search my soul and probably strike me dead when he discovered I was unforgivably horrible.

Sunlight splintered through leaded glass into prisms of red, green, blue, gold, shining all the way down to my soul. I was making peace: with the church that I couldn't get my arms around anymore, and with the past that flooded into rivers of tears for what was lost, what was found.

Driving along Old Highway 80 in Margaret's Cadillac, heading toward Marshall and lunch with my father, I felt too satisfied to feel worried, scared or even to care much what happened. The whole of this pilgrimage swept me along — past, present and future — emptying into an alchemical cauldron of forgiveness.

"A Mexican restaurant, Margaret? Why a Mexican restaurant?"

"It's what he wanted, Sandy. There he is. You see him?

Standing on the sidewalk by the front door." She gestured and pointed to the old man, much shorter and wider than I remembered, collapsed into a white shirt and khaki pants with a shock of white hair severely slicked back, making his ruddy and deeply lined Ernest Hemingway face appear startling by contrast. My father had aged beyond recognition and walked with a limp, lurching toward us as we approached.

Facing him I was instantly tongue-tied, frozen with embarrassment as I realized that my fashion choices — a red flowered print dress with white hose and white Mary Jane pumps — belonged in childhood. I never wore white shoes anymore. I bought them especially for today, to go with my new Easter outfit.

Margaret stepped forward and broke the awkward silence. "Well, George. Here we are. Let's go in." Once inside Margaret went mum, sat back and watched...although there was not much to see...or hear.

"How are you?" I asked.

Gruffly he answered, "All right."

I tried again. "So you live here in Marshall?"

He nodded and grumbled, "*Um huh,*" as he surveyed me through greasy lenses in crooked wire-rimmed frames.

I kept trying. "What do you recommend? Do you eat here often?"

"No. I don't," he growled.

I shot a panicked look in Margaret's direction. She smiled and blinked her eyes once as if to say, "I warned you."

God! This is horrible! Now what should I do? I didn't expect much, but I wasn't prepared for open hostility. Blaring mariachi music, my father's icy reptilian stare and the odor of enchiladas and tamales made me queasy.

Mother — whom I had forgotten — quickly responded to my question. "George feels ashamed, Sandy. He knows he hasn't been a father to you or Jo. Don't make it hard on him."

I felt furious. *Him? What about his daughters? What about me, for instance?*

She was relentless. "I knew you would feel this way. You needed to see him, and now you have. You're not going to get much out of him. Let it go."

I wished I could. Just let it go. It wasn't working for me. I felt disappointed and hurt. On the drive back to Hughes Springs, every inch of my body felt tired, old and heavy. Margaret could tell. She drove without saying a word while I stared from the window in shock. After a reasonable amount of silence, she spoke. "You sure were trying hard. He's like that, Sandy. He just doesn't talk."

She tried to help, but nothing could. All I could think of was a nap…outside…in the sunshine. And I'm not a napper. The minute I hit the door I flew toward the guest bedroom, chased by ghosts from childhood and the ghastly specter of a father who couldn't claim me. *Nor will I ever — swear to God — claim him.* Shedding the dress, wriggling out of the hose and dumping the whole unholy mess into a heap, I pulled on shorts and a T, promising myself: *I will never ever wear that outfit again.*

Hair on fire, I rounded the corner to Margaret's sitting room. "Margaret, do you have a cotton blanket? I'd like to nap on the grass in the sun. Do you mind?"

"Of course not. That's a wonderful idea." Rummaging in a cedar chest, she produced a Dresden Plate patterned quilt sewn in pastels on a white background. Reverentially, yet with a twinkle in her eye, Margaret stretched the quilt across my arms. "Here. Your grandmother quilted this herself."

Out in the back yard, with tracks a mere football-field length away from where I spread the quilt, a freight train roared past. "It's a railroading town," Margaret had explained. "Boy, was it busy in the day!" I forced myself to lie still, stretched out, became one with the roar of the train — *clackety-*

clack, clackety-clack — and scream of the whistle. The ripening spring earth filled my nostrils and sunshine warmed the bare backs of my legs. Eventually, I slipped into restless slumber. Content to rest my face on my hands, I felt like a small ant, an infinitesimal speck in a vast world.

I drowsed, only to be awakened by the rumbling vibration and shrill whistle of the next freight train screaming past, not far from my fingertips. I opened my eyes and my senses came alive to the cedar-chest scent of the quilt. Fuzzy colors — celadon green and sapphire blue — came into focus. My heart thumped against my chest and I gasped with recognition.

I was on my feet, grabbing the quilt around me, running toward the house, shouting like a small child. "Margaret! Margaret!" I busted through the back door.

"Well, what, Sandy?" Startled, Margaret dropped the book she was reading onto her lap.

"Could I have slept on this quilt when I was a tiny baby?"

Margaret frowned with concentration, and then an expression of joy spread across her face. "Why, yes, Sandy. Of course you could. Mother kept you all the time when you were a baby. And she put you to sleep on a quilt just such as this. Certainly you might have slept on this very quilt, Sandy."

I was back to the love again, crumbling into happiness, brick by brick my walls falling down. After a lifetime of separation, this time together was not nearly enough. Too soon, it was time to go.

Margaret walked me to the Jeep. She wasn't much for overt affection — this I had seen — but I kissed her cheek anyway. "Margaret, this isn't the last you'll see of me, you know. I'll be back. In the meantime, call me. We'll talk."

Gently, she pressed my shoulder; then hesitated. "Okay, my little blond Sandy." She winked and smiled. "I'll call you just like we've been doing. I need to." She grimaced and her expression turned dark as she struggled with something she'd rather not voice. "I'm worried about George. You see how he is. He doesn't take care of himself. I don't know how much longer he can go on like he is going."

The specter of death clouded the air. Margaret looked small and lonely. I threw my arms around her and squeezed tight. "I know. I agree. This is a miserable situation." With both hands on her shoulders, I searched her face. Nothing felt awkward now. We had traveled far enough in these few days to feel some measure of safety in our tender new relationship. It was time for straight talk. "No matter what happens I want you to know that I'm here. Just say when and how. Jo will probably be onboard, too. No way are you going through this alone. We're family. After all this time, you can't get rid of me now."

As I backed out of the curving drive, I heard Mother softly say, "This is the first day of the rest of your life, Sandy. You now perceive life through different lenses. Clearer, so the beauty shines through."

IV

GATEKEEPERS

Elizabeth Flewellen Miller with daughters,
Wilma and Louise

A SHOWER OF YELLOW notched-wing butterflies
fluttering north on their yearly migration from the Yucatan
Peninsula baptized my return from East Texas. Tiny creatures
sacrificed themselves across my windshield, risking their lives
to live again in their final northeast destination. I felt brand-
new, washed clean, blessed with new life. Gently as butterfly
wings, face-time with Margaret had rearranged my DNA.
Mother was right. Childhood prejudice had blinded me. But
this was past. Just north of Ore City, Pittsburg and Lone Star,
healing into wholeness had begun.

Many weeks after this life-giving journey, I staked my
claim on the farmhouse front porch, allowing the wonder of
the Hughes Springs pilgrimage to seep into my cells. I felt
open, face to the sun like a juicy tomato ripening on the vine.
In truth, my full family tree didn't grow strong and sturdy
branches like the Flewellen oak Mother wistfully represented.
I was a vine, fragile but flexible, a meandering wanderer
crawling toward the sun.

I grinned, laughing at my metaphor as I remembered the
tenacious tomato caper we experienced when Lacie and Sarah
were small. After Trey left us, we hung on in Larchmont for a
year. It was important. There was much to heal. But then
Sarah's birth brought new life, and we moved to a vintage old
brick with antique plumbing in a lovely suburb. The tired clay
pipes eventually backed up once and for all, demanding
excavation of the whole side yard and upgrade to PVC pipes.
Water wasn't the only thing that flowed freely. Summer heat
roused dormant tomato seeds, slumbering for eons past, now

bestowing a veritable forest of tomato plants — swear to God — growing as high as the roofline. If *E. coli* hung out in the soil, it was apparently too old to do digestive damage, but did provide highly effective fertilizer.

"Well, that's a bit earthy for my taste, but I get your point," Mother said with a chuckle. "You do have a way with words. Which, by the way, are growing in you every day. Have you noticed?"

Wow. You're here all the time, aren't you? Never missing a thing. And your point would be?

"You can't help yourself, Sandy. You will tell my story…which is your story…our story…in case you didn't know. I'll help. You'll see."

Bantering with Mother felt comfortable, more complete and real than our earthly relationship had ever felt. It did occur to me, however — probably because I didn't like where she was leading — that I might be imagining her visitations. Then did Lacie and Sarah also imagine Mother's visits? Did the computer and clock just happen to stop at the same moment the last time I attempted writing Mother's Story? Was it coincidence that the old guy crashed into us on the way to Mother's funeral? And even if imagination had run amok, where did imagination come from, anyway? Was it all in our minds, or were our minds connected to a vast universal flow of creativity that flung the planets and stars into orbit?

No matter whether her visits were dreamed up or actual reality, I had to take Mother seriously. My spiritual beliefs led me to conclude that she had in fact escaped the Other Side and was right here, right now, interacting in my life and the life of the girls. What was belief anyway but settling on a standpoint that made sense? How could I not believe in the Unseen? Even if God's reassuring hand on my shoulder originated in illusion, would I ever willingly turn away from the immense love I felt that day…and still felt? Maybe the otherworldly experience of God was only fantasy, but if so, it was accompanied with certainty.

And still, I knew better than to float along airy-fairy without grounding my beliefs in traditional wisdom. Mamo's secretary in the corner of my farmhouse front room was stuffed with volumes of contemporary wisdom, purchased from Amazon and Barnes & Noble, and wisdom of the ages, evidenced by the well-worn and crumpled spine and blue cloth cover of my Scofield Reference Bible. Torn pages and a road-map of scribbles in the margins of Scofield bear witness to six years of intense Bible study and turbulent determination to put Trey's death in perspective…and find direction for the rest of my life.

Besides Bible study, through the years I grazed through *Memories, Dream and Reflections, Man and His Symbols* and a number of Jung's paradigm-bending books. Still hungry, I devoured others' commentary about this prescient human being, including Segal's *The Gnostic Jung*.

My foraging expedition — which by now I'm certain will be lifelong — led me to deeply satisfying scholarship of Elaine Pagels, Harvard Ph.D. and Columbia professor of religious studies — translator of the Nag Hammadi Gospels. *The Gnostic Gospels* describes Pagels's research into the origins and core beliefs of the writers of gospels hidden for two thousand years. Her deliciously heretical scholarship — and radical alternative to orthodox doctrine — resonates and rocks my spiritual world with *ah-ha* after *ah-ha*.

The back story reveals that time-worn and bug-eaten leather-bound books were unearthed in Egypt in the 1940s by Arab boys who considered them only useful for kindling. Originally there were thirteen papyrus books, but just twelve survived by the time Indiana Jones-ish adventures delivered the Coptic writings into the hands of spiritual intellectuals who understood the world-shaking implication of heretofore unknown gospels — dated as contemporary with the four orthodox Biblical Gospels.

The surviving set of twelve books are diverse, ranging from secret teachings, poems, esoteric descriptions of the origins of the universe, myths, magic and instructions for mystical practice. All of which point to a far-reaching core belief found in the fifty-two texts that Pagels concisely thumbnails: "Self-knowledge is knowledge of God; the self and the divine are identical."

By the fourth century in ancient Rome gnostic beliefs suggesting that spiritual knowledge can be attained *only* through insights originating from the God-within were embraced under penalty of death. The Romanized structure of church hierarchy made up of pope, bishop, cardinal and priest — all believing that superior knowledge of God was attained through the intellect, rather than intuition — became the religion we call Christianity. Gnostic leaders and their texts were destroyed, but not before keepers of the gnostic faith buried their sacred writings in a red earthenware jar, hidden within a high cave in Upper Egypt.

Digesting gnostic beliefs brought me full-circle. From Joseph Campbell to Jung to Gnosticism, I was already here, paying attention to inner guidance without the support of "the one holy catholic and apostolic church," as the Nicene Creed goes. Now, suddenly, I felt like a member of an ancient and profound psychospiritual club whose insightful beliefs encompassed divinity common to all faiths.

Nothing stays the same and everything changes. Jung describes the natural order of change with a handy word — *enantiodromia* — suggesting that every force eventually swings to its opposite. When we're a-swingin', homeostatic balance eventually results. But sometimes, wouldn't it be nice to hang out in balanced bliss for awhile? We call that a vacation. And that's not life.

Only weeks after I returned from Hughes Springs, Lacie made one of her suspicious calls, "Mom. I'm coming to see you. I have a surprise. Call it an early Mother's Day present."

It didn't take a genius to decipher a transparent lead-in like that.

Lacie wriggled with pleasure as she delivered a cutesy gift bag. Under layers of tissue paper I uncovered a baby bib with the lettering My Favorite Grandma. Lacie's announcement of her first pregnancy — as hostess to Mother's reincarnation — was so shocking I couldn't feel my own feelings. Now I could. I hugged Lacie enthusiastically, while the scene from *Terms of Endearment* in which Aurora screams "I'm too young to be a grandmother!" flashed before my eyes.

Further signaling that another phase of life hovered just beyond the threshold, Sarah ripped through college and was a senior at UT before I could part with her Chocolate Soup pinafores. Her on-and-off boyfriend seemed like the one, especially since they spent the weekend together for her dad's out-of-town wedding. What began as a liberal-arts degree ended up in elementary ed. I knew how that turned out: early marriage and a white picket fence around the corner from family.

The staunch gentleman who owned these many acres slipped away while still living independently in the big house just up the hill. We were practically family. I loved who he was and would miss his spunky energy. When the will was read, surely his son would accept my terms. Maybe — as soon as another month — this land would truly, once and for all, belong to me and mine. Lacie even dreamed that she and John built their own house on the property.

Changes were undeniably afoot, but from my front porch there was high cotton as far as the eye could see. Caressing this family with kindness, the fates were abundantly generous the summer before everything changed. We didn't even have to worry about the normal Texas-sized drought. With the windows of my postage-stamp farmhouse flung wide open, I smelled the coming storm. Grasshoppers quit their fiddling, birds stilled their song; nothing stirred. Up and down my curving roadway, dust devils danced. The sky turned gray, then charry black. A shiver ran up my spine; like an animal I stopped in my tracks and sniffed at the wind. As lightning streaked across the sky I counted — one, one thousand; two, two thousand; three, three thousand…rolling thunder rattled the walls. For days torrents of rain fell without let up, poured in cascading sheets until the rivers roared out of their banks, consuming the countryside.

Mesmerized by the enchantment of simple abundance, I caught myself spinning Flewellen myths in my head. The fantasy of writing Mother's Story took on a life of its own. Much as I disliked admitting she was right, telling her story just might be a good thing. At least it would bring closure to her physical death. Wouldn't it? And now I could tell a kinder version than the original purge begun a few months before. I might even squeeze out a generous woman-to-woman revelation. You know the genre: Indestructible bond overcomes even the meanest family tragedy. I even talked with God about it and asked for help. He said: "As you wish," several times, short and sweet but clearly onboard. Who knew how it would go once I began writing? Maybe I would channel the whole thing — like many writers apparently do. The words tumble out effortlessly and you simply transcribe what you hear. This would be my preference.

It didn't happen. Like gleeful brown sparrows bathing in puddles left by rainstorms, I immersed myself in simple pleasures. Splashed and twirled, covered myself, rolled and twisted, all the while forcing the arduous idea of writing a book out toward the ends of the universe as far as my mind could possibly push.

Hannah was born in January. Unfortunately for Mama Lacie, her birth went into extra innings. Yet Hannah was perfect in every way. I was there the whole time, on third base acting as a leg stirrup while a nurse filled in on first. John preferred to coach center field at Lacie's shoulder, suggesting that holding down the southern end guaranteed he would never look at his wife in the same way. It was a bonding experience beyond any I imagined, and phenomenal relief to slide home to grandmother-hood without disaster. February, however, would be a whole 'nother creature.

I knew as I watched him loitering along the path. Men don't walk with their legs dragging unless they have something dreadful to say. He had tears in his eyes as he drifted past the white picket gate, up the stone walkway and onto my front porch. A gray winter wind whipped around the isolated farmhouse, sitting lonely in the midst of frozen earth stripped of growth. With compassion in his eyes, the elder heir faced me squarely. "Sandy…I have good news and bad news." Every time a man spoke those words, hurt was soon to follow.

"You know I've gotten married. That's the good news. The bad news is my daughter is unhappy about it. She never got over losing her mother to cancer. Because my new wife is moving in with me, my daughter is moving out and she wants your place. I'm sorry. I know I told you I wanted you here forever." His chin dropped to his chest. "When Dad died he only willed me a life estate in the property. He gave my kids ownership of these eight hundred acres and every building that sits on the land. My hands are tied. Both you and I are at the mercy of teenagers." Tears pooled in his eyes and he awkwardly wiped them away with the back of his hand.

"Oh…." I stumbled backward and braced myself against the sturdy porch column. "I expected to live here forever." His face twisted with discomfort. "I'm sorry," I said. "I didn't mean to make it worse. I understand. Really I do. It's not your fault. You're a kind and decent man. I've always seen that."

His face crinkled into a half-hearted smile. "I appreciate how you are taking this. No need to rush. Take all the time you want. This must be a shock. Just so you know, I tried, but the kids won't hear of selling even an acre of this land."

I was devastated. But like Dorothy tossed out of Kansas, I got my head together and searched for the next right move. I knew where to turn for guidance. I actually possessed a wealth of fortifying beliefs and impeccable principles: Things happen for a reason. No effort is wasted. Every hardship strengthens character. Love is stronger than hate and overcomes fear. Good triumphs over evil. Life follows the natural flow of change: spring, summer, fall, winter. I would never effing get used to it.

Dammit God! I have a serious bone to pick. The land was mine. I was certain. You told me. Didn't you? Where have I been? Where are you? On second thought, erase that. To tell you the truth, I'm so confused and hurt I can't hear anything you have to say. Let me get over this first….then maybe we can talk.

In my mind I heard a soft response: "As you wish."

I listened with indifference. I had turned off the holy spigot. Mother got through anyway. "You think this is evil. But God meant it for good."

Really, Mother? Now you're going all Jesus on me and quoting Genesis. This is proof. I'm totally losing it. Just leave me alone…please.

A month after I lost the farm, I signed a year's lease on an Alamo Heights bungalow just off Broadway, and office space in a delightful old Victorian converted into therapist office space on Avenue B, bordering Brackenridge Park and Zoo. Both arrangements became available at the opportune moment and were lovely to look at, but hardly delightful. Returning to Alamo Heights felt like crawling backward into the womb.

I still felt angry with Mother-Father God but identified my fury as projection of the rage I felt toward myself. For what, I didn't know. Surely there was something.

Amie had been neurotic since I strong-armed her into a collar and leash. She hung her head, refused to make eye contact, and slunk around with her normally perky tail dragging. I chose this cottage because of the doggy door and fenced yard, but a little freedom didn't go a long way. Amie's spirit was so low I felt like a murderer.

Maxy and Pookie were on the loose with traffic whizzing past. Pookie began her life as a city cat and had smarts about cars, but Maxy was a mouse-hunting, wildcat extraordinare. They both took to alley-catting ways, vanishing for days on end. I felt anxious about their safety, morning, noon and night.

At least sleep wasn't a problem. I readjusted to the city sounds of traffic, the wail of police-car and fire-truck sirens, the *pop, pop-pop* of rifle shots fired from the shooting range on the downside of Alamo Heights hills and the distant whistle of a train as it cut across the valley floor…reminding me of all things home.

I tried making peace with my suburban front porch, but nagging discontent stood in the way of anything close to a Zen state of mind. Like me, my clients were in a state of mutiny. One-third of them were incapable of reverse navigation. I didn't blame them, but felt the loss just the same. Not so much for the income, which was significant, but for them personally…as human beings I loved and respected.

One schlumpy autumn morning I wandered south on

Broadway destined for a noon client at the office, took a right at the Witte Museum and a left on Avenue B, not thinking about anything but a coffee fix. My energy was lower than a flea's belly but my magical mind was out there, bounce-diving in deep water. *God, you really burned me, you know. You're God, all right? You can move mountains if you want. Heal the sick. Raise the dead. What's wrong with you, giving me mixed messages? One minute we walk and talk together, celebrating the blessings of the farm. The next, it's a plague of locusts? The least you could have done was send a sign to warn that the end was near.* Striking up a deep conversation with God would have to be an accident. I trusted my spiritual insight less than I trusted the Divine.

"Do you want to talk?" The clear thought shot into my head, equally as riveting as the stark sunlight.

My mind stood at attention. *Oh! It's you. Well, actually I wasn't looking for you. You know I've been avoiding you ever since we lost the farm.*

"I know," God said. "I have missed you as much as you miss your clients."

I've missed you, too. Sorry for being so irreverent. I'm ashamed of myself. Sorry I pushed you away when all this came down. You know me. It's what I do. I've been miserable without you.

"You are changeable as sunrises and sunsets. This is the natural order of Creation. You always light up my life, Little One. Misery does not become you. Let it go.

Thank you. I needed that. I feel better already. Changing? Is that what I've been doing?

"So to speak. Be neither afraid nor ashamed. You simply altered your priorities. This is the nature of growth, a value you embrace. Upon return from the home of your ancestors, you requested assistance in sharing your family story, and asked less for ownership of the land, or to enhance your healing work. Is this correct?"

Oh, my God! Oh…oh…sorry. I didn't mean to be disrespectful.

But…oh, God! You're right. I talked about writing Mother's Story to whomever would listen, but got wrapped up in birthdays and funerals, clients and babies…one baby, anyway. Truth be known, I didn't want to turn off the joy when there were cows to watch, breezes to catch my hair and flowers to grow. So I did this to myself?

"You did. As a woman thinks, so is she. Change your mind. Change your life. Once you form a specific and heartfelt plea, all that does not serve deepest soul-purpose fades into background. Your country lifestyle became a stumbling block. It is not necessarily lost forever. Only placed in reserve.

"Your soul seeks to share the story of your ancestors. Some of my children bear greater fruit from fields plowed with austerity. You drive the tractor, so to speak. Abundance did not support your primary request. Nothing will be lost. Nothing else will satisfy. In sharing the story…you…ancestors past…and generations to come will become one. Fret not, Little One. All is well. You will see. For so it must be."

I want to believe you, God. I'm fairly depressed, you know. Will I feel better soon?

"Eventually. Not necessarily soon. Be gentle with yourself. Many pathways will be revealed within the coming months. Days of simple joys open before you. There are roads yet to cross. Be at peace. Once this is accomplished the next step will become clear."

"See, Sandy!" With a decisive lilt in her voice, Mother chimed in. "What did I tell you? Everything is unfolding exactly as it should."

All right Mother Socrates. Now you're sounding like me. No more. Pretty please?

She was on a roll. As I trudged up the steps to my office, I heard Mother quietly humming the tune to a Carpenters song she adored. "Make your own kind of music. Sing your own special song. Make your own kind of music. Even if no-bo-dy else sings along…."

THE SUMMER OF 1998 I skulked around Alamo Heights feeling like I wore Eighties clothes dragged from the back of my closet. Every street, every block of the old neighborhood reminded me of my married-lady lifetime. The leased Arts and Crafts bungalow with oak floors and vintage cabinets and woodwork even smelled like our old house looming a few blocks away, which I avoided driving past at all costs. Being Grandmother Nana to Baby Hannah, playing roses (rubbing noses) and butterflies (batting eyelashes together) and strolling along tree-lined streets with Amie prancing alongside expanded my heart with overwhelming love-seizures. So why did gut instincts insist that Alamo Heights was only a way-station to my somewhere?

Should I look for land in the Hill Country? Buy instead of lease? In the God-chat about losing the farm I heard that a Thoreau-esque lifestyle was "placed in reserve." What did that mean? God riddles drive me nuts. Was it time to start over with the security of a mortgage? Thinking of a mortgage as security somehow didn't resonate. But then, Mark Twain did say: "Buy land, they're not making it anymore."

I flat wasn't ready. I still ached for the three-year paradise of burgundy fields, waving grasses, oak groves and Herefords grazing against barbed wire. Country-lonely hurt so deep I couldn't talk myself into driving out Highway 281, much less fall in love all over again. Besides, a burning bush hadn't spoken.

Staying steady and persevering until the heartache lifted seemed the most sensible approach. Whether I felt inspired or not, I showed up on my front porch every morning, sucked in oxygen, and scribbled in a journal. I scheduled body work, yoga, aromatherapy and nutritional counseling, meditated with a Buddhist *sangha* and took long contemplative walks along La Jara Boulevard beneath an arbor of mystical oaks. By far, the monthly workshops in Austin with co-therapist and soul-sister friend Connie were the most healing events of the month. For clients — of course. For myself — without a doubt.

On Saturdays at the close of a full workshop day, we retreated to Connie's deck overlooking an inlet of Lake Travis. Sailboat rigging rhythmically slapped against masts as pink-and-purple sunsets stirred a twilight breeze whispering across lake waters. Her place began as a weekend house, and when Connie bought it years ago she undertook major reconstruction. My friend mirrored her one-of-a-kind home decorated with unique folk art and vivid splashes of color against neutral upholstery. She often wore signature hand-knits splashed with wild color and bold patterns, which only a tall woman could carry off.

I craved hearing stories about the Boston of Connie's childhood because it fanned my secret love affair with the Northeast. I loved Texas, but ever since reading *Little Women* I leaned north. Reading Thoreau touched off a similar, only grown-up, longing for natural serenity and transcendent peace, finally satiated at my farm. I wanted more. I would have it again, but yes, there were many roads to travel before I reached that destination.

In the meantime, Connie's sunset deck and easy conversation made me feel closer to that day. My dream life had become bizarre, and this sisterhood allowed letting it all hang out. "What do you make of this, Connie? It's an involved dream about a rodeo with lots of cowboys roping calves, and throwing steers to the ground. Then in the last part of the dream, I climb down steps into a dimly lit underground dressing room with lockers assigned to each contender. As my eyes adjust to the light, a small woman dressed in blue enters from a door at the far end. In her hand she carries a shovel. Suddenly the scene changes and I realize these aren't lockers but individual burial crypts. Just then I hear the announcer over the PA system bark, 'And they went out and began burying the dead!' Is that creepy or what?"

Connie frowned and answered in her Texafied, but still clipped, Yankee accent. "Yeah. Sounds pretty dark. What do you think it means?"

"Well. Death for sure. And the lady in blue is how I think of Aunt Margaret when we first met at Mother's funeral."

"Makes sense. But that's past. Something is dying right now…and has died." She hesitated, with sadness in her eyes. "I still miss your place."

"Me too, Connie. You know how much. No doubt, a big dream died when I lost my farm. Scary thing is, this nighttime dream seems plural — went out and buried *the dead* — like there are bunches of bodies. I suspect it means actual death, not only symbolic death. Who else but my father? Mother has been gone for two years, and Margaret is more concerned about George every time we talk. She feels his death is near."

"You don't sound upset."

"I'm not. It's inevitable. I'm prepared. Actually, I'll feel relieved when it happens. It's just hanging there, tying Margaret to a promise she made to her mother that she would take care of her brother. They don't have a real relationship. Nobody can. He's lost. Honestly, his death should be a blessing for all of us."

"Well, then. Your dream agrees the time has come."

"So it does. That feels right. And there's another, clearer and better dream. It's short. After this, enough about me. So, in this dream I'm the observer watching what's going on, but not being part of the action. I see a bed with George in it. He's thin and frail, struggling to take the next breath. It hurts to watch. Suddenly Mother is hovering over his bed like she's an angel, only she doesn't have wings. She floats down and reaches for George's hand, lifting him from what seems to be his deathbed. As she carries him higher and higher, he transforms into a teddy bear. Isn't that precious?"

"Oh, Sandy. That's beautiful." Connie paused, her eyes glistening. "It's all good, you know."

"I do. Birth, death and all that, but lemme tell ya, I'll be thankful to get to rebirth."

Connie smiled and nodded. "We all are!"

I laughed. "Ain't it the truth. It will be interesting to see what happens…."

Holding on is pointless when the future is on the move. With college behind her and anticipating inspiration for the next step in her now adult life, Sarah moved home and found an office job just for the summer. She and her boyfriend dated but couldn't keep it together. They broke up and to deal with her emotions, Sarah took frequent long drives out Highway 281. Ever since she first climbed behind the wheel when she was sixteen, this had been her healing ritual. One night she was gone for an especially long time. I knew she was working something out for herself so I wasn't afraid, but I was still awake when I heard the door slam.

"Mom? Are you asleep yet?" Sarah called out.

"No. Come on in. What's up, honey?"

Sarah sat on the foot of the bed. She was smiling, instead of crying as I had anticipated. "Mom…I've made a decision. I don't know how I got here, but suddenly I realize what I really want. You remember, I told you my friends moved to the Upper East Side?"

My heart picked up the pace. "You did. And…."

"I'm going, Mom. I can't do San Antonio. I don't want to teach. There's space in one of the apartments. I can buy in. Pay my part of the furniture. It sounds a little crazy, but feels right."

Before I could feel devastated, excitement ran through my body. "Oh, honey. Fantastic! What a big beautiful dream. I wish it were me!" And then with some concern, I asked, "But how will you support yourself?"

"Easy, they say. You work temp. Only take assignments in jobs you'd want. All my friends did it. That's how they got permanent jobs."

"Wow. Wow. Wow." We both jumped to our feet and hugged. "I'm so happy for you, baby. This is incredible. Manhattan. I can't wait to visit!"

"Thank you, Mom." Sarah's face looked soft and warm with happy tears shining in her eyes. "You've given me wings." Two weeks later — the first week of September — she was gone.

Two weeks after Sarah settled in with her friends at Ninetieth and *Lex* — Big Apple lingo for Lexington Avenue — Margaret called. "Sandy. I'm on the way to Marshall. George didn't show up for his chicken salad sandwich. I called 911. They found his body lying on the floor. Said he had been dead less than twenty-four hours. Fell on the way to the phone, they suspect. Bled to death from a head wound. I'm on my cellphone, on the way to the house right now."

Feeling lightheaded, I sucked in a gulp of air. "Margaret. We'll be there. Jo and I will be there." Within a couple of days we were on the road, tooling along in Jo's BMW, talking nonstop, sharing memories in preparation for burying a stranger who had been a bit player in our lives.

Every time we talked about our early childhood, the

differences in our recollection stood out in stark contrast. Our five years' age separation meant Jo and I grew out of different families. My sister actually idealized George — the fantasy-father — based on Mother's romantic stories. She reflected an odd tenderness toward him and didn't recall — or remember experiencing — any abusive incidents. This wasn't my reality. With me, it was all booze and bruises. But I kept my comments to a minimum, mostly because feeling resentful had lost its charm. Whether Jo viewed our father through rose-colored glasses or from the depths of hell, this man belonged to us, and because of him, we belong to each other.

As Margaret told it, since Grandmother passed away sixteen years ago, George had lived in that house all by his lonesome. Because he "never saw that it was cleaned," Margaret explained that she just quit going, rather than feel duty-bound to "clean up his mess." I remembered the house. In 1970 I traipsed up those front porch steps anticipating a reunion with my grandmother. But I got more than I bargained for.

My husband and I were on vacation at Lake of the Pines in Harrison County, close to Marshall. With proximity to the Foster habitat rustling like a bird in the bush, my man's hunter instinct took over. "That blood runs in our children's veins," he argued convincingly. He had a point there. To date there had been zero Foster sightings, and we had been married six years. I suspected Grandmother Foster still lived somewhere in Marshall, and a gritty filling-station phone book coughed up the address and phone number. A phone call would terminate the hunt — I hoped — but it rang and rang with no answer. This couldn't be the end of it. A drive-by was the suggested stalking tactic.

My insides churned even thinking about the Fosters, but it was true that all of our children would carry Foster DNA. Trey already did. It was a little out-there not to know what this side of the family looked like. I was seven months pregnant and wearing a 1970s yellow-ribbed polyester maternity pants outfit with a tent top when I waddled up the steps of a quaint Victorian cottage with sweet roses spilling from flower beds, and pressed the doorbell.

Within the house, a musical chime sounded. Five minutes is quite long enough for a rotund pregnant woman to stand in sweltering heat, shrouded in polyester all the way to puffy ankles and swollen tootsies. As I turned my back and prepared to evacuate via the front steps, thrilled to soon reclaim Trey from Mother in Longview, the door cracked open. It was mid-morning, and a man gathered a dirty blue robe around his middle as he peered at us suspiciously. Three-day scruff covered his jowls, and unruly tufts of gray hair sprang in all directions even though he roughly raked his fingers through the tangles, attempting to correct his rumpled appearance. From behind the latched screen, he growled, "Whaddaya want?"

Blame mommy-brain, but I didn't see it coming. Ratcheting my most personable smile, I said, "I've come to see Mrs. Foster." The scruffy stranger scowled and appeared hostile. Who knew who he was? What if something devious was going on and we arrived just in time to save my grandmother? "I'm her granddaughter," I prissily declared with fire in my eyes and a challenging — near-threatening, I hoped — tone in my voice.

"No, you're not," He growled.

Then I knew. "Yes, Mrs. Foster is my grandmother," I said, defiantly tossing my head. "And you're my father."

Grandmother Foster was away visiting a sister. The house was dark and creepy, and my father had clearly been drinking. His first question was, "How's my baby Jo?" It went downhill from there. Ten minutes was entirely enough, but we stayed an hour because my husband played the role of bone-gnawing hound dog, jerking conversation from the skeleton of a relationship. It was altogether depressing.

Now my father was gone and here we were again, twenty-eight years later, without once laying eyes on him until Easter a year ago at the Mexican restaurant. Margaret opened that same screen door and seemed exceedingly more cheerful that I felt. "Well, hello. Come on in this house. So glad you're here." I tripped over four cartons of Camels stacked at the doorway and stumbled along a narrow pathway of junk unending, piled to the ceiling. I made it as far as the den, took one look at the blood-stained carpet, clutched my stomach and bolted for the door.

The fallen-down front porch felt like the Garden of Eden. Cupping my hands against the rusted screen and craning my neck to see them, I challenged Margaret and Jo's seemingly Teflon-coated ability to endure vermin and filth. "What are y'all doing in there? We can't do this. No human being should deal with such squalor. Can't we hire a demolition crew and be done with it? Give me a number. I'm on it."

Dry, breathless heat scorched my face. Despite the blast furnace, this was September, a few weeks shy of the anniversary of Mother's death two years earlier. I melted in the last gasp of summer, imagining a yellow angel of wrath — claw-jawed Caterpillar — ruthlessly devouring the house. Wasps from a nest treacherously dangling beneath the porch eaves buzzed around my head. Flower beds that overflowed with blooming roses twenty-eight years ago now strangled on weeds and rot. I sucked gulps of air and grabbed hold of myself. There was no choice. This had to be done.

The next few days burned indelible imprints into my gray matter. Margaret had mentioned that George had another daughter, but for some reason, I didn't expect her to poke her head through the front door. "Well, hi, I'm Peggy. Your sister." Who wouldn't recognize her on first sight? Strangers on the street could knock us off as sisters. Her drawl was even the same. "Are you Sandy, or Jo?" The father's identity was not in question with this sister from another mother. A tall man ducked in the doorway, close on Peggy's heels. "Meet Ron. My husband."

All five of us crowded into the dank and dusty drawing room with only one functional light and heavy drapes drawn, still the cleanest spot in the house. John had stayed behind in San Antonio with Baby Hannah, who was only eight months old. The day before, Jo and I drove to the Shreveport Airport to retrieve Lacie. My first cousin Bill had driven in this morning, but his wife, Emily, taught first grade and had a good excuse for staying behind in Houston. Sarah had an easy out, too. No way could she turn around and fly back to Texas after being a New Yorker for only two weeks. Margaret charged into the room grinning from ear to ear. "Peggy! Ron! So glad you're here." We stood around with our arms dangling and swiveling our head from face to face, struck dumb by the amazing resemblance. Loopy with excitement that can't be bought in a bottle, Margaret chortled. "Mother would love this. All her girls...together at last."

It was a lot to take in. "Okay y'all," Peggy finally broke the spell. "We've got our two boys and my daughter taken care of, so we'll be here for a few days. We'll get to know each other as we go along, don't ya think? Come on! Time's a-wasting. Let's get to work!"

Grandmother's side of the house had been sealed since her death sixteen years before. Sifting through the dust and debris I wondered if archeologists who opened King Tut's tomb felt this amazed...and yet environmentally challenged. Now that I think of it, wasn't there some pernicious bacteria — most likely fatal — which imperiled them after breathing tomb air?

Lacie was the first up the ladder, tackling a gritty stack of boxes on the top shelf of Grandmother's closet. I advanced toward her clothes, which were neatly folded in dresser drawers, and sparkly jewelry boxes, combs, brushes and a plethora of girly goods arranged with an orderly eye along the crocheted doily-topped dresser.

Layer upon layer, our dig progressed. From George's area of the house, Peggy hollered, "Y'all, come here. Look at this." She ghoulishly grinned and gestured toward the broken-down chair positioned in front of a new television, where George clearly spent most of his time. "Lift it," Peggy dared as we crowded around. Peeling the threadbare rag rug from the chair seat revealed thick metal springs which protruded from the swayed frame like dinosaur bones in a peat bog. The leather upholstery and stuffing were worn completely away. It got worse. The brass standing ashtray beside the chair was mounded with cigarette butts almost a foot high, and in front of the chair, the precise impression of two manly footprints had worn through the carpet and pad, all the way to the wood floor. The eerie vibe was inescapable."Oh, my God!" I moaned. "It's the Bates Motel! Psycho!"

A shriek of agreement erupted as our newly forged family collapsed into horrified moans and giggles. Our liberally utilized rallying cry — Remember the Chair — energized continued progress through grim discoveries that kept on coming.

The kitchen staggered the senses. The refrigerator reminded me of high-school biology lab. Just tell me, how long does it take to grow mold? On everything? Even pickles?

The moldy-particulates gag-factor of the toilet in the adjoining bathroom prohibits explicit description. Backing away after a numbing stare, I flashed on the humiliating toilet stoop out in Mamo's garage built especially for *the help* — my other mother and father, Annie and Anderson. We could use help...and soon. But what person in their right mind would be willing?

From Grandmother's bedroom, Peggy — running neck-and-neck with Lacie's spirit for adventure — alerted us to discovery of another stunner. "Sandy, come here. You've got to see this!" Her eyes looked like an alligator's, rising from the deep. She extended a pink deckled sheet of writing paper inscribed with a schoolteacher's precise hand, dated in the 1970s:

> Dearest Sandy,
>
> I have been so happy to correspond with you since your visit to Marshall. I will always regret that I was away at my sister's house, but as I look up at the pictures of your precious family hanging on the wall here beside my bed, I recall all the wonderful times we shared. I still hope for that visit.
>
> It pleases me to hear that you have forgiven your father. You shared some bad times, but I want you to know that I never stopped loving you, precious Jo or your mother. I am so glad that we are speaking again, and I look forward to being with you.
>
> I have shared with George that I am writing to you and he has something to say:

The rest of the page was blank — the letter unsigned.

I felt overwhelmed with regret, ashamed that I wimped out and didn't visit Grandmother, even though she lived many years after that lackluster reunion with my father, when I was pregnant with Lacie. I had allowed fear to overcome love.

Margaret, Peggy, Ron, Bill, Jo and Lacie, had crowded around as I read the note out loud. They watched my face...but none of us spoke. The sadness was too big for words. I folded the note and returned it to the fabric bag which hung on the bedpost of Grandmother's bed. "Aren't you going to keep it?" Jo asked.

"No…what's done is done. I need to feel this. Lonely for what could have been…and absolutely miserable that I didn't come." Attempting to throw off the sadness, I coached a smile to my lips. "You're so right, Margaret. Grandmother would love being with us now. I promise…y'all too…this can't happen to any of us. Okay? I don't want to ever lose y'all again."

At graveside, an American flag draped my father's casket. A brittle fall drought sent grasshoppers noisily scavenging for any morsel. I felt dry and lifeless as burnt grass, detached and removed, going through the motions and peculiarly out of place seated in the front row, with my *two* sisters and long-lost aunt. In my head I struggled to understand whether or not this stranger we had come to remember did in fact earn the honor a flag-draped casket implies.

Margaret did say George served in WWII. I knew about that…but Korea and Vietnam, too…new information. That's a lot of bridge building under fire. I remember how starched, board-straight and proud he looked in that uniform. The military…finally a father figure that acknowledged his accomplishments…no wonder he kept returning.

And who is that attractive older woman sitting in the back row trying to hide herself from view? This group is too small to go unnoticed. Give her space. She's probably a girlfriend who knew more about him than any of us sitting here in the front row.

Listen to me. Being so judgmental. Not attractive. So unkind. Who am I to evaluate his honor? What do I know of his battles? Does he look down on us? Is he sad that he missed sharing life with us? I am. I can't cry for who he was to me. But I feel tears for who he wasn't.

The reception following our father's burial went on for days, with Peggy, Jo and I staying on in Hughes Springs at Margaret's request, for the reading of the will. But we weren't an imposition, Margaret promised. "Somebody has got to eat all this food!" Her dining table groaned beneath down-home dishes prepared by her many friends — ham, cornbread, candied yams, mushroom soup green beans dressed with French's onion rings, late-producing fall tomatoes warm off the vine, pasta, rice, potatoes, pickled peaches, buttery pecan and cinnamony apple pies.

Feeling impelled, I couldn't resist lifting a clear glass baking dish and craning my neck to see if the cook's signature was taped to the bottom. There it was — girlfriends still showed love as I remembered. After Trey left us, the explosion of Pyrex baking dishes was so intense we had to beg Larchmont neighbors for freezer space.

"You can have anything here, Sandy. You don't need to look and see if your name is on the green beans. Help yourself." My cousin Bill — as I was learning — could be counted on to lighten the mood.

"Just checking!" With a full heart and no explanation, I slid the dish back into place. Maybe someday I could explain that Scotch tape feels stronger than grief. Scotch tape makes life worth living. Scotch tape is the language of love. Right now I would cry old tears, and this was not the time or place for that conversation. It was my solitary secret and uniquely beautiful time for experiencing love coming full circle.

I once dismissed Norman Rockwell's paintings as sentimental poster art, conceived through imagination but surely not real. But then I would feel this way, since his subjects portrayed small-town caring, dogs and families, lovely sentimentalities absent from Jo's or my childhood…at least our Longview childhood. Just now, I thought of Rockwell…and imagined he would feel drawn to this unpretentious town with one main street…the spectacle of friends knocking on the kitchen door, struggling beneath the weight of glass baking dishes; red, green and blue serving bowls.

Glancing toward the china cabinet, I recognized Grandmother's good china winking behind glass. I reached to hold, but couldn't quite touch the picture of that house on the hill in the Marshall, Texas, of my early, barely recalled childhood…*almost, though…I hear the echo in bone. The love and laughter, no-holds-barred, no-subject-sacred, free-flowing conversations spreading around the table, the values: higher education, the accomplishments of every generation surpassing those of the one that came before. The seeds were planted around Grandmother's table…watered by stories of Papaw and his Puritan Work Ethic…and matured in the sunshine of my own family, my husband and children. Far away, long ago, disconnected all these years, these are my values…they are who I've become.*

In a tastefully subdued office on Marshall's town square, along either side of an oblong table, Margaret, Peggy, Jo and I sat down with the middle-aged, gently rounded attorney. Speaking with the familiar East Texas drawl, he swept us with his gaze. "And so you pretty girls are Mr. Foster's heirs?"

I nodded and wondered what the attorney saw when he looked at us. Did he think we were close to our father? Or did he understand how unkind the years had been? I don't know what Jo and Peggy felt, but I struggled to reckon the surreal reality. *Yes, I do have a father…did have a father. His name was George Porter Foster. I am his child. His blood runs in my veins…and I am no longer afraid to claim him.*

Paying attention to the lawyer's words felt less

compelling than identifying the melody that rippled through my mind. The barrister smiled broadly. "I think you should know that Mr. Foster loved you girls very much. The evaluation of his properties runs upwards of five figures…" He paused to allow the unfathomable largesse to register. "…that will be divided equally among you girls. And there is the house. And the possessions which I assume will accrue to Mr. Foster's girls? Is that correct?" He nodded toward Margaret, and she nodded back. "I can recommend an excellent estate-sale outfit. They come in. Clean. Sell everything right down to the toilet paper. Those proceeds are to be divided equally among you girls, as well."

I stifled a sob as I suddenly grasped what Margaret had implied: "George is saving something for you girls." All the pieces slid into place. Poor tortured soul. He denied himself, hoarded what he had, existed at the poverty level, lived into a future someday when his daughters would know his love. My father did have a heart, but it was too bruised to open. I didn't want the money. All I wanted was him. I wept for the father I would never have and for the broken man I never knew. While in my imagination Neil Diamond sang:

This is a fantasy. A pure fantasy. It is a dream. A dream about an old man who dies alone and leaves a gift behind.

Morning sighed, the old man died. And no one cried. They simply turned away. And when he died, he left a table made of nails and pride. And with his hands he carved these words inside: For My Children.

Morning light, morning bright, I spent the night with dreams that make you weep. Morning time, wash away the sadness from these eyes of mine. For I recall the words an old man signed: For My Children.

DREAMS ARE POWERFUL. Sometimes they leak out and somebody standing close by picks one up and runs with it…before you get your socks pulled on and Nike laces tied. By 1999, my whole family was gone. Each and every one claimed *my* magical place of longing — the Northeast.

Of course it made sense. When he was a toddler, John had been separated from his New York father and raised in Texas. His engineering dad and pie-baking, roast-searing stepmom still lived in a verdant valley with a river running through it, the Catskills and Adirondacks not far away. Of course it was beautiful, a sparkling white blanket in the winter. After all, Lacie's high-school guy friends called her Hot Dog because they couldn't keep her off black-diamond slopes when her church youth group went on Christmas skiing trips to Colorado. Of course it was outrageously green in the summer. "Planting a garden as soon as we're settled," John said. Of course it was the right thing to do. "Mom, this is your thing, you know. Come on. We're just getting here first," Lacie said.

My refrigerator and I were bare. I felt cold. Ice cubes left too long, smelly from leftover takeout, two-day-old enchiladas and a moldy onion shriveling in the back of the hydrator. Nothing made sense anymore. Nothing was exactly bad. There was just nothing new. No spark. Over is over. Empty is empty.

Overworked and soul-weary, I stared from the second-story window of my office and attempted to decide where — and if — I should bother to eat lunch. Instead I became mesmerized by lyrical patterns of red, orange and yellow oak leaves swept up in the hot autumn breeze, dancing to earth within my transfixed gaze. Almost four years now since Mother died; two since Sarah graduated from the University of Texas and moved to Manhattan; one since Lacie and John, and my baby-girl granddaughter, Hannah, moved to upstate New York. My exterior life and I sat here, swept clean and waiting. *For what?*

Faintly within my mind I heard a startling response. *If you stay here you will be dead within five years.*

"Dead?" This didn't sound right. Usually my inner voice was a God-thing, definitely not scary. On alert to call up God-magic and send this likely bad guy out into the universe where they couldn't hurt anyone, especially me, I protested out loud. "Hey! Who's talking?"

I apologize for the shock value, but you haven't been listening. It is I. Your True Self. Your essence. Your soul. Your God Self. Are you feeling joy in your work? Where is excitement and love of life? In these eighteen years since you've lived here, have you fallen in love with San Antonio? The time for change has come. Pack your bags.

Oh, I said inside my head. *You mean, like* emotionally *dead, unhappy and just plain bored?*

That's it…exactly.

Internally, I complained to my Self. *Just wait a minute. I do love San Antonio. It's funky, easy, laid-back, ethnically diverse, beautiful and totally cool. Just like that I'm supposed to bail? How can I leave my clients? I'll miss them. I'll be devastated…once again. The goodbyes are bunching up already. You know what meaningful work means to me. You don't just establish a practice overnight. To go where? The idea of relocation is impractical.*

Inner dialogue continued from me to my Self: *The Northeast, of course. That's your obvious destination. The clues have been evident all your life. Clients? Get real, Sandy. You may love and revere them, but do you believe a healthy therapist lives only for her clients? In truth, you're worried about chasing after your children. You're not. At least not totally. Something draws you to the Northeast…always has. You have work to do there. Lacie knows it…Sarah knows it. Your daughters don't possess exclusive rights to that real estate. You don't have to climb into their lap. It's a big place.*

What are you waiting for? Come on…you're torturing yourself day and night because you aren't doing any deep writing on the story about your family and your life. How do you think you're going to do that and be a therapist, too?

Anticipating my building resistance, my Self cut me off at the crossroads. *I don't care if J.K. Rowling wrote* Harry Potter *on a busy London commute. You're not that kind of writer. Get over it.*

Follow your heart! Isn't this what you insist your clients do? You understand how the spiritual journey works: God always gives you what you need at just the right moment. Have you considered that maybe your ancestors left you an inheritance so you would have this freedom? And anyway, it doesn't have to be forever. Think of it as a sabbatical. After all these years as a therapist you deserve a break. Do it. Pack up and go. You know you will never forgive yourself if you don't write the book.

Immediately, I felt alive and vibrant. For months, my losses had piled up like snowdrifts from a New England blizzard. Now, instantaneously I blew past self-doubt and uncertainly that had haunted me since I lost the farm, and Sarah moved, and Lacie's family moved…and…and…and.

Tucked in the bookcase across the room, the black office phone almost shouted my name. In a flash of inspiration I grabbed it, fumbled in my appointment book for a number and placed a life-altering call.

"Bud. Is that you? This is Sandy."

"I know who it is. Hi, cousin. How are *y'all?*"

"Good. 'Bout the same as *y'all* are," I giggled.

"Well that's good that we are all good. What can I do for y'all?"

"For starters, enough already with the *y'all*! And then tell me about your offer of your summer home on Cape Cod. I just had the crazy idea I might close down my office, store my stuff and move up there for a while. What do you think?"

"Well, come on! July begins the summer season, so you've got until then."

It took several months to make it happen, but with a rush of energy I closed the door on all of it, stored my life, packed my bags, backed out of Texas and headed for the Cape. A Yankee at last, if only for a time, here on a sliver of New England land engulfed on all sides by ocean and bay, I cast my lot aware I walked where Thoreau had walked. The land of Louisa May Alcott echoed with the poets and writers I modeled my life after. Far from Texas, I came home to myself.

A roaring fire crackled in the fireplace. Maxy and Pookie were curled up, blissfully asleep on the rug in front of the hearth. Wearing black sweats and a fleece hoodie, I slouched on one of a pair of soft green, cotton sofas arranged before the raised hearth. Even though it was April — and springtime in Texas — here on the Cape, snow had begun falling during the night. I glanced through a broad picture window and felt encouraged to see light snow flurries, instead of the plump, wet flakes that came down most of the morning. Beneath a dusting of powdery white, thick Rhododendron bushes sprouted fat buds on the tips of leafy branches. So much about the Cape felt foreign, including these glossy leaved, rotund bushes I had never seen before. Yesterday, the barista in an Orleans coffee shop — a middle-aged woman and year-round resident of the Cape — had supplied their name. She was a fount of knowledge. "Don't worry, Tex…" she laughingly assured me when I had asked about the weather, "...spring is on its way. Happens every year." This was my second week at Bud's house in Brewster and ripening Rhododendron blossoms were the only discernable sign that she might know what she was talking about.

Map in hand, I had already reconnoitered the lay of the land, crisscrossing this skinny jester's-boot peninsula — really an island connected to the mainland by bridges — Cape Cod Bay to the west and open Atlantic to the east and south. Scrumptious coffee shops and restaurants lousy with ambiance dotted quaint village streets strung out all along the island. I had no idea there were so many townships. Traveling toward the tip of the boot I had discovered the hamlets of Orleans, Chatham, Eastham and Provincetown. In the opposite direction heading toward the mainland I found the villages of Dennis, Harwich, Hyannis, Barnstable, and those were only the ones I explored so far. There were more, plus the islands of Nantucket and Martha's Vineyard. Not to mention Boston, a ferry ride across Cape Cod Bay.

Even though I was alone — except for my furry companions — and besides the lady in the coffee shop, knew no one, this adventure was far too magical to feel lonely. I did miss Mother, though. She was never far from my thoughts now that I had acted on impulse, and cut myself off from my Texas life. My intent for this sabbatical rested heavily on my determination to start that book I felt she wanted me to write. But where was she? Since two years ago just before George's death when I had the dream of Angel Mother raising him from his deathbed , there had been zero Mother sightings — or hearings. Last night though, I had a fairly stunning dream:

A number of psychospiritual healers and teachers — some living and some dead — are milling around my friend Alison's house. In the ethnic sea of colorfully clothed luminaries, I recognize the Tibetan monks, Black Elk, Thomas Merton, Edgar Cayce, Carl

Jung and Joseph Campbell, the Dalai Lama, Thich Nhat Hanh, Jacquelyn Small, Eckhart Tolle, Marian Woodman and endless more. The seemingly limitless congregation of spiritually wise men and women is staggering. Brushing against these deeply loving human beings, I feel overwhelmed with joy.

Taking me by surprise — since she famously disdained religion as too spooky and metaphysical teachers for the same reason — Mother descends a staircase. She looks astoundingly young and radiant, and is uncharacteristically clothed in an earth-toned caftan — like a High Priestess — which billows around her as she floats into the room, emanating a pulsating glimmer. No one speaks. Words are unnecessary. We read each other's thoughts.

Mother transmits the impression that I should come to her side as she reclines on a carved daybed in the center of the room. Immediately she is encircled by a colorful variety of beings, meditatively laying hands on her body as if some prearranged signal has been heard. I am drawn toward Mother and join the healers, closing my eyes and gently touching. Mother smiles, her eyelids close and golden energy flows through healing hands. In my mind I hear Mother's thoughts: Thank you, Sandy. I am whole. It is done.

This morning I awakened from the dream sobbing, but my tears quickly turned into giggles. My San Antonio friend Alison makes a career of gathering spiritual knowledge and experience. She's a feng shui practitioner by profession, but her real job seems to be tirelessly hostessing spiritual events. I tease Ali, suggesting she lives at Alison's Ashram. The Tibetan monks do stay with her when they are in town. When Mother walked on earth — regarding spirituality with equal parts fear and revulsion — she would never darken Alison's door, any more than she would cross a church threshold. Yet I had just experienced her as a High Priestess, in the company of angels, healed at last and thanking me. After this circuit-blowing dream how could I feel any less thankful for our life together? And now, the real work began.

I opened the fireplace screen and rearranged smoldering red embers on the grate before I tossed three more cedar logs on top of the pyre. The bed of coals banking the floor of the hearth glowed white-hot. Instantly the dried wood caught and blazed into flame. Momentarily disturbed, Pookie and Maxy yawned and stretched, regarded me with disinterest, and curled into tighter orange-and-white and black-and-white fuzzballs. Amie rose from her fleece bed beside the hearth, stretched and looked at me expectantly. Wondering, I suspected, if it was time for a walk. "Not yet, Me-Me. In a little bit. Maybe the snow will slack off soon." *Precious loyal dog,* I thought. Amie sneezed a couple of times, scratched at her bed, then settled down with a moan. *I shouldn't put her off much longer. Just a little more…and then I'll be ready.*

Snowflakes swirled on gusts of wind and frost gathered on the corner of windowpanes like fake snow Mother sprayed on our tepid Texas windows at Christmastime. This day had fulfilled everything I imagined a breather from my everyday life could be: lounging in front of the fire, not answering to anyone or anything, slowly unpacking the contents of Mother's treasure box, unopened since she left the earth. The box was deceptively shallow, with oil paints tracing pink roses and dahlias across the cream-colored lid embellished with gold scrolls. *Gold-leaf?* I wondered. *Actual gold hammered into thin sheets used for decoration? Probably not, but the gilt-framed portraits of the ancestors which hung on The Dead People's Wall must have been.*

As the day unfolded, contents of the far-from-shallow box mounted into stacks of paper, emotionally charged…. *Cute little thing.* Mother's picture stared back at me from the pages of an old scrapbook with photographs taken at the seashore. Mamo and Aunt Bodie were perched in the bow of a small boat, ocean waters crawling onshore in the background, vast sky above. Bodie held a parasol over two little girls. Their bathing suits were baggy bloomers in the style of the Twenties. *This must be Mother and Louise. Of course. Roaring Twenties style. Mother was born in 1923. Louise is older, maybe six. Mother is probably four, blond hair cropped and left hand on her hip. Mother once asked, "Do you think I look like Daddy?" I see that she did, wide-eyed, mischievous.*

Two formal studio photographs revealed clearer facial features. Little Wilma had laughing eyes, a face that must have attracted attention even then — strangers probably stopped, stooped down and smiled. *I'm sure she drove Louise crazy. Attitude. Mother had attitude no matter the circumstance.* Louise by comparison looked uncomfortable, stiff, not happy having to pose. *I know they fought, both sharing the same high bed where Jo and I later slept. Mother told me about Louise drawing an imaginary line in the sheets and saying, "Stay on your side!" Of course that never happened.*

Mamo — the slender young woman with a patrician nose, deep-set dark eyes, Mona Lisa smile and etched features reminiscent of Roman coins — posed serenely with her small daughters. I am drawn to her face. She was luminous like a woman in love, at home in her skin. *And that hat! Black straw with a broad brim the width of her shoulders.* Flipping the photograph in search of Mother's careful lettering, I wanted to be certain this was actually my grandmother, wife of Angus, mother of these two girls. *Yes! Unbelievable! I never saw Mamo look this satisfied and happy.* Magnetized to these faces, my heart ached, longing took hold. I missed who they were, wanted to turn back the clock, make them smile again.

Wow. Look at this…two pictures of Mamo's house at 815 Charlotte Drive. The older one with white square columns across the front porch. The newer one, with New Orleans-style wrought-iron filigree. I remember Mamo replacing those columns. Because of termites, I think.

And here's that iconic black and white photo of the Old Home

Place, rambling Victorian angled caddywampus across a corner lot. I remember exactly how it looked. Every school day after we moved from Mamo's she still chauffeured me along Green Street past the Old Home Place on the way to junior high…always telling me stories about how it all came to be. I almost hear her explain why the house stretched out that way…at odd angles. In hard times Mamuvah and Papaw built additional wings, adding space so children and grandchildren could return home.

The Old Home Place…so much a part of this family…the good part. And then it was over. The house just sat there for years: deserted, shuttered and empty. I had lost sight of it when I moved on to high school and Mamo and I no longer drove down Green Street every day. Then, one weekend home from college, I took the car and without thought steered toward the Old Home Place. Cut adrift from roots and needing to find my own way, I felt homesick for the talisman that personified worlds of meaning. The house was gone. The corner lot lay bare, arching pine, sweetgum and oak trees taller than I remembered and unkempt, with only the wrought-iron fence standing sentinel to what was.

Doubtful I could maneuver past unmanageable feelings seeping through each tender memento — yellowed photographs, scraps of poetry, letters written in flowing script or bold strokes, certificates of marriage and death — late in the afternoon I stacked the contents of Mother's treasure box into haphazard categories, reverently closed the lid and vowed to the ethers, "God, if I'm supposed to write a book about all this, you've got to help. I can't locate an objective, detached or sensible bone in my body. This is beyond overwhelming."

Inundated by a storm of protest toward this self-inflicted project, I steered the Jeep along 6a, threaded through meandering streets lined with iconic Cape Cod cottages, and finally parked at Red River Beach on Nantucket Sound. I pulled out a favorite CD and zipped my jacket. "Come on Me-Me." I grabbed Amie's leash and together we faced the fierce storm, hoping — I suppose — to obliterate my emotional tempest with the roiling seas and gale-force winds.

Through the strains of *Braveheart* I entered portals of fantasy. *Did our ancestors laugh, love, dance and weep to sister melodies?* I walked at the end of the world, out beyond knowing or sense-making, grounding one boot in the sand following the one before. *Step on a crack. Break your mother's back....*

Turning around to scan the sliver of beach behind, I shivered with awareness that Amie and I were alone on this chilly contour of land. Only weathered gray plank walkways protruded into the waterline, interspersed between tumbled granite jetties, robust boulders hauled to this shoreline during Colonial times. Packet ships had sailed the Cape coast from the West Indies and Great Britain, bringing supplies to Pilgrim shores. Still a destination for sturdy stock, this slender beach would once again be invaded — within a matter of months — by the tourist trade, families, dogs, laughter and warmth. But now only I, Wolf Spirit Amie, and ancestors populating my heart and mind sidestepped delicate pink, yellow and white shells as we navigated the moraine between tide line and ocean waters tumbling toward shore.

In her element, Amie occasionally jerked at the leash, her keen nose sensing potential scavenged delicacy, tender crustaceans washed ashore. With unease loosed by the storm's wrath, I gladly hesitated, humoring Amie's culinary taste while scanning increasingly vicious seas and mounting cloudbanks. Smoky puffs of breath obscured my vision as I measured the gathering intensity and thickness of the squall swirling around me.

Have I done a fool thing wandering to the ocean? The TV weatherman when I tuned-in last night forecast a late-season

Nor'easter. What did that mean, anyway? And what time is it? It's getting black as night. Feeling panic beginning to rise, I estimated how much daylight remained before absolute darkness fell beneath the storm. Beyond the roiling ocean and all along the shore, nothing stirred, not even ever-present gulls. All other life forms seemed to know to seek shelter.

Resolving to turn around and head toward the protective womb of the Jeep, I realized Amie was on point, as she used to be when she sniffed a herd of sheep, or a polecat nearby. She stood stock-still, pointed ears set back, winds flattening her bushy coat, tail curled rigidly over her back. "What, Amie? Come on, we're going home." Imagining she felt terrified by the storm, I knelt down, murmured encouragement, my hand gliding over her head and down the full-length of her fluffy coat. She remained on point, not making eye contact, even as I continued to pet her and murmur, "It's okay, Me-Me. I'm here. You're okay." Getting nowhere, I rose and pulled gently on her leash. She ignored me. *Obstinate. She can be so stubborn when she wants. Well, hello. She's my dog.* Tugging again, I started feeling downright impatient. Snapping off the *Braveheart* CD and dragging earphones from my ears, I straightened up and reared to my full height, representing — I hoped — an alpha-dog posture. "Amie. Come on. Now!"

Disregarding a forceful yank, she determinedly balked. In a tide of frustration with chilling fear creeping up my spine and instinctual herding mentality grabbing hold, one last time I implored my dadburned-stubborn-four-legged animal. "What, Amie?" Magnifying the snowy maelstrom, a gray fog skimmed over ocean waters and raced toward shore. I squinted to focus beyond the swirling mists, aiming my gaze toward Amie's fixed stare. "That's only a granite rock. Enough!"

Beyond the tide line an enormous mottled charcoal boulder lay at a distance from the craggy jetty. *Odd. Guess that stone was dropped by accident long ago and over the years was never relocated along the jetty wall.* Giving up, I stooped to scoop Amie in my arms, willing to carry her all the way back…but just then…the rock turned to gaze into my eyes.

I froze. Enormous soulful brown eyes almost filling the baby seal's face fixed me with a penetrating gaze. Time stood away, leaving us in a soulful dance of wonder. Creature to creature our eyes met and locked in searching recognition. Tears filled my eyes as I whispered in reverence, "You are so beautiful."

Smooth, sleek, sentient, the seal's vast stare met mine, watched in the stillness at length, then seemingly satisfied, turned and swam effortlessly into the oncoming wave. In those eyes I knew God, my Self, all lives past and all to come. Releasing bottomless grief, with tears now rolling uncontrollably down icy-cold cheeks, my Wolfish-Wise Friend and I relented, turning away, retracing our steps along the shell-strewn moraine.

Awestruck, transported to another space and time by the seal's magical gaze, I miraculously envisioned the spirits of my ancestors massed in forgiving benediction. Holding fast to this storm-blessed moment my heart sprang open, drawing the whole of my human experience to me. A liturgical prayer involuntarily rose from some quiet place inside as if it had been there waiting to be spoken, feelings so powerful I chanted into the wind: "Blessed be Father, Son and Holy Spirit and the Great Mother from whom they all came. What God has brought together let no man…or woman cast asunder. As it was in the beginning is now and will be forever and ever…for so it must be."

The ferocious windstorm snatched my puffs of breath and swirled them away, flowing as one breath into the maelstrom. Out beyond the edge of forever a shiver of anticipation rippled up my spine. Beyond any doubt, ancestral spirits crowded around, their voices raised, whispering my name above the stormy din. "Sandy…Sandy…sister… daughter…child." I ached to reach out and touch their skin and hair, to smell and feel them. In fiber and bone every cell vibrated with their seed, captive to their past and our unfathomable future. *Gatekeepers…these generations of my blood are the portal through which I come and by whose leave I must now go.*

Straining against the whirlwind, I implored these intimately present, fully alive spirits whose number challenged belief, *How can I serve you?* In my imagination I heard a muted response, chorus of voices drenched with love, generation upon generation upon generation, before America, before European place names, before there were places to name, spoken in fervent union: "Respect and understanding. We ask only this. And more will be revealed…."

Frigid winds tore at my heart, but could not weaken the gentle, constant warmth emanating from true center…where wisdom is ever known. *I've been an unconscious fool. Please forgive me for not knowing you…not respecting you…not understanding who you are. You've been here from the beginning, looking down on me from the picture wall, from endless generations past…speaking to my heart. Loving me more than any human being ever could. Respect and understanding? Oh, God…yes. But most of all…I love you…all of you…past…present and future. And more will be revealed….ever and always…for so we must be.*

ABOUT THE AUTHOR

Publishing *Just Because You're Dead Doesn't Mean You're Gone* – December, 2011 — was the next obvious direction for Sandy's work, begun first as a teacher, then mom, inner city volunteer and for the past thirty years, holistic psychotherapist.

Born in Elmhurst, Illinois and raised in Texas from three months on, Sandy graduated from The University of Texas in Austin and then at midlife, from St. Mary's University in San Antonio. Valuable as a college education may be, Sandy claims the experience of "being raised in a *colorful* family," as her greatest teacher and source of inexhaustible inspiration for stories to come.

Since 2000, beginning with her cousin's loaned cottage on Cape Cod — where *Just Because You're Dead Doesn't Mean You're Gone* ends – Sandy has been on a *walkabout,* a spiritual journey of sorts, researching and retracing the footsteps of the ancestors and seeking answers to soul questions most of us eventually ask: Who am I? Where have I come from? Where am I going?

This first story was created on writing sabbaticals in New England, Upstate NY, Houston, and in-between, a return to private practice and the San Antonio Riverwalk. Now the pieced fragments for a novel and a slender self-help are gathering into a sizeable pile. The next stories wait to be told.

Sandy looks forward to ongoing conversation with readers and friends. She can be contacted through:

Website:	http://www.sandyfostermorrison.com/
Facebook:	Sandy Foster Morrison / Author & Psychotherapist
Mailing address:	5150 Broadway, PMB 199, San Antonio, Texas 78209

Made in the USA
Columbia, SC
13 February 2018